# Essentials of Information Systems

**C.E. Tapie Rohm, Jr.**

**Walter T. Stewart, Jr.**

*Mitchell Publishing, Inc.*
*Innovators in Computer Education*
915 River Street • Santa Cruz, California 95060
(800) 435-2665 • In California (408) 425-3851
*"A Random House Company"*

Composition: *Freedmen's Organization*
Cover Design: *John Edeen*
Printed By: *R. R. Donnelley*
Production Management: *Hal Lockwood*
Sponsoring Editor: *Erika Berg*
Text Design: *John Edeen*

Printed in the United States of America

10 9 8 7 6 5 4 3 2 1

library of Congress Card Catalog No.: 87-51541

ISBN: 0-394-39362-7

# Brief Contents

# Detailed Contents

## Chapter 4    Word Processing Systems    68

## Chapter 8   Data Communications Systems   170

UNIT ⠿  **HARDWARE AND SOFTWARE:
CONCEPTS AND APPLICATIONS**    197

UNIT **IV**    **COMPUTER INFORMATION SYSTEMS**    293

**Chapter 13**    **Systems Development**    294

# Preface

Welcome to the Information Age—the exciting world of computers, information systems, and their applications in business and society. Advancements in computer technology have led to some of the greatest discoveries of this century.

One of our greatest challenges while developing this textbook was to keep in perspective what was, what is, and what will be. The computer field is changing so rapidly that presenting current information in a relevant and practical manner takes a lot of hard work.

*Essentials of Information Systems* is designed to bridge the gap between today and tomorrow, to provide a solid foundation, to prepare students to become effective users of information. In essence, the purpose is to increase their own professional and personal productivity through better decision making.

## ■ Who Should Use This Book, and Why?

The book is designed for students taking an introductory course in computers and information systems. *Essentials of Information Systems* meets the guidelines of the Data Processing Management Association (DPMA), the Association for Computing Machinery (ACM), the American Assembly of Collegiate Schools of Business (AACSB), and the International Information Management Association (IIMA). Both the authors and the publisher of this text believe in the necessity and importance of these standards.

## ■ Organization and Scope of the Text

*Essentials* is divided into 13 chapters organized into four units. Unit I provides students with an overview of information systems, computers, and their applications. Unit II covers the concepts and applications of word processing, electronic spreadsheets, presentation graphics and desktop publishing, databases, and data communications. Unit III provides a general understanding of input/output devices, secondary storage, and the central processing unit. Finally, Unit IV discusses systems development from a user perspective.

After Unit I, which sets the stage for the remainder of the text, Units II, III, and IV can be covered in any order. If application software is a component of your course, Unit II can provide an early conceptual ''springboard'' into your hands-on instruction. (The publisher offers a wide selection of manuals, summarized at the end of this Preface, to support your specific course objectives.) If you would rather follow Unit I with an emphasis on hardware and software concepts, you may prefer to cover Unit III before Unit II. In any case, the units and chapters within units are modular; you can tailor use of the text to meet your specific course objectives.

## Primary Features of the Text

*Essentials* is designed for ease of teaching and learning. This text provides a range of unique features, including:

- **Flexibility.** Covering only the essentials of information systems, *Essentials* leaves time for the lab. And, because the chapters are self-contained, teachers can cover the material in any order that meets student needs.

- **End-User Perspective.** *Essentials* focuses on what today's end user needs to understand to be productive in today's information age. A wealth of real-world examples and applications make the material interesting and personally relevant.

- **Decision Making and Productivity Themes.** These two themes drive *Essentials*. This is not a glorified glossary. Technology is never presented for its own sake, in isolation. It is introduced only when and where it is applicable to the end user—to solve problems, make decisions, and increase productivity.

- **Information as an Asset.** Throughout the book, information is presented as a need, a resource, and an opportunity—an asset that needs to be managed carefully to assure productivity and effectiveness.

- **Learning Tools.** Each chapter contains the following features to support student understanding and stimulate interest.

- **Chapter Outline and Briefing Memo.** An outline and memo to the students gives a preview of what will be covered in the chapter.

- **End-User Perspective** and **The Point.** An opening scenario illustrates the key issue that will be discussed in the chapter. The Point, a brief explanation that follows, identifies and discusses the key issue.

- **Insights** and **Impacts.** Boxed inserts supplement the text with practical information, e.g., how to select a spreadsheet package, how to ''upgrade.''

- A wealth of **Illustrations.** Photos, illustrations, and tables enhance the text. In addition, after Chapter 6 (on graphics), a full-color photo essay on ''Business Computer Graphics: Persuasive Power at Your Fingertips'' is featured.

- **Chapter Review** and **Key Terms.** These aids provide a quick summary of the main points of the chapter.

- **Questions for Review.** These questions give students an opportunity to test their understanding of the chapter material.

- **Questions for Thought.** These questions are designed to stimulate thought and class discussion.

- **Minicase** and **Decision Making: Your Turn.** Each Minicase is based on an actual event from the authors' experiences, and illustrates a problem. The questions that follow under Decision Making encourage the students to apply what they've learned in the chapter to solve the problem.

- **Projects.** The successful completion of the three projects at the end of each chapter requires that students identify and use resources in the field.

## Extensive Support Package

*Essentials* is backed by a wide array of supporting materials designed to help both student and instructor. These materials include the following:

- **Instructor's Manual** contains Key Terms, Detailed Lecture Outlines, Answers to Review Questions and Thought Questions, Teaching Tips, and References.

- **Lecture Notes on Disk and PC-OUTLINE** help instructors to administer their course. PC-OUTLINE is an outlining program that, in conjunction with the lecture notes, enables instructors to tailor their notes to meet their individual course objectives or teaching style.

- **Transparency Masters** consist of illustrations from the text plus original illustrations on key state-of-the-art topics.

- **Computerized Test Bank** contains more than 1,300 T/F, multiple choice, and fill-in-the-blank questions. The computerized version is available for the IBM PC.

- **Videocourse** entitled "Computers at Work" is a set of broadcast-quality videotapes in documentary style.

- **A CAI BASIC Turorial** is available to supplement the text.

- **Application Software and Manuals** also are available to supplement *Essentials.* Your choices:

- USING APPLICATION SOFTWARE: WORDPERFECT, VP-PLANNER, AND DBASE III PLUS, Pitter. Includes software. Available "shrink-wrapped" with *Essentials* at a special package price.

- APPLICATION SOFTWARE FOR THE IBM PC: PC-TYPE+, PC-CALC+, AND PC-FILE III+, Shuman. Includes software and data diskette. Available "shrinkwrapped" with *Essentials* at a special package price.

- BUSINESS APPLICATIONS USING THE IBM PC: WORDSTAR, LOTUS 1-2-3, DBASE II/III/III PLUS, AND DATA TRANSFER BETWEEN APPLICATIONS, Meinhardt and Verno. Includes data diskette.

- SPREADSHEET SOFTWARE! USING VP-PLANNER, Pitter. Available with or without software.

- WORD PROCESSING SOFTWARE! USING WORDSTAR, Topham. Available with or without software.

- USING APPLEWORKS, Pitter. Available with or without BASIC programming module.

- INTEGRATED SOFTWARE! USING ENABLE, Barnes. Includes software.

- DEVELOPING EXPERT SYSTEM USING 1ST-CLASS, Ruth and Ruth. Includes software and instructor's solutions disk.

## Special Acknowledgments

We could have never completed this project without the help of many people. We owe a very special thanks for those who have been involved extensively since the beginning

First, and foremost, we thank Erika Berg of Mitchell Publishing for her outstanding job as our editor. She has been an enthusiastic motivator of the project since the beginning. Her tireless energies are greatly appreciated.

We also would like to thank C. Brian Honess, University of South Carolina, for his extensive reviews and insights.

The reviewers who helped to bring our thoughts and writings into focus cannot be forgotten: William Cornette, Southwestern Missouri State University; Caroline Curtis, Lorain County College; Steve Deam, Milwaukee Area Community College; Pat Fenton, West Valley College; Peter MacGregor; Peter Irwin, Richland College; Christopher Pidgeon; Keiko Pitter, Truckee Meadows Community Collge; Leonard Schwab, California State University, Hayward; Charles Silcox; and Tony Verstraete, Pennsylvania State University.

A special thanks also must go to our wives and families who tolerated our absence for long periods.

We gratefully dedicate this textbook to our children, who are the future of the Information Age and current users—Tapie, Trevor, Tucker, Terrell, Ty, Kirsti and Taylor; Elizabeth, Ann, Emily, Karin, Jill, Michael and Kathryn.

C. E. Tapie Rohm, Jr.
Walter T. Stewart, Jr.

# Photo Credits

We are indebted to the many people and organizations who contributed photographs to this book. The page numbers and contributors are listed below.

# Information Systems: An Overview

This Unit establishes a starting point for your study of information systems and your role as an end user. Chapter 1 is designed to help make you aware of that fact that you already depend on information and that, by learning some basics, you can increase the quality, timeliness, and value of the information that you receive. Chapter 2 discusses how computers and the information they provide serve users and their organizations. Also featured is a process that you can apply to help reach effective decisions and become more productive as a user of computer-generated information.

## Chapter Outline

## CHAPTER 1

# Welcome to the Information Age

**Briefing Memo**

TO:       Information Users
FROM:   T. Rohm, W. Stewart

Information has become one of life's essentials!

As a student, you already are an information user. Your academic program, your studying, and your test taking all are instances of information gathering and application. You need information to identify and capitalize on opportunities, to function and succeed in today's society.

This chapter is designed to illustrate that both the quantity and the quality of your information affect your actions and decisions. We hope you will come to appreciate that information is a vital business resource—a resource that must be managed, generally through application of computers. There also should be some personal benefits as you learn about how computers can contribute to your future growth, personally and professionally.

## End-User Perspective

"Don't worry," the mechanic said, "we'll have you back on the road in no time. The computer has isolated your problem. The part you need is a compressor for the air conditioner. It's under warranty."

The mechanic went on to explain to Cindy that troubleshooting on automotive problems used to be a matter of trial and error. Now, the mechanic simply plugs some computer cables into connections on the engine. The computer not only figures out what is wrong, but checks to see if needed parts are in stock and orders them.

"If what you say is true," Cindy said, "we can have lunch and you should have the car ready for us to get back on the road before we finish."

"Just think," Cindy's father commented, "in my day we were happy to drive without air conditioning in our cars. Now we treat them as necessities and feel we can't make a long trip without it. The more technology we get, the more we seem to need."

## The Point: Information is an Asset

Cindy's problem—and particularly its solution—serves to illustrate the extent and the degree to which computers impact today's population. The mechanic who solved her car problem did so by using a computerized tool. He is a

Diagnosing problems with automotive engines can be efficient and reliable when computers are used for automatic, programmed checkouts.

direct *user* of information system capabilities. The mechanic benefits because he saves time in diagnosing and solving customer problems. For him, time saved translates into a potential for greater earnings. Cindy represents a different kind of user, the person who receives results or benefits from the availability of information.

The situation described above identifies two kinds of information *end users:*

- Some users receive and apply information produced by computers.
- Some users actually work at computers to access information.

Both types of end users need a common background and knowledge base to deal with the requirements and challenges of their lives and jobs.

## Information for Solving Problems

Living and succeeding in an information-dependent society is about identifying and solving problems. Where people are involved, solutions have led to growing fields and branches of technology. Information technologies and computers represent just one of the ways in which ideas and innovations have served both to help people solve old problems and to present them with new ones. Other technologies have reshaped people's lives over long periods of time.

To illustrate this trend, consider the automobile. The car gave people freedom to move individually and over long distances. With the automobile, people no longer had to include stables alongside their homes. As cities became crowded, keeping and caring for horses, the main means of transportation, had become a major problem. Automobiles demanded less space. They could be parked on streets without requiring overnight care. Transportation gained flexibility. People even could think about and develop new lifestyles that involved living in suburbs and working in town.

The car also presented new needs and challenges. Billions of dollars had to be spent on roads. And millions of people, the great majority of the adult population, had to learn how to operate a car.

In the future, the population of computers will rival that of automobiles. This will have an impact on most people. Like most adults, you probably have learned to operate an automobile. The automobile is the main technology for meeting people's transportation needs. In the same way, the computer has become the main vehicle for dealing with increasing demands for information. The parallel of technologies is straightforward. Just as people have recognized the necessity of learning to drive a car, so also are they in the process of learning to become comfortable with computers and their use.

Your dependence on computers and information systems is established so firmly that you may be unaware of all the ways in which you use computers.

Consider an everyday experience: You pick up a phone and punch some buttons. You hear tones, then a buzzing sound, and the party you are calling answers. You take this for granted. To realize this convenience, however, you have entered instructions into a massive set of linked computers that connect your telephone to millions of other instruments around the world.

The touch-tone phone you take for granted has, in actuality, solved the latest in a long succession of problems associated with growing telecommunication demands. Initially, telephone connections were made manually, at switchboards. Had this practice continued, it was estimated that more than half of all high school graduates would have had to become telephone operators. The dial telephone proved an interim solution by enabling subscribers to make connections directly. Eventually, mechanical switching devices couldn't keep up and telephone switching was computerized. Thus, when you dial a number today, you are operating a computer. The computers that support today's massive, computerized telecommunications system can identify and connect two telephones out of more than 100 million installed throughout the country. If you had wished, you could have dialed any of tens of millions of other phones throughout the world.

As you talk, this network of computers stands by, keeping track of the time you are connected. When you hang up, the computer notes the time and the point-to-point information on the call. Other computers follow up at the end of the month and send you a bill for these services. Or, if you wish, the telephone company's computer can be authorized to withdraw money from your bank account to pay its bill.

This everyday experience makes a point: *The time has come when you and the great majority of people are information-dependent.*

## Information as a Need: Lessons From History

Information systems have been needed for centuries. The size of modern volumes of information made the difference that called for development and use of computers as information tools. Just as cars needed roads to make them useful, information systems ultimately needed the capacity that computers could deliver.

The growing emphasis on and need for information has evolved throughout the history of the United States. Volumes of information and problem solving needs were modified at each major period in the development of the country. As the country became more populous and life became more complex, the nature of information needs changed. In general, the scope of the problem has tended to dictate the scope of the solution. This principle can be traced through the historic periods tracked in the account that follows.

## Agricultural-Crafts Period

During the early days of the United States—from the Colonial period through the mid-1800s—information dependence was minimal. The main business was agriculture. Some 90 percent of the working population were farmers, simply because it took this many people to meet basic requirements for food. As businesses, the early farms tended to be small, chiefly because an individual farmer couldn't till and work much land with a horse or mule and a single-blade plow.

## The Industrial Age

With a growth in scale in farming, manufacturing, and commerce, the demand for information grew. Large companies employed workers in factories and trading or banking organizations. Materials were traded in quantities by mid-dlemen, people who bought and sold products. The sellers, in turn, built organizations that were based upon providing information—information on availabilities, prices, and deliveries of needed goods. Transaction volumes multiplied to a level at which simple record keeping was no longer adequate. In this sense, a *transaction* is a basic act of doing business, the exchange of goods or services for a value such as money. Transactions are the main source for information on which decisions are based and plans are formed.

Technology gave machinery to factories. Technology also addressed itself to the development of information about businesses. Information processing

Computers were developed to answer a need for increased information processing capabilities. Early computers like this one occupied entire rooms but provided less capacity than today's desktop microcomputers.

machines began to appear in parallel with the industrial development of the country. On the industrial side, the steam engine, the railroads, and automatic weaving equipment meant growth. On the information side, inventions like the adding machine, the cash register, the typewriter, and the calculator provided the capacity to keep up with the growth in information volumes resulting from increases in numbers of business transactions.

The industrial period of growth started in the mid-1800s and continued through to the mid-1900s. Changes were dramatic. By the twentieth century, the United States was the technology capital of the world. American factories experienced worldwide demands for automobiles and machinery. Manufacturing plants became the main provider of jobs for a growing population. Technology became a guiding force in the lives of most of the country's population. As manufacturing and transportation systems grew to dominance, information needs expanded as well. Eventually, technology was needed to solve problems of people who were swamped in efforts to keep up with paperwork and information demands.

## The Information Explosion

With industrial growth, organizations grew larger. So did the need for information to keep up with growing organizations and mountains of paperwork generated by multiplying volumes of business transactions. Growing companies devised assembly lines for paperwork to match the assembly lines that manufactured products. Major companies created separate accounting departments to collect and handle business operations. Accounting departments grew to levels at which problems of scale began to set in. The amount of information to be recorded and handled became too great for the pen-and-ink methods of existing information systems.

### ■ The 1890 Census.

A major breakthrough in information processing came with the growing job of counting and analyzing the country's population. By law, the United States Bureau of Census is required to count and report on the makeup of the population every 10 years. This got to be a massive job. In 1880, the population of the United States reached 40 million. The census reports for 1880 took seven and one-half years to compile. As 1890 approached, the census takers were looking at a population of 50 million. Using 1880 methods, 1900 would have arrived before the results of the 1890 census were complete.

This sequence of events demonstrates a basic trait of information processing: Progress follows recognition of a need. The demands of people stimulate application of technology. Change takes place as a way of dealing with the problem. In the instances of the U. S. Census, the solution came with the hiring of a young scientist to deal with the recognized problems. Dr. Herman Hollerith, a Census Bureau employee, devised a series of machines to solve the problem.

Hollerith viewed the census problem as resulting from the need to enter and reenter the same numbers repeatedly. Each time a new report was needed, it was necessary to search through the collected figures and create entirely new records. Hollerith reasoned that machines could be developed to capture information once. This information could be reused many times without requiring rerecording. Hollerith's invention was a series of machines that could enter data into cards. The cards then could be sorted and tallied by other machines. With these machines, the results of the 1890 census were ready by mid-1892. Twenty-five percent more information had been processed in one-third the time. Hollerith had devised a solution to match the size of the problem.

**The Payroll Work Load.**    Starting January 1, 1936, the great majority of workers were taxed for contributions to a Social Security system that would pay benefits when they retired from jobs at age 65. The concept of Social Security attacked the problem of survival for the elderly. But these benefits had a price. One of the costs came in the form of a new information explosion.

Under Social Security laws, employers had to calculate percentages of earnings that were withheld from workers' pay. This money, along with percentage contributions from employers, had to be paid periodically to the federal government. Large companies could not handle the extra volumes of payroll

The 1890 census provided the impetus for mechanization of information processing. Punched card accounting machines like the units at the right were developed by Dr. Herman Hollerith (above).

processing work with existing methods. Again, punched-card techniques provided a scale of solution to match the scope of the problem. Use of punched-card accounting machines grew explosively. The growth continued as the United States tooled up for World War II and created organizations of sheer size that had never before existed in all of human history. During World War II, some 10 million men and women were processed through the armed forces. Without mechanized information handling equipment, the work load would have been impossible to handle.

After the war, demands for information continued to expand as companies leaped at opportunities to produce goods that had been unavailable during the war. Demands for capabilities to handle more information continued to build. Society and its organizations—at least in an informational sense—were waiting for the computer to be invented and put to use.

## Today's Information Society

The information explosion, like earlier problems resulting from growth, called for technological solutions. This is where computers came in. Computers do the same things that people used to do with pencils, or that electrical machines used to do on a motorized basis. An important difference is that computers do the same things many thousands of times faster. Speed and the ability to handle volumes of information represent just one of the major benefits of computers. In addition, computers deliver accuracy and reliability because they check their own work, both electronically and under control of instructions created by people. Also, computers enable users to store and retrieve desired items from vast collections of information.

These capabilities became necessities as the scale of transactions among people and organizations multiplied. Consider these examples:

- People and companies now write more than 40 billion checks annually. This much paper could not have been shuffled—and the information contained in the checks could not have been handled—without the electronic capabilities of computers.
- During the 1950s, the New York Stock Exchange used to experience buy-and-sell volumes of perhaps 20 to 30 million shares daily. Today, volumes regularly exceed 200 million shares a day. This level of business could not have been handled without computers.
- During the 1950s, major food chains used to realize sales of perhaps $25,000 to $30,000 per week through each checkstand. Today, volumes in stores with computerized registers are 200 to 300 percent greater. If automation had not come to supermarkets, the food you eat would be a lot more costly.

These are just a few examples of scale. Today's large volumes of business transactions require high-speed capabilities for solutions. However, where computers are concerned, this is only the beginning of the story of the real values

Computers have become standard tools in the modern workplace. Examples of present-day applications include securities trading (near right) and the reading of package labels at supermarket checkout counters (far right).

that have been realized. To be used as tools, information results generated by computers also have to be accurate, reliable, and available on a timely basis. These are the needs that have challenged technology throughout human development, from agricultural societies, to an industrial environment, and into a world dominated by needs for information.

## Information as a Resource

As information demands have increased, people have acquired new tools of information technology—computers and sets of directions for their use. The new techologies of the information age, in turn, have led to creation of new kinds of jobs and opportunities.

### The Computer: An Information Tool

In business organizations, most information sources stem from transactions. This is basic. A business is an organization established to conduct transactions, or do business, with specific people or markets. Information on transactions causes changes in the state, or status, of a business. For example, you buy a compact disc in a music store. The store now has your money and you have a disc to enjoy. An exchange of value has taken place. But, for the business, the value of the information generated by the transaction has just begun.

When information on your purchase is combined by computers with information on thousands or millions of other transactions, the results become tools for running the business. Computers combine transaction information to describe what items customers want to buy. Store managers are faced with the problem of determining what customers want and meeting those demands. Information tools monitor buying trends and guide managers toward decisions about how to run the business. Managers use computer-generated information to decide what goods to buy or which services to offer. At higher levels, executives use computer-generated information to decide where to open stores, whether to close existing stores, and how many people to hire.

Through computer processing, raw facts about transactions, known as *data items,* are combined. Processed data items become information. Information, in turn, is a tool that has become vital to decision making and planning for the continuing development of individual businesses, of governmental agencies, and for society as a whole.

As the number of computers in use have soared into the millions, it has become apparent that major values and payoffs are derived from the ability to accumulate data and generate information that can be analyzed and used as a basis for decisions. In the modern view, a manager's job is to evaluate information and make decisions about operations and plans. Computers are tools that accumulate more information than people can deal with in their heads. Success requires information. Accurate and reliable information has to be available when and where it is needed.

This book assumes that you are just getting started, that you are being introduced to the concepts and realities of information as a resource and to the computer as a means of generating information. Whatever career decision you make, a basic knowledge about information systems and the capabilities of computers will be valuable to you as an active and responsible participant in an information society.

## Applying Information to Solve Problems

Think of what happens when you buy a hamburger at a fast-food outlet. This market is dominated by large national chains supplied and managed through regional and/or central offices. Think about what happens: You buy a hamburger and other items, possibly french fries and a soft drink. In the process you establish a need for the fast-food chain. The purchases you make use supplies that have to be replaced. Replenishment of supplies to possibly 2,000 outlets is a major undertaking. If too much meat and too many buns are shipped, the items can spoil or become stale. If replenishment supplies are too low, business will be lost because local outlets are unable to fill orders.

Under computerized techniques, you, in effect, order the replacement supplies for tomorrow's customers through your purchases. The cash registers at the counters of fast-food outlets actually are computer terminals. Each day, sales of every food item are tallied and reported to a supply center. Replenishment and service quality are assured.

## The Information Processing Cycle

The example above links thousands of sales points into a single, integrated computer information system. This demonstrates that a *computer* is a coordinated, connected set of devices that follow instructions supplied by people to process data and deliver information. Computers process data and produce information in a sequence that includes four basic steps:

- Input
- Processing
- Output
- Storage.

■ **Input.**   Methods are needed to capture information and present it to the computer for processing. A variety of equipment devices are used to accomplish input.

■ **Processing.**   This is the work of actual calculation and handling of data and text. Processing takes place within a single portion of an overall computer system—the *central processing unit (CPU)*. All processing occurs through a combination of on-off signals handled by electrical and electronic devices. The power of the computer lies in its ability to do simple tasks rapidly. Sequences of single tasks executed at rates of millions per second can accomplish the massive processing needed to develop and handle information.

■ **Output.**   To be useful, computers must be able to deliver the results of processing in forms that can be understood and used by people. The main outputs generated by computers are displays on screens or reports printed on paper.

■ **Storage.**   Computers need massive capabilities to store sets of instructions called *programs* for their own operation, and to accumulate information that supports operating and planning decisions. Storage devices are to information systems what bank vaults are to financial systems. These are the places where assets are kept and protected.

Everyone should be as familiar with the basic functions of computer systems as they are with the facts that automobiles need engines, transmissions, steering systems, and brakes. You will encounter the elements of input, process-

Computers process data and produce results by following a four-step cycle: input, processing, output, and storage. This diagram shows the relationships of the steps, with storage depicted as a processing resource while the other three steps occur in sequence.

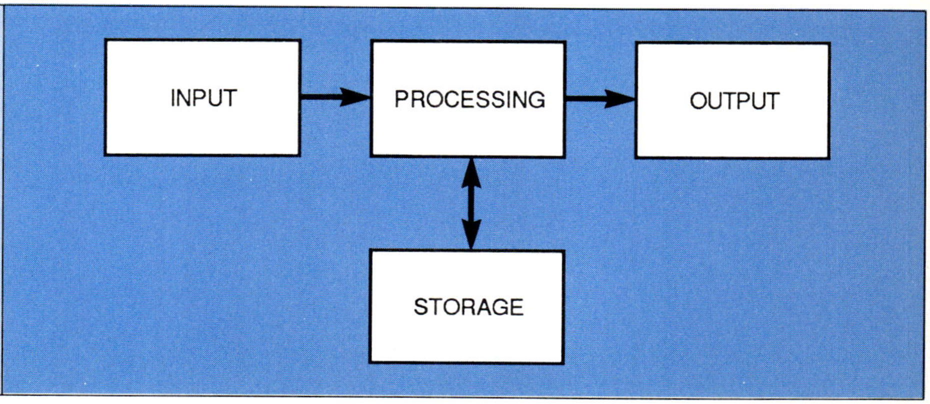

INPUT → PROCESSING → OUTPUT

PROCESSING ↕ STORAGE

ing, output, and storage in all computer applications with which you are associated. Additional information on this processing cycle is presented throughout this book.

## Users of Information

Computers are powerful and automatic tools. But computers are machines that meet needs defined and described by people. As machines, computers are no better or more valuable in meeting the needs of people than the accuracy, reliability, and timeliness of the information that is produced. In turn, the quality and quantity of information are no better than the knowledge and skills of the people who operate computers and use their information.

Use of information is the work and the concern of people. People are the key ingredient of information systems. Within the information system environment, you and other information users, as well as computer professionals, play a number of roles, including:

- End users
- Managers
- Computer professionals.

**End Users.**   These are people who require information, generally for problem solving and decision making in connection with jobs that are not directly involved in building or operating information systems. End users, however, are working at computer keyboards in increasing numbers to develop their own information resources or to tap into collections of information created by others. In an environment that rewards people who appreciate the value of information and know how to access and use it, a level of comfort with computers and the systems they implement can be a valuable competitive edge. A main purpose of this text is to lead you along the path to become such a sophisticated end user.

**Managers.**   *Managers* are information end users who plan, organize, and operate business enterprises. The responsibilities of these people center around identifying, defining, and solving problems, or making decisions that implement plans or achieve goals. To do their jobs, managers depend upon information as support and, therefore, they depend upon computerized information systems. For this reason, management expectations drive the development and operation of information systems.

**Computer Professionals.**   People who use information depend on *computer professionals*. These people develop systems, operate equipment, and deliver results in the form of computer outputs. Computer professionals are end users of computers and developers of information outputs, whose jobs center around a number of established specialties. *Systems analysts* determine user and management needs and interact with technicians to build systems. *Programmers* write the instructions that operate computers. *Operations personnel* actually run most large- and medium-sized computers.

People at all levels collaborate and cooperate to make information available. Information systems operated by professionals become delivery systems for essentials required by groups of users who include executives, managers, and the vast majority of workers who depend on information to be effective and efficient in their lives and on their jobs. If you become interested in a career that involves computing, this text will help orient you toward selection of a profession to pursue.

## Information as an Opportunity

This chapter establishes that the need for and reliance upon information is universal. This message has a personal dimension: Information is power! You rely on information and will increase this reliance as you pursue future goals. This is the time to build an understanding of the reliance that is both an inevitability and an opportunity. That is, you know you will need to understand information processing and information values. The opportunity lies in the constructive thought and serious effort you apply as an information and/or computer user. Information is a competitive tool. You are a competitor and probably will become more involved in competitive situations in the future. Skill in identifying and meeting information needs can make a direct contribution to your success.

**Impact**

## Can the Real World be Placed in Your Computer?

Can your computer help to solve practical, everyday problems? Can the real world be placed in a computer? Stated another way: Can the computer simulate, or imitate, realities as you define them?

When the question is rephrased in this way, the answer is *yes*. As long as you can define what reality means to you through information a computer can process, the computer can reflect your image of reality.

Consider a typical business example. Using a quantitative (numeric) representation of operating conditions that reflect customer service demands, a bank could determine the number of automatic teller machines to install. First, the bank would have to decide on how long a customer would be willing to wait in line. Other decisions would center on how many customers would use the automatic tellers, and other details. These decisions would be represented numerically to simulate operating conditions for ATM services. From results of computer processing, the bank could determine the number of ATM units that should be installed.

Through use of information under techniques of this type, a computer can help to simulate the real world, and to determine the most efficient ways to operate in the real world.

## Chapter Summary

- Computers exist to provide information required by end users. Two types of information users include those who require and receive information outputs and those who actually interact with computers. Both groups of users apply information to meet needs and/or to solve problems.

- People have needed information throughout history. Information needs have expanded dramatically as people advanced through a series of historic periods—from agrarian, to industrial, to information societies. The modern era has been marked by a continuing information explosion.

- A major breakthrough in the mechanization of information processing occurred when Dr. Herman Hollerith developed punched-card data processing capabilities to handle the figurework associated with the 1890 census.

- Another key event in the information explosion that built demand for computing power occurred with implementation of the Social Security Act at the beginning of 1936. Payroll computations became many times more complex than under previous requirements, creating demands for mechanization of information processing and multiplying demand for punched-card equipment. This demand continued to multiply during World War II.

- All information processing follows a standard process, or series of steps. These steps are input, processing, output, and storage.

- The time has come when everyone must acquire some level of knowledge about computers and their use. Levels of need vary according to the type of job performed by each individual. General categories of computer-knowledgeable people include information end users, managers who commit resources to the building of information system capabilities, and computer professionals who develop and operate information systems.

## Questions for Review

1. Identify two types of information users and describe the similarities and differences between them.

2. How is information used to solve problems and reach decisions?

3. How do the growth and development of the computer industry parallel the growth and development in the automotive field?

4. Describe the contribution of Dr. Herman Hollerith to the field of information processing.

5. What problems associated with payroll processing led to growth in acceptance of mechanized information processing?

6. What is a business transaction and what is its role in the generation of information?

7. What are the basic steps of the information processing cycle?

8. How do the steps in the information processing cycle interact to deliver information for users?

9. Why and how do managers of business organizations and computer professionals qualify as information end users?

10. Describe the roles of information as both a necessity and an opportunity.

## Questions for Thought

1. This chapter makes the point that, as a student, you already are an information user. Think about your situation and describe the major ways in which you use and apply information in your life. Can you think of ways in which a computer might help you as an information user? Describe.

2. As an information user, you perform the functions of input, processing, output, and storage. Think of a typical experience, such as a class lecture and a quiz during the semester. How do you perform the functions of the information processing cycle to succeed as a student?

3. Do you drive a car? What would your life be like if you did not have personal transportation available? Now think about your objectives as a student and worker. Compare the ability to interact with computers with the ability to drive a car. Describe similarities and differences.

4. Define an information society and explain your present role within an information society.

5. When you make a purchase in a retail store, how do you think the information generated might help management of the store to operate the business?

## Terms

| | |
|---|---|
| central processing unit (CPU) | operations personnel |
| computer | program |
| computer professional | programmer |
| data item | systems analyst |
| end user | transaction |
| manager | user |

# MINICASE

**Situation:**

The company is hypothetic. But the experience is real and has been shared by scores, perhaps hundreds, of organizations across the country. Call the organization the Composite Manufacturing Company. The family-owned company used to employ more than 100 persons in a small town in western Pennsylvania. The company made work clothes. Its products were established. There was a loyal organization of dealers in place who ordered the company products regularly.

Tim Duster was president. He was fond of saying that he had inherited a solid business as the third generation in his family to run the company. "We are in a region of working people, all of whom wear clothes every day," Tim would say. 'Our position is solid."

Tim also was happy with the semirural setting in which Composite had its plant. The factory was right alongside a small river. Tim's grandfather had chosen the location for the convenience of using water power to weave cloth and conduct other manufacturing operations. After electricity came to the area, the family added landscaping to give the location a rustic feeling.

One day nature took over. The river misbehaved. The Composite Manufacturing computer room and all its business documents were wiped out by rains and a flood of historic proportions for that region. Tim and the other managers checked the manufacturing equipment first and were relieved to find that damage and loss were minimal.

"I thought we could get back into production in a few days," Tim recalled. "We thought it would be routine to restart computer operations. We went to the file cabinets where we had kept our computer storage units and our records. That's when we realized the mistake of putting our information center in a part of the plant overlooking the river.

"Our records were gone. Before it rained, we had reviewed figures that said our customers owed us more than $1 million. Without our records, virtually all of this money was uncollectable. Also, we had an order backlog of close to $3 million. That was gone too. Payroll records we needed for government reporting—they also were down the river somewhere. My family wound up having to close the business."

**Decision Making: Your Turn**

1. From the information you have and from Tim's viewpoint, identify and describe the problem to be solved.

2. Identify alternatives that could be followed to avoid or solve the problem.

3. On the basis of the limited information you have: a) Identify additional information you would gather if you were dealing with this problem in a real situation. b) Identify the solution that appears best on the basis of the information that is available and explain your reasons for this selection.

4. What lessons are to be learned from this situation?

# Projects

1. Obtain copies of at least two of the following magazines: *Time, Newsweek, Business Week, U. S. News and World Report, Byte, PCWeek* or other, similar publications. Look for articles on the new breed of sophisticated end user of information and computers.

2. Interview at least two computer professionals: one who is involved with operation of a large computer system, and another who uses a microcomputer regularly. Find out what jobs are done on their computers. Find out how much each individual has had to learn about computer hardware and software. Discuss the relationships between computer professionals and information users. Prepare a report on your findings.

3. Interview relatives, friends, and acquaintances who use computers or computer-generated information in their jobs. Ask what their jobs would be like, or whether their jobs would exist at all, if computers were not available.

# Chapter Outline

## CHAPTER 2

# Computers in Organizations

## Briefing Memo

TO:      Information Users
FROM:   T. Rohm, W. Stewart

Information serves users. The main users of information, in turn, are people who work for organizations. For information systems to be effective, therefore, they must fit into and support organizations of people whose efforts must be coordinated.

This chapter discusses the interrelationships and interactions between computers and organizations. Presentations also cover the relevance of information for decision making that affects the operations and plans for business organizations. The decision-making approach presented in this chapter also is appropriate for your current situation and future career challenges.

## End-User Perspective

As she had been instructed, Samantha stopped at the information desk in the main lobby. It was her first day of work, on her first part-time job. "I'm a bundle of excitement and nervousness," she had told her roommate as she left home. But she felt good about her prospects at Global Enterprises. Her plan was to complete her degree in Computer Information Systems during the coming school year, paying her way from earnings at Global. Samantha had been encouraged about the prospects of full-time work in the Global's Information Systems department following graduation.

At the information desk, Samantha told the receptionist that she was reporting for work. The receptionist checked a list in front of him, picked up a telephone, dialed, and spoke briefly. Then he asked Samantha to wait just a moment.

A young woman appeared through a door at the back of the lobby, asked Samantha's name, then asked for a driver's license to confirm her identity. After that, Samantha was taken to a small room off the lobby and seated in front of a Polaroid camera.

"This will take just a minute," explained the young woman, who introduced herself as Jan. "You'll need a badge to get around the building and to let yourself into your work area." As she assembled the badge, Jan showed Samantha how her badge had been prepared to include access codes. A photograph was needed for identification.

Jan demonstrated how the badge was to be inserted into slots alongside doors throughout the Global building complex. One of the access-code imprints would get Samantha through the front door in the lobby or through an entrance from the employee's parking lot. Another permitted access to the Information Systems department, where Samantha would work.

Jan explained that, each time the badge was used, one of Global's computers checked the access code to be sure Samantha was authorized to enter. Also, each time the badge was used, the time and location were entered into a computer log.

"I came to work with computers," Samantha noted. "Now I've encountered them right at the front door."

 ## The Point: Successful Organizations Need Computers

From her first day on the job, Samantha experienced the impact of computers in organizations. She was hired as a computer professional; she was to write programs to implement business applications. However, as she learned quickly, her own actions within the organization were to be supported, directed, and sometimes controlled by computers.

Security in the workplace is promoted through computer-operated devices like this electronic combination lock that restricts access to a parking lot. The combinations that permit entry are given only to authorized persons. A computer validates each entry before the barrier is opened.

Many organizations, small as well as large, are capitalizing on the power, accuracy, and speed of computers to process avalanches of information. It is true that information is a necessity. Unfortunately, information presently is being generated at rates beyond the capabilities of manual processing. Volumes and complexities of data can create problems. For problems involving the need for and production of information, computers provide the primary solutions for most business organizations.

Much of the rest of this chapter, and of the entire book, is devoted to describing the role that information systems play in supporting the organizations in which they are used. The organizations themselves are systems of people, equipment, procedures, data, and other resources. Organizational systems need information systems for current operations and future planning.

# ■   The Nature and Value of Systems

Information is a tool for users who are part of people-oriented systems called *organizations*. An organization, as a system, is a structure established to produce specific results from application of resources. For an organization, the resources include personnel, materials, equipment, money, and information. Through management of these resources, an organization seeks to serve an identified market or group of customers by delivering specific products or services.

A business organization typically is a system that is made up of smaller, contributory systems, called *subsystems*, each with a purpose. Typical functions performed by organizational subsystems include finance, manufacturing, distribution, information resources, and personnel. Systems and their subsystems are related closely and are dependent upon one another. If the linkage among subsystems is disturbed, or if a subsystems fails, the entire system is in danger of failing. In fact, the combination of subsystems is the system.

For each business system, a set of procedures is applied to manage resources and produce targeted results. The steps in implementation of a system for running a business include planning, organization, coordination, and control. The sequencing and relationships among these functions are as follows:

- Each business requires a plan that identifies markets and products and sets goals to be achieved.
- On the basis of organizational objectives, managers establish an organization structure that integrates the efforts of people, procedures, data, and equipment to achieve the identified objectives.

Computers play key roles in business organizations. At the left, a computer-generated display provides visual interest at a conference. At the right is an executive work station at which hands-on use of a computer provides direct access to information resources.

- The resources of each organization must be deployed and coordinated to assure efficiency and effectiveness of operations.
- The organization implements an operational system through a series of controls that involve processing of information and initiating action on the basis of that information.

As indicated, information is an essential of an organizational system. Information has been called the glue that binds and holds a business organization together. People communicate and coordinate their activities on the basis of the information sources on which they rely. The structure of subsystems needed to produce and deliver information, described below, is essentially the same as those for organizational systems.

## Information Systems

All systems that produce information, regardless of whether computers are involved, share certain common features:

- Each system should support a specific organization function and/or group of users.
- Each system is made up of a series of interrelated subsystems.
- Each system is carried out in a series of steps that involve input, processing, output, and storage.

An information system is an organized set of people, equipment, procedures, and data. Information systems are designed by people to produce usable information that meets established needs on reliable schedules. Information systems can exist with or without computers, but almost all businesses use computers as essential information processing tools.

## Computer Information Systems

In the information processing area, a number of subsystems exist that reflect the role of computers as information processing tools.

**What is a Computer?**    A *computer* is a collection of equipment devices connected to one another for coordinated use in supporting information processing. However, a computer by itself cannot process or deliver information. A computer is a collection of inanimate equipment.

## What is a Computer System?

A *computer system* includes computer equipment, plus sets of instructions, called *programs*, that enable a computer to perform and complete processing jobs to deliver information needed by people. A computer system includes programs and equipment. But a key ingredient for information development and delivery still is missing.

## What is a Computer Information System?

A *computer information system* includes the people, procedures (including programs), data, and equipment needed to accept data as input and to deliver information required by users. In this context, procedures include both instructions for human users and operators and also programs that instruct the computer equipment.

The subsystems of computer information systems, and also of organizational systems are described below.

**People.**  Computer information systems are designed by people, are operated by people, and exist for the benefit of people. Through the years, the growing need for information has led to demands that have been met through use of technology. The basis for the very existence of information systems, then, is the needs and goals of people. These needs have been met by people, computer professionals, who have developed the equipment and procedures. Other people, managers, have invested the money needed to develop systems that make needed information available for other people, information users.

Computer information systems encompass capabilities that range from microcomputer work stations for individual employees to massive computer complexes that consolidate information for entire organizations.

This flowchart diagrams what happens in a computer information system. Source data result from manual procedures. The data are entered into a computer, which draws on stored programs and data, and produces documents and/or displays as outputs. The outputs from computer processing then support activities and decisions by users.

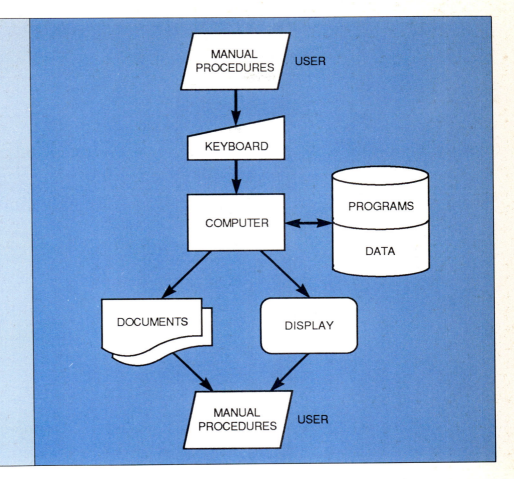

■ **Equipment.** Computers are part of the equipment used to process data and develop information. Other kinds of equipment also support information systems. Information tools range from the humble lead pencil to sophisticated office copiers, telephones, typewriters, file cabinets, and any other devices capable of performing input, processing, output, or storage. Computers, however, play special roles because of their power to execute complete processing sequences and to deliver information that is accurate, reliable, and timely. All units of computer equipment, collectively, are known as *hardware*.

■ **Procedures.** Procedures encompass both the programs for operating the computer and the directions followed by people who operate and use computer information systems. Some of the procedures for information processing are stored within a computer. These sets of instructions, called programs, direct operation of equipment. All of the programs that implement computer infor-

The elements of a computer information system are identified in this illustration, which also covers the relationships among those elements. People interact with procedures and data. Data and procedures, in turn, interact with one another and with equipment.

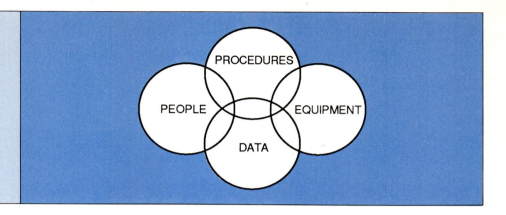

mation systems are known, collectively or individually, as *software*. Other procedures cover human functions required to enter data into a computer, set up computers for processing, handle outputs generated by computers, and protect data and hardware.

■ **Data.**   Within a computer information system, data are the raw materials that are processed. Every productive system needs some sort of raw material. To make automobiles, the raw materials include steel, plastics, rubber, and upholstery materials. To produce information, raw facts and figures are needed. These are the data processed to generate information. To illustrate, data items such as 5′ 1′′ tall, 108 lb., blue eyes, blond hair, born 10/29/70 might be data items that add up to Sally Jones. Additional data items that identify street address, city, state, and ZIP code would add to the information that identifies Sally.

## Computer Information System: An Example

Coordination of the components of a computer information system identified above is the essential key that makes it possible to process data and produce information. In other words, a computer information system illustrates the principle that the whole must produce a result with greater value than the sum of the parts. The parts of a computer information system, in themselves, have no value. Combined, they can deliver the power of accurate, reliable, timely information.

To illustrate, consider the functioning of a computer information system for which you may be an active user. If you have a bank account, you also may have a card that entitles you to withdraw or deposit money at computer terminals called automatic teller machines (ATMs).

The *people* associated with this system include bank customers like you, bank managers who decide where to put the machines and what services they should provide, and computer professionals who program and support ATM services.

*Equipment* in this situation is extensive and complex. Included are the actual work stations that customers use, communication lines that tie the terminals to large computers, the computers themselves, the devices that store customer account information, and the printers that generate reports on account status.

*Procedures* range from instructions on putting money into and taking deposits out of ATMs to operation of central computers that maintain customer records. Procedures also include programs that control operation of ATM units, communication links, and central computers.

*Data* items include all entries by terminal users, as well as content of customer files. Other data are developed for operational use. For example, each ATM produces data on how much money it has available. This data item is set when money is placed into the dispenser. Then the figure is adjusted when customers withdraw money.

## Computers: Enhancing Productivity in Organizations

As tools, computers make it possible for people at all levels of organizations, from top-level executives to individual employees in offices and factories, to be more efficient and effective.

### Computers: Increasing Efficiency

Today's giant national and international enterprises could not function without the speed and productive capacity of computers. Banks could not process all the checks their customers write. Airlines could not process all the reservations and fill all the seats on their planes. A single retail chain could not have developed capabilities to handle sales volumes in excess of $30 billion annually. Penal institutions could not keep track of more than a quarter of a million prisoners.

Even for smaller businesses, computers can contribute to increased efficiency. Many small businesses have found it profitable to employ desk-top computers, or *microcomputers*, to relieve overburdened employees. As an example, consider a videocassette rental store. A microcomputer is an ideal tool for setting up customer accounts, checking to be sure that cassettes are returned by customers, keeping track of customer deposits, and other tasks. Handling this work with pencil and paper could produce burdens that could lead to mistakes or could reduce the quality of service.

All of these applications share common denominators of size and volume. Business managers were faced with a paperwork avalanche in the 1950s and 1960s. Computers were the devices that enabled people to cut the mountains of paperwork to manageable size, to increase productivity.

Computers now are used to help operate factories that build computers. In production situations, computers contribute to efficiency and effectiveness of their organizations.

## Computers: Increasing Effectiveness

Volume of work is only one of the reasons for using computers in business. Another is the ability to grasp and deal with business complexities that were not even imagined a few decades ago. Business organizations have expanded into new ventures and into new geographic regions. Computers have supported the ability to make decisions more effectively.

Computers supply the power to deal with volumes of data and to deliver information relevant to the decisions being made. With computer-generated information, managers can make knowledgeable decisions and act more quickly—with a greater level of confidence. This means that managers have an opportunity to be more effective in the jobs of guiding and planning.

Considering the responsibilities carried by top managers, productivity increases at this level are high-yield benefits because these decisions impact entire organizations. To illustrate, think of the implications of decisions made by the manager of a national retail chain. Management of the organization may decide to build and operate stores in a region in which the chain has not previously done business. A decision of this type leads to the purchase of hundreds of millions of dollars worth of merchandise, tens of millions of dollars in purchases or construction of buildings, and creation of thousands of new jobs. If the decision is wrong, the money is wasted and the jobs disappear. If the decision works, the organization and the economy of the region grow. The soundness of the decision becomes greater and the confidence of the decision maker is increased if the information used is accurate and reliable. When computers promote this kind of business productivity, everyone benefits.

The same types of benefits can be realized, proportionately, by smaller businesses that use microcomputers. A good example can be seen in the use of microcomputers to manage local insurance agencies. Devising insurance coverage and calculating rates for policies is a complex business. Local agents used to provide interim coverage to clients while actual computation associated with the issuing of policies took place on large computers in home offices. Today, thousands of local agents who use microcomputers serve clients directly.

## Standard Applications in Business

When computers first were introduced, each system had to be programmed individually, from scratch. The work was slow and expensive. Not many companies could afford computers because of the time and expense required to create systems. Gradually, suppliers of computers with an interest in expanding their markets found ways to convert general-purpose computers into specialized business tools. The need was met through the discovery that large

Common information processing needs of many business organizations are being solved by standard application packages. These standard programs and operating instructions make it relatively easy to create information systems to support needs of individual organizations.

numbers of businesses share the same kinds of information needs. That is, most business organizations use computers for similar jobs, or *applications*. Accordingly, suppliers of computers began to ''package'' hardware and software to perform these common, or standard, jobs.

These applications are related to the running of virtually all businesses. With standard applications, general-purpose computers have become affordable for most business organizations. By enabling businesses to increase efficiency and effectiveness, computers make people more productive and businesses more profitable.

## The Decision Maker and the Decision-Making Approach

Within business organizations, computers are tools that help meet two major needs of people. First, information users must deal with and manage large volumes of data to produce meaningful information. The other need is analysis. People must be able to access information to build an understanding of

Impact

## The Microcomputer as a Tool

The microcomputer, supported by inexpensive software, has become a major business tool. Since its introduction in the late 1970s, the popularity of the microcomputer has continued to grow.

At first, the microcomputer was looked upon as a novelty intended for home use by hobbyists. The advent of affordable, ''user friendly'' business software provided one stimulus for rapid growth. Another occurred with IBM's entry into the market in 1981 with its Personal Computer (PC). The IBM designs provided standards around which manufacturers could unite, and for which software houses could develop an endless stream of products. Shortly after IBM's entry into the field, microcomputer deliveries spurted to a high point estimated at more than 1 million per month. By 1988, it was estimated that more than 20 million microcomputers were in use in business, with 4 million

more being delivered each year.

The rapid spread of microcomputers throughout organizations has caused concern and alarm in some quarters. Computers once were under the control of computer professionals in data processing centers. The microcomputer fell outside the jurisdiction of most data processing centers. As the number of microcomputers increased and software became more ''user friendly,'' users and managers began to use this new tool. Soon, these individuals discovered that the power of a computer on a desk top would allow them to do things faster, more reliably, and with greater flexibility and accuracy than through the use of central facilities.

The word was out and the microcomputer became the business tool of the twentieth century. The microcomputer is the main force behind the continuing information revolution.

what is happening within the organization and its environment to support effective decision making by managers.

Computers process information, but they don't make decisions. People do. People use the information generated by computers, but people ultimately make the decisions. And, because decisions can have large price tags and consequences, people need a systematic approach to guide their decision-making efforts. This decision-making approach is implemented through a series of orderly steps, identified and discussed below.

- Step 1: Identify and define the problem or need.
- Step 2: Gather information and evaluate alternatives.
- Step 3: Select the best course of action.
- Step 4: Implement the decision and evaluate results.

## Step 1: Identify and Define the Problem or Need

Major decisions can involve multiple sources of information and many opinions can be involved. People who participate in a decision-making process will tend to offer suggestions or solutions on the basis of their own experiences.

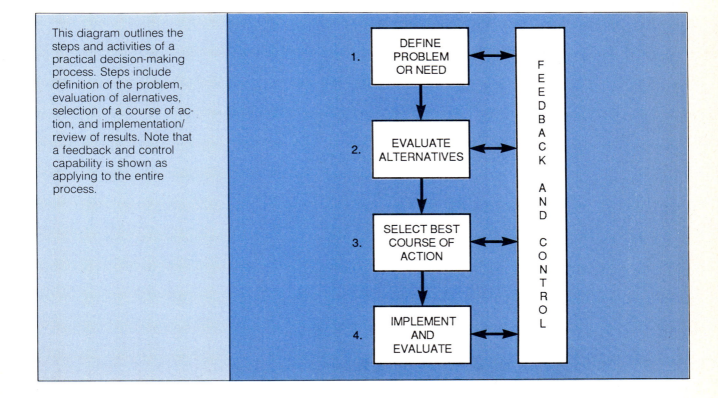

This diagram outlines the steps and activities of a practical decision-making process. Steps include definition of the problem, evaluation of alernatives, selection of a course of action, and implementation/ review of results. Note that a feedback and control capability is shown as applying to the entire process.

That is, people who have past experiences in specific situations tend to want to apply the solutions evolved elsewhere to any current dilemma they encounter.

To establish coordination for the efforts of participants, it is generally best to start each decision-making effort with a clear statement of the problem to be solved and the need to be met through the targeted results. Activities that follow to reach the decision should focus upon the problem. But efforts of decision makers should be goal oriented and should reflect the limitations on resources that may be available.

■  **Case Example.**   To demonstrate how this systematic approach works, consider an example based upon a real business situation. Electronics, Inc., is a major manufacturer and distributor of microchips, switches, circuit boards, and a wide range of electronics parts and subsystems. For years, distribution has been through a series of regional warehouses located at six dispersed points around the country. Company headquarters is near Boston.

Information generated by the company's computers indicates that about half the warehouses are not cost-effective. That is, the profits on the parts they ship do not always cover operating costs. Management has been aware for some time that some of the warehouses are not profitable, but has elected to keep all of the warehouses open in the belief that they are necessary as a basis for customer service, particularly in support of government programs.

The distribution manager, Juan Mirro, has received a proposal that could change this outlook. He goes to top management with a proposal from an air freight company recommending that distribution be consolidated at the home office and that shipments of all orders be done by overnight air express. The argument is that customers will still get next-day service. Orders could be handled by providing customer access through 800 numbers. Shipments could be expedited out of the central location, which would be stocked completely with all of the company's parts. Major customers and company sales representatives could have direct access to the company's computer system for immediate confirmations of orders.

Management decides this opportunity is worth exploring. A team is assembled and a problem statement is prepared:

> Determine whether it is necessary to continue to operate some distribution facilities at a loss to maintain customer service or whether another approach can stem losses and improve efficiency.

## Step 2: Gather Information and Evaluate Alternatives

With a problem defined, decision makers should be encouraged to consider as many solutions as possible. This is among the most creative opportunities open to businesspeople. Markets and companies can be shaped and reshaped through application of imagination to produce new and innovative solutions to existing problems.

Within a problem-solving context, alternatives are potential solutions to be evaluated. Alternatives come from the consideration of information available within the organization and additional facts gathered from external sources. In dealing with a major problem, decision makers might look at market and economic trend figures from government sources, note strategies of competitors, check with suppliers for suggestions, and try to think up new approaches from scratch.

For each alternative considered, consequences should be evaluated. Some projections of consequences will predict favorable results, such as better customer service or reduction of expenses. For the same alternative, there also may be adverse consequences. An approach that saves money for the company may offend and cause loss of customers. Care should be taken to project both positive and negative results of each alternative, then to weigh the advantages against the disadvantages.

■ **Case Example.**  In the situation at Electronics, Inc., managers would get operating figures on existing warehouses. They would talk to distribution personnel to identify existing problems and methods for their handling. For example, what do local warehouses do when they are out of stock of an ordered item? Costs of shipping stocks to separate warehouses would be accumulated and compared with the expense of shipping all orders individually from the home office.

Assume that the studies show that costs of air shipment at volume discounts would represent savings of more than $10 million annually.

This is a favorable consequence. Potential unfavorable consequences also appear. One is that air shipments may be impossible during bad weather, leading to delays in deliveries and possible customer irritation. Another potential adverse consequence is that direct contact between customers and company personnel at local service points would be lost. Customers are concerned that strangers who serve them from the home office will not be familiar with their individual needs. There also are operational considerations. The central warehouse now ships in bulk to satellite distribution points. Entirely new systems will have to be developed to support the addressing, packing, and shipping of individual orders from the home office. There also is a question of whether it would be best to consign all air shipments to a single freight service or to seek a number of shippers. This is not a complete list of benefits and adverse consequences. But this description indicates the thought processes that are applied.

## Step 3: Select the Best Course of Action

It is time to make a choice, to select the alternative that will best solve the problem or meet the need—and to commit the resources necessary to implement that decision.

Decision makers must recognize that one commitment leads to others. There can be large-scale changes that lead to loss of jobs, to the hiring of new people, and to changes in the work routines of established employees. When

The combination of air freight shipment and computerized processing of orders and shipping documents makes it feasible for a large organization to consider centralizing its customer services. Without the capacity of computers, it has been standard practice to set up multiple warehouses at geographically dispersed locations.

management decides to adopt a course of action, extensive efforts may be necessary to plan for and introduce inevitable changes. This is one of the major challenges of operating managers. People tend to get used to things the way they are. Many people feel threatened by proposed changes that would affect them and resist or actively block the implementation of changes perceived as threats.

The challenge of change lies in involving and seeking participation of people who will be impacted. Management should have good reasons for major changes. Before changes are implemented, these reasons and the benefits expected should be shared with the people who will have to implement those changes. All affected personnel should be encouraged to make suggestions. Consensus is a vital element of smooth implementation of a decision.

**Case Example.**    For Electronics, Inc., the proposed change would require a major reshaping of the company. Management has been tempted with the prospect of saving more than $10 million. Other alternatives might be partial implementation of the plan, shutting down some satellite warehouses and retaining others, with each of the remaining facilities gaining volume and potential profitability.

The cost savings from centralization proved so great that the other alternatives were overpowered. However, the step-by-step approach had beneficial results in that management was alerted to a series of requirements associated with implementation of this alternative. Because they focused on negative consequences in reviewing the centralization alternative, managers were aware that it would be necessary to establish a major data communication network to support central distribution. This involved hiring and training people to handle high volumes of orders. Managers realized also that studies would be necessary to determine requirements for loading trucks and getting shipments to airports. Benefits were high, but problems were not eliminated by the decision commitment. Rather, when one decision has been made, other problems or needs that require further decisions often are uncovered.

**Step 4: Implement the Decision and Evaluate Results**

Implementation of major changes in information and organizational systems involves a wide range of complex factors. The implementation plan must, of course, be tailored to the specific changes to be undertaken. All involved parties, both within and outside of the company must be made aware that the change is coming and, in turn, should be accorded the courtesy of an explanation about what is going to happen. Affected individuals should be trained and prepared for the new policies and procedures they will be responsible for implementing. In addition, provisions must be made to monitor and, as necessary, react to problems, particularly unexpected problems, that result from change.

This last point is critical. Benefits are confirmed only after the chosen course of action has been implemented and the results have been reviewed and evaluated. The reason for a followup review also is significant: Managers should study results of their actions and should learn from the review process. A business is ongoing. Success in a competitive world requires continuing attention to forces for change and adjustment to problems or opportunities as they are presented.

The systematic approach to decision making described above is a general-purpose business tool that can be applied to a wide range of situations. The focus in this book is upon use of this approach for the development and effective use of information resources. As an information user, you will have many opportunities to think about information requirements and to use this technique to meet your needs.

## Chapter Summary

- Information systems are tools for organizations which, in themselves, are systems within which people establish goals, organize to achieve those goals, and apply monitoring and control techniques to evaluate results and make any necessary adjustments.
- Systems consist of interrelated subsystems coordinated to produce expected results. Each system is carried out in a series of steps that involve input, processing, output, and storage.
- An information system is an organized set of people, equipment, procedures, and data coordinated to deliver results required by users.

- A computer is a collection of equipment devices connected and coordinated to support information processing.
- A computer system includes processing equipment and programs that direct configuration and operation of the interconnected devices.
- A computer information system includes the people, procedures (including programs), data, and equipment needed to process data and deliver information.
- Computers help organizations to function more effectively and efficiently. Thus, computers contribute to organizational productivity.
- Decision making is implemented through a four-step approach: 1) Identify and define the problem or need. 2) Gather information and evaluate alternatives. 3) Select the best course of action. 4) Implement the decision and evaluate results.

## Questions for Review

1. What overall benefits do organizations expect to derive from use of computers?
2. In what ways does an organization qualify as a system?
3. What are the relationships among systems and subsystems?
4. Define an information system, then identify its parts and describe their functions.
5. What is a computer system? Of what does a computer system consist and what is its role?
6. What is a computer information system and what are its subsystems?
7. What are the differences and relationships between data and information?
8. What contributions do computer information systems make to the efficiency, effectiveness, and productivity of organizations?
9. Identify the steps in an organized decision-making approach and describe the way in which they build upon one another.
10. What are the special reasons for considering adverse consequences of alternatives for solving any given problem?

## Questions for Thought

1. Could a computer produce problems or negative results within a business organization? How?
2. Think of the United States government as an organizational system. What are its subsystems? What are the informational links between each subsystem and the overall system?

3. The decision-making process discussed in this chapter recommends consideration of multiple alternatives to meet each need or to solve each problem. Why are multiple alternatives recommended? How would results compare if only one alternative were considered?

4. This chapter identifies four elements for information systems. It is stated that people are the key to making an information system work. However, some people are afraid that computers are putting people down. What people can benefit from expanded use of computers? How?

5. What are the pros and cons of computers in the workplace?

## Terms

| | |
|---|---|
| application | microcomputer |
| computer | organization |
| computer information system | people |
| computer system | procedure |
| data | program |
| equipment | software |
| hardware | subsystem |

## MINICASE

**Situation:**

Sarah Schulhof has decided to work her way through college by operating a stenographic service. She reasons that she can do most of the work on a personal computer that was a high school graduation gift from her parents. She has a cassette player that can be used to take dictation from clients by phone or on cassettes that the clients bring to her.

To start her business, Sarah bought pads of standard forms from her office supply store, including pads of invoices, account statements, and receipts for money received. Sarah posted notices on bulletin boards around the school and received assignments from several faculty members who were working on journal articles, books, and book reviews.

One day a business professor for whom Sarah had worked said only half jokingly: "Here you are using a computer to provide services and giving us handwritten invoices. When we pay, we get a handwritten receipt. What's the matter? Don't you believe in computers? Why don't you produce your invoices on computers?"

The professor laughed. But Sarah thought she detected a serious undertone to the questions. She had decided earlier that her volumes of document production were too low to warrant using a computer. When she mentioned this to the professor, he replied that software for these applications had become easier to use and far less expensive. He recommended serious consideration of this option. Sarah decided to study the possibilities of computerizing her transaction documents.

**Decision Making: Your Turn**

1. From the information you have and from Sarah's viewpoint, identify and describe the problem to be solved or need to be met and its related benefits.

2. Identify alternatives that could be followed to produce best results for Sarah's need.

3. On the basis of the limited information you have: a) Identify additional information you would gather if you were dealing with this problem in a real situation. b) Identify the solution that appears best on the basis of the information that is available and explain your reasons for this selection.

4. What lessons are to be learned from this situation?

# Projects

1. Find a magazine or journal article that describes the extent of reliance upon computers by business organizations. Write a summary of your findings and explain how this information might affect your role in the workplace.

2. Think about how you would use the steps of the decision-making process outlined in this chapter to select a computer system, car, or other major purchase. Would this systematic approach help you to get better value for your investment? How?

3. Interview a businessperson whose job includes decision-making responsibilities. Determine how he or she applies information to meet decision-making assignments. Does the approach described to you differ from the systematic approach described in this chapter? If so, how?

# Tools for Using Information

Information systems are developed and used through the application of a series of information tools, including the six described in this Unit. Chapter 3 overviews the basic components of a computer system—the hardware and software required to use application software. Chapter 4 provides in-depth coverage of the concepts and applications of word processing software. The manipulation of numeric data through electronic spreadsheets is the focus of Chapter 5. Chapter 6 overviews the many and increasing uses of graphics and desktop publishing in business. The database programs discussed in Chapter 7 illustrate how data are organized and cross-referenced to provide useful information to database users. Chapter 8 concludes this unit with an in-depth examination of data communications applications and technology. A special feature of Unit II is a full-color photo essay illustrating graphically the persuasive power of presentation graphics. This photo essay follows Chapter 6.

# Chapter Outline

End-User Perspective

The Point: Computer Systems are Combinations of Components

The ABCs of Computer Hardware
*Input Hardware, Processing Hardware, Output Hardware, Storage Hardware, Communications Hardware*

The XYZs of Computer Software
*Operating Systems, Programming Languages, Application Programs*

The 1, 2, 3s of Computer Applications

The Value of Computer Tools

Chapter Summary

Questions for Review

Questions for Thought

Terms

Minicase

Projects

## CHAPTER 3

# Computer Systems: Getting Started

**Briefing Memo**

TO:      Information Users
FROM:   T. Rohm, W. Stewart

The tools of information systems consist of computer hardware and software. Most of the rest of this book describes these tools and explains their value to information users. This chapter is designed to get you started in your understanding of computer hardware and software by providing an overview of computer information systems.

As you read and assimilate the content of this chapter, you will gain an understanding of how hardware and software elements combine to form the systems that deliver the information outputs on which you rely.

**End-User Perspective**

"You told me this would be simple!" Herman was shocked. Several cartons of assorted sizes and shapes were piled in the outer office, making it necessary for him to sidestep his way to his desk. 'I expected that we would just be able to plug the new computer in and begin to get results. It looks as though you've got to have a crash course in engineering simply to assemble this thing."

"Not to worry," Harriet said. 'It all plugs together. As long as the right cords go to the right sockets, it really is simple." Harriet, Herman's assistant, had completed a course on microcomputer equipment and applications sponsored by the company's management training group. Her enthusiasm showed as she continued: "Every computer is a series of parts that have to be assembled and coordinated to meet the needs of a specific user.

"Once you understand the components of a computer system and what each does, it isn't hard at all," Harriet continued. 'We have the computer itself in this box. That big box contains a monitor. Then, here's a modem. That's the keyboard. The computer plugs into this surge protector to guard it against damage from electrical power problems. All these parts go together to make the computer system we decided we needed."

Harriet laughed as she told Herman: "Why don't you have lunch while I put this together. We'll be ready for a demonstration in an hour or so."

 **The Point: Computer Systems are Combinations of Components**

The office in this scenario, like millions of others around the world, is going through a transition to direct computer use. Harriet and Herman have decided that their volume of administrative work and their need for information analysis and decision making can be aided by a microcomputer system. Their study has shown that the benefits from the new system will deliver values worth more than its cost. An important principle in such situations is that computer systems should be tailored to the needs of individual users.

A computer is a series of hardware components selected to meet specific needs or solve identified problems. The preceding chapters establish the value of information as an end product required by users. User needs form the framework within which information systems are created. Within this frame-work, computers are the tools of information handling and delivery. The hardware and software components that form computer systems make it possible to deliver accurate, reliable information on a timely basis.

Computer hardware configurations are individual collections of standard components. Each work station or computer facility is assembled to meet needs of individual users. Throughout an organization, however, there should be compatibility in organizing, processing, and delivering information to users.

## ■  The ABCs of Computer Hardware

The term hardware applies to any piece of equipment that can become part of a computer system. Every computer consists of a set of parts. As a rule, computer system components are designed to support individual functions of the information processing cycle—input, processing, output, and storage.

Additional, auxiliary hardware components can be added as necessary to adapt computers to meet specific user needs. For example, devices can be attached that link computers into telecommunication lines of the public telephone network for transmission and receipt of data. Computers also can be attached to instruments that control temperatures, operate burglar alarms, turn off lights, and perform other functions. All these auxiliary devices rely on the same basic capabilities of input, processing, output, and storage. These components and their functions are reviewed below, along with the function of communication among computers.

## Input Hardware

Input is the starting point for a computer's ability to process data and deliver information. Input hardware encompasses the equipment with which users enter data into a system. The single most popular input device is the *keyboard*. Every microcomputer and user terminal has a keyboard. Other systems have special keyboards to handle specific jobs. The cash register is one example. Another example can be seen in the keyboards included in automatic teller machine (ATM) units at banks. Still another input device that you may en-

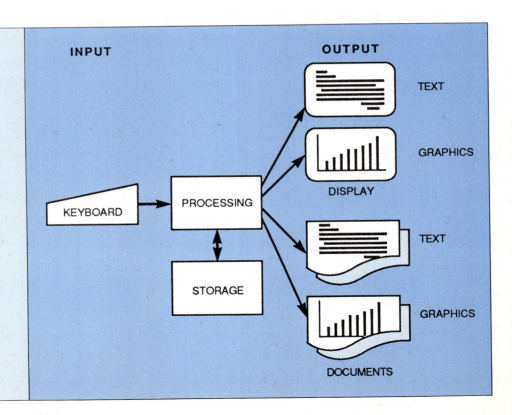

This diagram shows a functional view of the information processing cycle. Input generated by a keyboard is processed with support of the storage function. Outputs include text and graphic displays and text and graphic documents.

Computer hardware is present in many routine activities of information users. In the near-right photo, a customer receives direct banking services from an automatic teller machine. At far right, a user performs computations with a calculator-equipped wristwatch.

counter regularly is the laser scanner used to enter product code information in supermarkets. Some input results from retrieval of stored information. Other inputs occur when documents are read by special sensing devices or when electrical or mechanical instruments are connected directly to computers. All of these methods accomplish the same general goal: They encode data into a format that can be accepted and processed by computers.

To illustrate input functions, consider what happens when you pick up a telephone and dial a number. You are a user who is providing direct input. As you turn a dial or press buttons on your phone, you generate signals that can be read into a computer in the telephone company's central office for further processing. Computers respond to your needs. In the case of a telephone, computerized systems meet the needs of people to contact and communicate with one another.

## Processing Hardware

Data processing occurs in multiple stages. The first step is acceptance of input from an external source by the processor. This occurs when entered data are stored in the *memory* of a computer *processor*. Computer memory functions as a holding area for data to be processed. The processor consists of a series of electrical circuits, some of which process, or *transform*, data items. Processing functions performed by computers are extremely simple, so much so that these capabilities often are described as *primitives*. The primitive functions of a typical computer consist mainly of basic arithmetic functions and comparisons of two values presented by computer programs.

Think of these simple capabilities and think of what you already know about electricity. Electricity can be turned off or on through the setting of switches. Electronic devices can have positive or negative settings. A positive setting has a value of 1, a negative setting a value of 0. To illustrate, a light bulb that is turned on reflects a positive electrical setting. With the switch turned off, a negative condition is created. This simple principle is the basis of all computer processing. Circuits that handle on and off electrical signals accomplish the arithmetic functions of addition, subtraction, multiplication, and division. Also, processor circuits are able to compare two values and guide operations on the basis of results. A computer can direct its own processing by determining whether two values are equal or whether one is greater than the other. Basic processor functions also include capabilities to accept inputs or to read data items within the system, and to follow instructions for their combination, movement, deletion, or other manipulative functions. These primitive capabilities then are combined under directions from people to deliver sophisticated results. Applications as complex as automated manufacturing or advanced purchasing procedures are carried out through large numbers of primitive functions.

In a processor, operating instructions and data items are retained in memory. Instructions and data are drawn into the processing circuits in small units that consist of one or two characters of data and a single primitive processing function. Each of these instructions is acted upon in millionths of a second, then sent back to memory. When units of work are completed, the computer follows instructions about transferring the electrical signals for output.

As an end user who dials a telephone, you call upon processing capabilities as soon as you enter a number. Your entries are accumulated in the memory of a computer at the telephone office that serves your phone. This computer checks the area code and exchange numbers that you enter. These entries are compared with sets of numeric values stored within the computer. The immediate processing that occurs results in the switching of your call to another computer—perhaps a series of computers in different switching centers and telephone offices.

The processing cycle continues throughout your call. The computer equipment in your telephone office records the time your call is placed. If the connection is made, the computer automatically creates a record that is retained for later processing, when output hardware generates your telephone bill. This example reveals an important characteristic of computer processing: Processing can involve a cycle of events that are completed in stages. The computer needs a capability to maintain jobs in memory—a key hardware component—and to follow up at intermediate stages until the processing cycle is completed.

## Output Hardware

The value of computers depends upon their ability to respond to user needs and instructions to deliver accurate, reliable information on a timely basis. To

This illustration presents a simplified view of the equipment and software support components of a computer, overlaid on a silhouette of a microcomputer. Input capabilities are represented by the keyboard, outputs by the display screen. The processor is shown as having communication, arithmetic, and comparison capabilities. Storage is presented by two disk devices. Memory holds programs, input data, working storage, and output content.

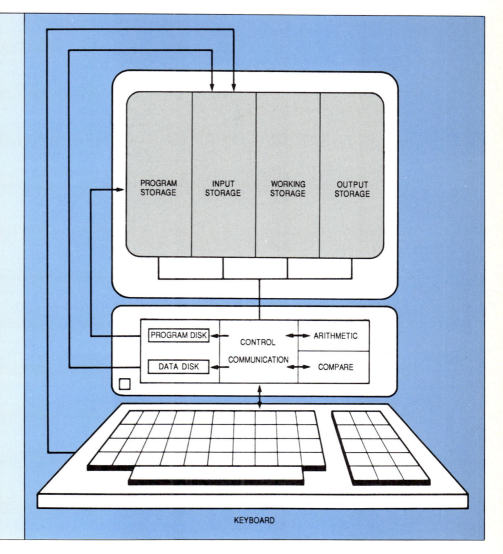

do this, computers need hardware components that can present information to users quickly and in forms that people can understand. The most common output devices are video displays and printers. By far the greatest amount of output from computers is delivered in the form of displays on video screens or printed documents. Other output units can draw pictures or present images on film.

A characteristic of computer outputs is the ability of equipment, following instructions from users and programmers, to handle and to generate massive volumes of information. Individual printers have operating speeds that go as high as 20,000 lines per minute. Pages of text or graphic images can be generated at speeds of more than 7,000 per hour. Recording on film can be even faster. At the other extreme, printers linked to microcomputers generate outputs at speeds measured in characters. Pages of reports are generated at rates of one each 30 to 60 seconds.

Outputs occur on a planned basis. Each output should deliver information to meet a user need or produce a planned result. An output can be as simple as a ringing telephone in response to a dialed number. A more formal, planned output occurs when you receive your telephone bill. The hardware devices that generate documents for delivery to users are printers. Computer printers come in a wide range of models that deliver different levels of speed and quality. Displays also have a number of variations. One option centers around the ability to show colors or to limit displays to a single color (monochrome). Size and image qualities are other hardware options.

## Storage Hardware

Without storage hardware, computers could not carry out business applications or make information available for future processing. Storage devices are guardians of information on which users depend. For actual processing support, a computer uses the memory within its processor. However, memory is temporary. On virtually all computers, memory goes blank when power is turned off. In addition, memory is expensive and, because of its cost, is limited.

**Secondary Storage.** Computers need additional capacity to store data. This additional, or *secondary storage,* capability must be available at low cost but must have high capacities to record and retrieve data. The most popular approach to meeting this storage need is to record data and programs magnetically by using the same principles you experience when you use audio or video cassettes. Magnetic storage is retained for long periods; information does not disappear when power is turned off. Magnetic devices also are relatively low in cost.

Magnetic storage devices interact with memory. After processing, the computer records, or *writes,* data to a magnetic device. Because these magnetic units are coordinated as backups to memory, they are called *secondary* or *peripheral* devices. Two types of magnetic peripherals are in general use: tape and disk.

**Tape and Disk Drives.** Tape storage devices are similar to those you probably have used in your car stereo or video recorder. That is, a long ribbon of plastic film is coated with a material that contains tiny pieces of iron. When the tape is processed over magnetic read/write *heads,* information can be recorded or previously recorded information can be played back.

The same principle is applied to the recording of data on disk devices, except that a disk contains coating on a round, rigid platter or a sheet of flexible plastic. Disks rotate under their magnetic heads, making it possible to record

Flexible, high-capacity output capabilities are situated in the center of this central computer facility. The printing unit in the center of the room is controlled from the work station at the right and is linked to computer processing and storage hardware in the background.

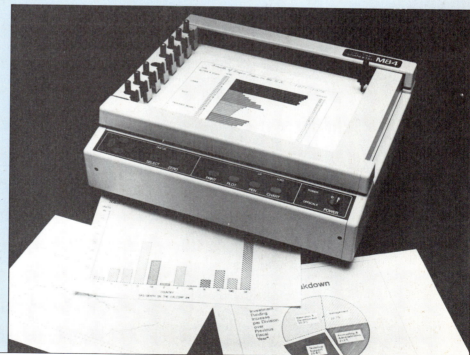

Graphic outputs from computer systems are generated by plotters like the one shown here. Images are formed through movement of pen-like devices over sheets of paper.

and write data one record at a time. By comparison, a tape passes under magnetic heads lengthwise, making it necessary to read or write all material recorded each time the tape is processed. The ability to record and read information one record at a time on disks made possible *random access* to individual data records without having to read stored files in sequence.

■    **Importance of Random Access.**    This represented a major breakthrough in the value of computers to business. Before random access, processing had to be done on groups, or *batches*, of data items. With random access and the ability to find and record individual records, direct support of business operations became possible. Businesses no longer had to group transaction records into batches for effective processing. Instead, records could be accessed, processed and rewritten to storage individually. When random access was introduced, businesses were able to process customer orders directly, during telephone calls or at service counters. Previously, it had been necessary to process orders manually and to update computer files in separate, later operations that handled groups, or batches, of documents.

With the introduction of microcomputers, the most widely used storage medium has become the flexible, or *floppy,* disk. A floppy disk uses round sheets of flexible plastic for recording. These recording media are encased in a protective sleeve to form a *diskette* that is easy to insert into disk drives of microcomputers. Diskettes are small enough to be stored in desk-top cabinets or even in file folders with corresponding documents.

Other storage methods also are available and are discussed in a later chapter that deals specifically with storage devices.

As a telephone user, you make use of truly massive storage capabilities. For one thing, each time you dial a call, you use a series of interconnected storage devices with records of more than 100 million telephone numbers. Massive disk files stand by to furnish the information needed to serve you. In addition, the records for your account—the data used to generate your telephone bill—also are stored on high-capacity disk devices.

## Communications Hardware

Many users who require information work in locations that are distant from the computers on which they depend. Also, user needs may require access to or exchanges of information among multiple computers. As a result of these requirements, *data communication*—the transmission and receipt of data specifically to support computer applications—has become a major factor in the telecommunications industry. Some experts in the field have predicted that more transmission time ultimately will be devoted to data transmission than to telephone conversations among people.

To make data communication possible, special adapter devices have been needed between telephone systems and computers. Originally, telephones were designed to carry voices. Voice service is carried by the same kind of signal used for radio broadcasts. That is, the signals carry variations of continuous tones that deliver outputs such as speech, music, etc. Data transmissions,

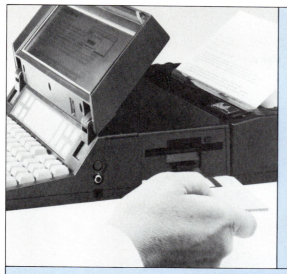

Storage hardware to maintain and provide access to computer resources comes in a number of forms and options. At the right is a group of tape drives that handle sequential files in support of applications on large computers. The microcomputer above uses diskettes, or floppy disks, to provide random access storage. At the upper right is a microcomputer with both hard disk and floppy disk storage capabilities.

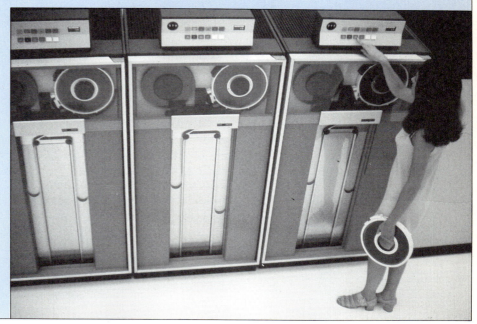

on the other hand, are carried in stop-start patterns that represent the electrical, or *binary*, language of computers that is based on the on-off states of electrical circuits. Thus, for computers to talk to one another over telephone lines, special devices are needed. These are called *modems*, an abbreviation for modulate-demodulate, the process that converts traditional telephone signals to the binary values required for computer processing. Modems and their functions are covered in greater depth in a later chapter.

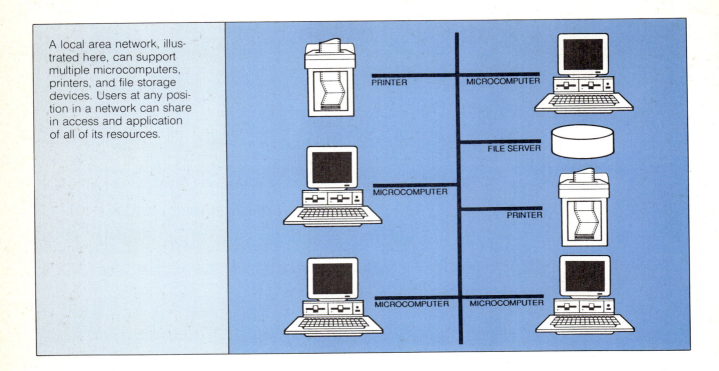

A local area network, illustrated here, can support multiple microcomputers, printers, and file storage devices. Users at any position in a network can share in access and application of all of its resources.

One widely used data communications service assembled from late-model data communications and computer hardware is the *local area network,* or *LAN.* LAN service generally is used to connect computers within a single building or on one or two floors of a large building. Direct hardware connections are established between microcomputers and large systems or between multiple microcomputers. A LAN makes it possible for multiple end users to share data resources through access to large storage devices or to communicate among computers in a type of service known as *electronic mail.*

## ■ The XYZs of Computer Software

As indicated above, hardware represents just one element of a computer information system. As far as users are concerned, the power of hardware processing requires intervening support from software and operating procedures.

Computers, no matter how large or small they may be, are inanimate. They are simply collections of cabinets and racks that hold circuits and mechanical devices such as disk drives. To become useful and to develop the power to generate information, computers need sets of instructions devised by people.

Information users and computer professionals prepare instructions in coding formats that are necessary for electronic processing. These sets of instructions, as you know, are called programs, or software. It takes multiple types of programs to support operation of a computer. The main categories of computer software include:

- Operating systems
- Programming languages
- Application programs.

Each type of software serves a separate purpose that is coordinated with the functions of other programs. Software categories relate to the user support that is provided. User instructions to a computer pass through two or more separate levels of programs between input and actual computer processing. Types of software are determined by the functional positions of the programs between the user and the computer.

## Operating Systems

*Operating system* software is closest to the computer and furthest from the user. These programs are so close to the functions of the computer itself and so distant from user involvement that computer users may not even be aware of their presence. To describe this relationship, many functions of operating systems often are described as being *transparent* to the casual user of a computer.

Packaged software is available for a wide range of uses that can meet virtually any need of a computer user, including operating system, programming language, and application programs. In addition, a variety of special-purpose options, including software integrators and communication packages, also are available.

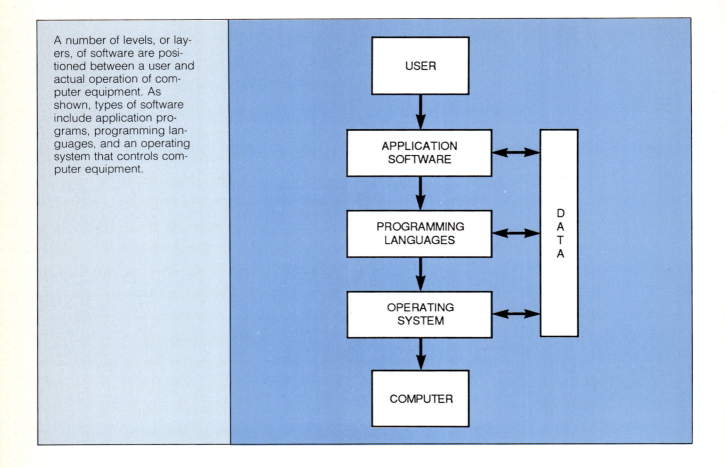

A number of levels, or layers, of software are positioned between a user and actual operation of computer equipment. As shown, types of software include application programs, programming languages, and an operating system that controls computer equipment.

An operating system consists of a series of programs that control computer hardware to make processing available to users. When a computer system is set up, the operating system must receive instructions that describe the *configuration,* or combination of components, that the software must control. For example, when a user enters an instruction to print a letter captured under a word processing program, the operating system checks to be sure that a printer is available, that it is connected, and that it is turned on and ready for use.

When a computer is turned on, the operating system is the first software loaded into memory. The operating system then makes the computer available for instructions from users or application programs. The operating system also provides a series of programs, called *utilities,* that perform basic, often-used functions. Utilities can be shared by all users and their programs.

To illustrate software functions and capabilities, consider the features of a typical microcomputer. You undoubtedly have been, or soon will be, introduced to use of a microcomputer. As a microcomputer user, you will load

Contents of an operating system are listed in this screen display. At the top line of the display, a user has entered a 'dir' command, which asks the system to list the directory in the A drive. The listed items are program names, with columns indicating, from left to right, the number of bytes in the file, the date of last update for the program, and the time of the last update.

```
A:\>dir

 Volume in drive A has no label
 Directory of  A:\

LDRTIME          1536    1-01-80   12:53a
PERFLABL          640    7-31-85   11:28a
PERFMBO           768    7-31-85   12:21p
SELECT1           256    1-01-80   12:12a
SELECT2          1408    1-01-80   12:02a
SUPVDAY1         2560   10-01-85    1:40p
SUPVDAY2         1792   10-08-85    1:44a
SUPVDAY3         3328   10-15-85    3:32p
SUPVDAY5         1792   10-29-85    5:44p
COMASGN2 WS2     1859   11-17-87    1:11a
COMMINV  WKS     4224    1-01-80   12:20a
COMASGN3 WS2     1500   11-24-87   12:19a
CASE     WS2    11165   12-07-87    4:56p
SPELROLE         5888    3-13-86    3:07p
COMMDAY3 WS2     4114   11-09-87    5:30p
COMMDAY4 WS2     2108   11-09-87    5:31p
COMASGN1 WS2     1014   11-09-87    6:01p
       17 File(s)     285696 bytes free

A:\>
```

a *disk operating system (DOS)* as part of the procedure for turning on the computer. You interact with the operating system in the course of setting up your computer for use. All of the application packages with which you interact as a microcomputer user are closely tied to DOS capabilities.

In effect, the operating system is an essential element of software needed to run any computer. As a user, you may call upon the operating system to help access information or programs you need. Or, you may depend on the operating system to support your application programs. Most application packages, for example, make use of at least some of the processing capabilities included in operating system software. Whether you use it directly or through application packages, the operating system will be there and will be necessary for your use of the computer.

## Programming Languages

The term *application* covers all of the programs, procedures, and instructions needed to cause a computer to process a specific job. Programs that cause computers to produce information specifically to meet user needs are called *application programs.* The instructions that make up application programs are written through use of software tools called *programming languages.* This means that programming languages form a middle level—between operating systems and applications—for the interactions of users and computers.

The purpose of a programming language is to make it easier for people to instruct computers. In the early days of computer use, programmers had to write instructions entirely in the 0 and 1 symbols of binary, *machine language* code. Each computer had its own machine language that was meaningless to any other computer. This work was tedious and error prone. To ease the job of programming computers, and to reduce costs of application development, software tools were developed. These tools, programming languages, made possible direct communication between professional programmers and computers.

As examples, commands for arithmetic functions can be used directly to generate programs in some languages. The words ADD, SUBTRACT, MULTIPLY, and DIVIDE may be used to produce program code. The term IF usually is used to instruct the computer to compare two terms. If the comparison is true, a THEN instruction leads to the next processing sequence. If the comparison is false, an ELSE instruction is followed. These instructions are processed by programming language software, which generates binary code for computer operation.

As a user, you may never have to write an application program. However, an understanding of the process of program development and the characteristics of programming languages can help you to make your requirements known if you deal with computer professionals in the future. You will find additional

Access to a BASIC language program is built into IBM PC and many compatible systems. If the computer is turned on without a diskette in the A drive or an operating system on a hard disk, this display appears. The list of commands on the bottom line in the display can be used to initiate or apply programs in the BASIC language.

```
The IBM Personal Computer Basic
Version A3.30 Copyright IBM Corp. 1981, 1982, 1983, 1984, 1985, 1986, 1987
60225 Bytes free

Ok
```

```
1LIST    2RUN    3LOAD"   4SAVE"   5CONT   6,"LPT1 7TRON   8TROFF 9KEY     0SCREEN
```

descriptions in Chapter 9.

## Application Programs

The results required by users are delivered under control of application programs. Each application program does a single job, or *task*. The idea is to keep individual programs small enough so that quality control and accuracy checks can be applied. The breaking down of applications into tasks is necessary partly because of the primitive nature of functions performed by computers. Multiple programs, or *systems of programs*, usually are required to generate the types and amounts of information needed by users.

To illustrate, a common application for which many companies use computers is payroll preparation. Completion of an entire payroll may require a

Users can access multiple applications on-line with software integration capabilities of packages like Symphony. With these capabilities, users can integrate content from word processing, spreadsheet, database, and graphics programs into the same report. Users also can move from one application program to another at will, relying on the integrator packages to keep track of their activities.

dozen or more separate, coordinated programs. Some of these programs may be run on computers every day while others may be run weekly, monthly, quarterly, or annually. The separate programs may be used to record employee working time on a daily basis, to figure gross pay on a weekly basis, to calculate deductions, to write checks, and to accumulate information for government agencies.

Organizations follow two basic approaches to acquire programs to process applications. One method is to write original, custom programs through use of a programming language. Another is to purchase existing *application packages* that include programs and sets of procedures manuals covering their use. Some users also might opt for purchase of a package that comes close to, but does not meet every requirement for, a given application. In such instances, a decision is made between the options of creating a custom program or buying and modifying a standard package. The approach selected can depend upon the nature of the problem being solved.

Options are evaluated on the basis of effort, cost, time lags, and the ability to meet user needs. A really large system of application programs may require many months of work by a dozen or more programmers. If the application is unique, this may be the only appropriate method. For example, programs to control operation of an automated warehouse would, at this time, have to be developed from scratch in a programming language. On the other hand, many application packages are available for payroll applications. Most of these programs are purchased and put to work with minimal adjustments or modifications. The payroll job can be standardized because of common requirements; all payrolls must conform to government regulations.

Today, application packages are a major factor in the information systems field. Literally hundreds of programs and associated procedures manuals are available to handle the standard jobs that most businesses have to perform in the course of routine operations. The section that follows describes some common application packages that you are likely to encounter as an end user.

## The 1, 2, 3s of Computer Applications

There was a time when it was assumed that each business and every application was unique. Procedures for developing a new computer information system began by describing needs, then went on to guide programmers in developing software to meet those needs. Over time, both users and computer professionals discovered that not all applications were unique and that every task did not require development of customer programs. Rather, certain functions were found to be common to many user applications. Standard software tools were developed that eliminated the need to program each application individually and thus reduced the cost. The resulting affordability, in turn, expanded markets.

At first, common denominators were discovered among functions found to exist in many application programs. This recognition led to creation of utility programs that now are part of most operating systems. These utility functions include control of input, recording data on storage devices, retrieving data from storage, and sorting data items in preparation for input and processing. Today, most application programs depend upon utility routines within the operating system to provide these capabilities.

Later, common requirements were identified for entire user applications. As an example, all payrolls must meet government regulations. Common denominators of requirements have made it possible for suppliers to develop and market a number of efficient, effective payroll applications. The great majority of payrolls now are processed with the aid of application packages that include report forms, paycheck form, programs, and instructions for users and computer operators. For similar reasons—government reporting regulations—application packages also have been prepared for the keeping of accounting records, the preparation of financial reports, and the computation of income taxes. All of these are operational, or administrative, requirements common to many business.

In addition, a number of general applications have been supported by specialized software packages. These applications satisfy common needs of users. The common responsibilities supported by these applications include:

- Correspondence and other documents require processing of text.
- Specialized reports, called spreadsheets, are used to meet the financial planning and operational reporting responsibilities of most managers.
- Programs that generate graphic outputs are used for situations in which pictures communicate more effectively than words and numbers.
- Information management tools are used to organize data for easy access, analysis, application support, or reporting requirements.
- Communication of data over telephone networks enhances the ability of managers to analyze data and reach decisions.

Text processing software has helped businesses to keep up with increasing work loads in the preparation of letters, memos, proposals, legal documents, and other reports. The software, described in the next chapter, makes it possible to create, edit, and maintain document files on computers. These files can be edited and new versions of documents can be produced with ease. Use of stored files eliminates the tedious and frustrating job of retyping documents repeatedly before they are ready for delivery. Major time and cost savings in document preparation have resulted from use of text processing software. In addition, users gain flexibility to revise documents to be sure that messages convey exact meanings and also to enhance the appearance of finished documents.

Spreadsheet software solves common problems faced by managers at all levels of businesses. Almost all managers with responsibilities for receiving or spending money on behalf of their companies are required to prepare financial plans, called *budgets,* and operating reports that compare those plans with actual results. For many years before computers were introduced, budgets and operating reports were handwritten on wide sheets with ruled spaces for financial entries—called spreadsheets.

To prepare spreadsheets manually, managers had to handwrite all entries and perform all computations individually. A recognition of the common nature of this problem led software suppliers to develop application packages that make it possible to prepare spreadsheets electronically, on computers. Data entries are made in spaces set up on computer displays. If computations are necessary, the user enters formulas and the computer completes the calculations and data entries. When changes are needed in existing spreadsheets, the computer displays can be edited, saving the need to rewrite entire documents.

## Impact

# What Is Upgrading?

What do you do when your computer becomes ''too slow?'' When you desire to add more memory? When you wish to have graphics capabilities?

These are typical questions asked by individual users. These types of questions have a single, rather simple answer: You take out the old and bring in the new. Computer manufacturers, from the beginning, have developed techniques to ''upgrade'' user systems. No matter what computer you may be using, design features are built in so that you can replace old components with new parts that will increase computer system capabilities and, in turn, your personal and professional productivity.

Years ago, upgrading hardware was quite expensive. However, with the advent of microcomputers built from standard components, a new breed of manufacturers, known as ''third-party vendors,'' have entered the marketplace. These companies specialize in providing components designed to add new features and to upgrade capabilities of existing systems. The presence of third-party vendors assures you that there is a group of companies trying to think up ways to enhance the value of your computer. A few examples of how to upgrade your computer:

Need more memory? Purchase an expansion board.

Want to add graphics capabilities? Add a graphics card and a high-resolution monitor, either color or monochrome.

Looking for increased processing speed? You need a co-processor, or accelerator card.

The more knowledgeable you become as a user, the more conscious you will be of potential benefits from added hardware features, and of the need to shop with caution. Ask some critical questions, such as the following:

Is the upgrade you are considering fully compatible with your existing computer system? You may find that you have to buy special connecting devices to use a given component with the system you have. You also may find that the manufacturer has neglected to state that an upgrade device is not compatible with your system.

Will service be available both for your computer and for the attachment? If your system has a mix of parts from different vendors, who will be responsible for service? Will any of the parties refuse service because you have attached ''foreign'' devices?

Look out for yourself! You are the customer. Know what you are buying.

For some time, businesspeople have enhanced communication by drawing charts and graphs to convey meaning of text and financial presentation. Computers have expedited this area of communication by providing graphics software that translates number values into pictures. Desk-top publishing software has made it possible to combine text and graphics outputs into attractive publications. Also, computer software has made electronic assistance available directly to artists. Many TV commercials and animated motion pictures are generated by computers that record their outputs on videotape or film.

The need for information management tools stems from the fact that all organizations that conduct business transactions accumulate large amounts of data. The information produced, in turn, becomes an important asset of the company. Managers review, analyze, and make important decisions on the basis of information accumulated and managed by computers. Requirements are common enough so that major markets have been developed for application packages that enable users to build databases to support information systems. These packages are known generally as *database management systems (DBMS)*.

For users who require capabilities for data communication, special hardware-software packages are provided. These include modem units that connect to communication channels and provide the encoding and decoding necessary for compatibility between computers and communication utilities.

## The Value of Computer Tools

A computer system, as described, is a combination of hardware and software components that can be interconnected to tailor information to the needs of users. Emphasis in discussions about computer hardware has been on their role as tools. Computers represent one way of providing information to users. There are other methods. But this book focuses on development and delivery of information through use of computers. The tools for implementing computer systems, of course, include several levels of software that make computers usable.

An important result of the growing popularity of software application packages has been that computers have become easier to master, or more *user friendly*. Most application packages, particularly those designed for use on microcomputers, can be operated effectively by people with little or no technical expertise. Software packages tend to be designed to meet needs or solve problems encountered in business situations. Qualifications for use of computers, then, no longer are highly technical. Instead, requirements center around a real understanding of the problems to be solved and the results expected. Documentation associated with application packages makes it possible to evaluate the suitability of a total, overall solution to a problem. Given a set of simple tools, almost any end user can take hold of and use a computer to solve problems and capitalize on career opportunities.

## Chapter Summary

- Computer systems are sets of devices, or components, assembled to meet the needs of specific users.

- All units of computer equipment are called hardware. Special hardware devices are available to handle the basic functions of the information processing cycle: input, processing, output, and storage.

- The most widely used input device is the keyboard. The most popular keyboard is the typewriter-style unit. Others include numeric keypads like those on telephones or cash registers.

- Processing occurs in a central processing unit (CPU) that includes a processor and main memory. The processing contains one unit that controls operations of the entire computer configuration and another that performs computations and logic operations. Memory supports processing by providing the data and program instructions required for execution.

- The primary methods of computer output are displays and printers. Other techniques include recording outputs on film and graphics devices.

- The most widely used storage media are magnetic tapes and disks.

- Hardware that supports data communication among computers must convert signals from the digital formats of computers to the tone, or analog, signals of telephone carriers.

- All programs that control operation of computers, collectively, are known as software. Three levels of software are identified: operating systems, programming languages, and application programs.

- Operating systems control the operation of computer equipment and also contain sets of utility programs that can be called upon by users or can be used to support application programs.

- Programming language software accepts instructions written by people and translates them into machine languages required by computers. Programming languages are used to code user applications for computer processing.

- Application programs control processing of user jobs. Many applications can be implemented through use of standard application packages that include programs and instructions for their use. Among the most popular application packages are word processing, spreadsheets, graphics, database managers, and communication controllers.

- The value of computers as tools lies in their ability to improve efficiency and effectiveness of people, thereby contributing to their productivity.

## Questions for Review

1. Describe the makeup of a computer system.
2. Why is it said that each computer is individual and unique?
3. What is the most popular technique for computer input?
4. What is the role of main memory, or primary storage, in the processing functions of a computer?
5. What processing functions are performed by a computer? Why are these functions described as primitive?
6. What is the role of the control unit of a computer's CPU?
7. What are the primary output methods? Describe the function and purpose of each.
8. What are the primary media used for data and program storage and what are the major advantages and disadvantages of each?
9. Identify and describe three types of programs that comprise computer software.
10. What are the major values of computers as tools for people who require and use information?

## Questions for Thought

1. Identify at least two activities in which you engage that result in computer input. What are the activities and how does computer input result?
2. A computer system is formed from a group of coordinated components. Describe the relationships between the purposes of main memory and secondary storage. Cover both the active processing of data and the need to retain data and information permanently.
3. Imagine that operating systems had never been developed. What would the absence of operating systems have meant to the ability of people to interact with and derive information from computers?
4. What are application packages and how did their development affect the acceptance and use of computers in business organizations and by individuals?
5. Define ''user friendly'' and describe at least three features of modern computer and software systems that make them friendly to users.

## Terms

| | |
|---|---|
| application | memory |
| application package | modem |
| application program | operating system |
| batch | peripheral |
| binary | primitive |
| budget | processor |
| configuration | programming language |
| data communication | random access |
| database management system (DBMS) | secondary |
| disk operating system (DOS) | secondary storage |
| diskette | system of programs |
| electronic mail | task |
| floppy | transform |
| head | transparent |
| keyboard | user friendly |
| local area network (LAN) | utility |
| machine language | write |

## MINICASE

**Situation:**

To buy a microcomputer, as Harriet did in the scenarios in this chapter, it is necessary to identify the outputs to be generated and the inputs to be provided. Assume your instructor has asked you to help configure a system for use in the computer information systems department. The system will use a microcomputer to produce lists of majors within the department and records of major course requirements completed, special work assignments for students, syllabus documents, and departmental budgets. All outputs will be printed. The department computer must be able to communicate with the campus computer over telephone lines.

**Decision Making: Your Turn**

1. From the information you have, identify and describe the problem to be solved.

2. Identify alternatives that could be followed to avoid or solve the problem.

3. On the basis of the limited information you have: a) Identify additional information you would gather if you were dealing with this problem in a real situation. b) Identify the solution that appears best on the basis of the information that is available and explain your reasons for this selection.

4. What lessons are to be learned from this situation?

## Projects

1. Develop a picture of a microcomputer by using an office copier to duplicate an existing illustration or by creating a simple drawing. Label the following components and explain how they interact: monitor, floppy disk drive, keyboard, processing unit, printer.

2. Go to the microcomputer lab in your school and obtain a DOS disk from an instructor or a lab assistant. Ask for instructions on how to: 1) start, or *boot up*, the DOS system, and 2) copy a file.

3. Page through two or more different computer magazines and/or journals. List at least 10 different titles of software packages that are advertised. Arrange your list into functional categories according to the application areas identified in this chapter.

## Chapter Outline

CHAPTER **4**

# Word Processing Systems

## Briefing Memo

TO:      Information Users
FROM:   T. Rohm, W. Stewart

Business organizations must produce written documents, words on paper. The documents can include letters or memos that convey information. Other written documents include contracts, product inquiries, and reports. The total demand comes to billions of documents monthly. Word processing systems are reducing the work connected with producing this mountain of paperwork and are permitting better document preparation.

As a student, you prepare written documents. You are, therefore, a prospective user of computers for preparing term papers and reports. This chapter describes the concepts and applications of word processing as they apply to all users, to you, and to users in business.

## End-User Perspective

"Excuse me," Josefina said, "but this is ridiculous."

Members of the advertising department of the school newspaper turned and looked at her in surprise. Morgan, the advertising manager, asked: "What's the problem, Jo?"

Josefina explained that she couldn't believe the procedures that Morgan had just described for soliciting ads from businesses in the area of the Central State campus. Morgan had indicated that form letters would be preprinted on an offset printing press. The staff would insert these in typewriters and enter the names of prospective advertisers. Also to be inserted were quotations of their advertising rates.

"We can do the whole thing on a word processing system in a fraction of the time and effort," Josefina explained. 'And it will come out looking more professional," she added.

Recently, Josefina had purchased a microcomputer, along with a word processing application package. With this software, she could enter names and addresses of prospective advertisers in one file and the text of one or more letters in another. The computer system allowed her automatically to combine the names and addresses with the body of a letter and generate personalized, individually typed letters that would make the recipients feel as if they were important enough to the staff of the college newspaper to receive personal attention. The computer would produce quality letters with less overall effort than filling in names and addresses on form letters.

"With a word processor," Josefina summarized, "we can produce professional-looking documents with less effort."

## The Point: Word Processing Enhances Written Communication

Traditional methods for preparing documents have become outdated. The same type of project described in the scenario above occurs among computer-using organizations. For applications ranging from the preparation of letters and memos to a wide range of other, more complex documents, computers and *word processing* application software are bringing about sweeping changes. Josefina has a point: When it comes to creating text or documents, computers enable people to work more effectively and efficiently, and to deliver superior quality.

Word processing work stations have replaced millions of typewriters in modern offices. Use of word processing techniques helps to increase productivity, enhance efficiency and effectiveness, and generate documents of high quality.

## ■ The Need for Word Processing

Word processing is a computer application in which text is captured and stored on a peripheral device and can be retrieved for revision at any time. Within a word processing system, the preparation and editing of text files generally is separated from the printing function, which can be used to create either interim drafts or finished documents.

Word processing applications take on special importance in business organizations because of the volume of written communication involved and the number of text documents that must be drafted. Word processing capabilities also are important because written communication is essential in the management of business organizations.

## The Need for Written Communication

Businesses write tens of millions of letters and memos every day. In addition, many other documents play key roles in business operations. These written communication applications are identified and described briefly in the discussion that follows.

■ **Letters and Memos.**   Letters and memos represent business transactions. A letter writer often presents an offer to buy or sell products or services. Letters written in response accept or reject the offers. Commitments are made through the exchange of letters.

■ **Requests for Proposal (RFP) and Proposals.**   A request for proposal, or RFP, precedes a purchasing decision. An RFP spells out all requirements and asks suppliers to describe their proposed solutions, including price quotations.

■ **Price Lists and Technical Reports.**   Price lists, marketing support materials, and technical reports are documents used in marketing products and services, and in responding to RFPs.

■ **Contracts.**   A contract is a document that describes terms and conditions of a formal commitment. Within a typical business cycle, contracts are drawn when proposals are accepted. A contract commits two or more parties to its stated terms and conditions. The ability of computers to process changes and to produce new drafts rapidly is critical to development of contracts.

Each type of document makes a different contribution to its business organization. Each, therefore, presents an application opportunity for effective, efficient use of computers. Because of the importance of written communication in business, word processing has been the most popular type of application software package sold for use with microcomputers. This situation exists because word processing is profitable for its organizations and its users. Specific advantages lie in the areas of improvements in efficiency and effectiveness of operations, as described below.

## Word Processing: Increasing Efficiency

In written communication, efficiency is a measure of the amount of text or the number of documents that the user can generate. Efficiency is a major benefit derived from word processing systems. Efficiencies are inherent in a number of standard features of word processing systems. Methods that contribute to efficiency include:

• During revision, unchanged portions of text can be reused.
• Standard paragraphs or sentences can be retrieved from storage and incorporated in new documents.
• Finished documents can be created by using the computer to merge addresses stored on one file with text elements stored separately. The

result is attractively typed, personalized letters generated at mass-production costs.

Business documents lend themselves well to preparation with the aid of computers. Letters may go through as many as seven drafts before they are considered ready for mailing. These revisions are necessary to be sure that all statements are correct, that all key points have been covered, and that the text is accurate and neat. Though these revisions are necessary to assure quality, the complete retyping of documents can be expensive and time consuming. The inherent efficiency of word processing makes a high level of quality affordable.

Many business documents include necessary portions of text that are repeated from other documents. For example, contracts or letters on legal matters need certain paragraphs that state conditions and terms. All letters have certain repeatable elements that include signature blocks for the persons who will sign them. Computers add productive power to office procedures by making it possible to store portions of messages and to include them in documents where they are needed. These standard elements can be maintained in files and called up for inclusion as needed. Considerable time is saved by using computer files and modifying them as necessary as compared with complete, original typing of each document.

Another popular feature of word processing packages is *mail/merge*. With the aid of this feature, users can create lists of addressees who are to receive a given letter. The text of the letter is stored in a separate file. The computer

Organization-wide efficiency can be achieved when users share access to files, application software, and other resources throughout an office or department.

merges the files by selecting one addressee at a time and incorporating name-and-address information with the text of the letter. The computer also has capabilities for inserting personal references, such as the first name of an addressee, into the salutation and also into designated positions within the body of the letter. Thus, personalized form letters can be created that have the impact of being individually typed.

## Word Processing: Increasing Effectiveness

In written communication, effectiveness is a measure of how well a document accomplishes its goal. Measures of effectiveness include several elements:

- Clarity in the use of words
- Completeness with which the topic is covered so as to avoid misunderstandings
- Appearance of the finished product.

To assure clarity and completeness, document preparation can require multiple drafts. In this context, a *draft* is a preliminary or intermediate version of the text of a document. Drafts are preliminary or rough steps toward completion of an acceptable, or final, document.

Drafting is an age-old practice in document preparation. Before computers were available, drafts were prepared by hand or on typewriters. Computers have introduced the ability to store the text of drafts and to retrieve those texts for rework. The need to rewrite entire documents, as was necessary

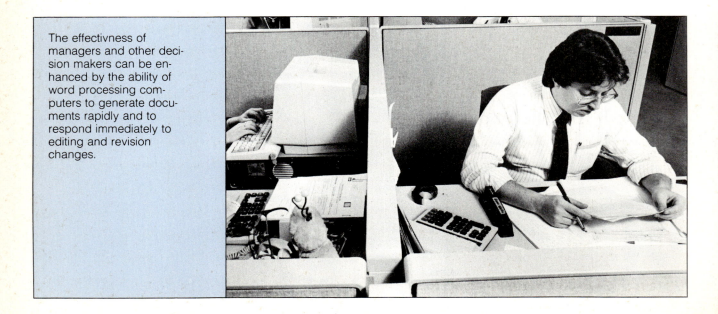

The effectivness of managers and other decision makers can be enhanced by the ability of word processing computers to generate documents rapidly and to respond immediately to editing and revision changes.

manually or on typewriters, is gone. Only the changes need be entered. The computer generates new drafts or final documents rapidly, accurately, and attractively.

The descriptions of business documents above stress an important characteristic about their creation: Frequent, careful revision is necessary to achieve precision in the wording and content of each document. In bygone days, each draft had to be retyped—then proofread—from start to finish. The cost in time and effort is obvious. Less obvious is a reticence that sets in: People aware of the work involved are hesitant about requiring a complete retyping of a document—and of running the risk that new errors will be introduced during the course of retyping.

When text files are stored within a computer system, users can preview final appearance by displaying the text on a video screen. Also, revisions in format can be made easily on printed drafts. Efforts are minimal and results are enhanced by the ability of a computer to retype a complete letter in seconds.

Word processing makes a big contribution to the effectiveness of business communication by providing quality assurance and flexibility at each stage of document preparation. The quality of correspondence is a major beneficiary from the word processing power of computers. As described below, word processing packages implement computer information systems and have the same basic components as any other system.

## Word Processing Systems

Note the word ''systems'' in the heading. Word processing systems involve a combination of people, procedures, data (text), and equipment to deliver expected information outputs to designated users:

- People
- Procedures
- Data (text)
- Equipment.

## People

The people who use word processing services and generate textual documents are employed at all levels within their organizations—including top executives and managers who originate documents and the people who implement the word processing systems to generate and distribute the resulting documents. Almost everyone in business receives and depends upon documents that contain text, particularly correspondence, the letters and memos used to promote a company and transact its business.

## Procedures

The procedures of word processing are a standard working routine in business organizations. Word processing software is part of these procedures. Software packages support the general steps for producing a document:

- Create a message.
- Capture text.
- Produce a draft.
- Review and edit a draft.
- Approve and distribute final document.

■ **Create a Message.**   Words capture information and ideas. People use words as tools to communicate what they mean, to promote their businesses, and to confirm commitments made to one another. Most documents within business

The steps followed to implement a word processing system are identified in this flowchart. Word processing procedures begin with creation of a message and proceeds to text capture, printing of a draft, review and edit of the draft, review and (if necessary) revision, and (on approval) output of finished documents.

CREATE MESSAGE

CAPTURE TEXT

PRODUCE DRAFT

REVIEW AND EDIT

APPROVE   NO

YES

FINISHED DOCUMENT

organizations are originated by managers who direct other employees and deal with outside companies or individuals.

To illustrate, consider the hypothetic case of Vera Abel, a mid-level manager responsible for purchasing fasteners (bolts, screws, rivets, etc.) for the High Flyer Aircraft Manufacturing Company. Vera travels frequently in the course of her job. Before she places a large order, she inspects the facilities and evaluates the capabilities of at least two or three potential suppliers.

Vera has found that it is best not to wait until she returns to her office from field trips to write agreement or confirmation letters. While she is away, so much work builds up at the office that it would be difficult to get everything done. ''I couldn't keep up or catch up if I wrote all of the letters at my desk,'' she explains.

To use time efficiently, Vera drafts her letters during her travels. Depending on the situation, she uses either of two methods. First, Vera carries a portable, lap-top computer on some trips. With this, she can draft letters right in

Document displays on screens of computer work stations provide efficiency and flexibility for document editing and revision by teams of managers and word processing operators. High-quality outputs can be derived quickly through these techniques.

supplier offices or can work in hotel rooms or on airplanes. This method is preferred because Vera can review and revise the wording of her drafts as they are written.

An alternate method is used when Vera travels to facilities in her own region or during the 30-minute drive to and from work each morning and evening. Vera carries a portable dictating machine on which she can dictate drafts of correspondence en route and have these transcribed to produce drafts she can review on her own computer screen. With either method, Vera meets her responsibility for originating correspondence that supports her company's manufacturing operations.

■ **Capture Text.**    The *capture* function involves keying the words into a computer keyboard. Vera performs this function directly when she uses a lap-top computer. When Vera dictates an initial draft, the capturing is done by her secretary, Roxanne, who transcribes the spoken words into a computer by using a transcription machine. Roxanne listens to the spoken draft and generates a text on her computer screen. Roxanne provides all of the punctuation, capitalization, sentence structuring, and paragraphing as she transcribes the dictated documents. Periodically, Roxanne uses a save function to cause the computer to record the text on a diskette for future retrieval and use.

■ **Produce a Draft.**    Under computerized word processing systems, the printing of documents is separated from the keying of text. Text is retrieved from storage and printed as often as needed. Even at high speeds, computer printers are able to produce quality documents in a matter of seconds per page. Draft copies of documents can be generated as the basis for review and revision.

In the case of Vera's commitment and confirmation letters, Roxanne may produce one or more drafts before the letter is presented to Vera. Vera, who worked as a secretary herself while she was going to college, notes a difference that has been introduced into the manager-secretary relationship by word processing systems. "When I started in business," Vera explains, "the manager was an editor and the secretary merely transcribed dictation or retyped drafts. Today, the volume of work and the capabilities of equipment have changed that relationship. Now, often the manager creates rough drafts directly on a word processing system and counts on a qualified secretary to edit and structure the finished documents."

■ **Review and Edit a Draft.**    This function holds the key to the extensive savings of time and money achievable through word processing tools. A document can be reviewed and revised as often and as extensively as needed. At each revision, only the actual changes need be entered. The parts of the document that are correct do not have to be keyed again. Thus, checking of work also becomes easier, since the unchanged portions of a document do not have to be checked repeatedly.

At High Flying Aircraft, electronic editing capabilities are especially important. As indicated, Roxanne does an initial edit of all documents as she completes transcription. Or, if Vera has done an initial draft, Roxanne displays the

Convenience and flexibility are inherent in microcomputer-based word processing systems that store text on diskettes. The storage media can be kept conveniently on desktops or can be held in the file folders that contain the corresponding documents.

text from the disk she receives. She checks spelling, sentence structure, and letter formatting before a draft is delivered to Vera. Vera herself may make some changes as she reviews each document. To ease the process, Vera asks Roxanne to provide a disk with each set of documents. Vera makes some of the changes herself and provides an updated disk for generation of new drafts. Once Vera is satisfied, the documents must be reviewed by product managers and also by the legal department. Additional changes may be specified. These are made quickly and new drafts can be produced in minutes.

■ **Approve and Distribute Final Document.**    The originator and any other responsible managers can check a document as often as needed until the wording and appearance are acceptable. When a document is approved for preparation of a final draft, the text is retrieved from storage and printed in final form for distribution.

Vera recognizes that the final draft of each letter requires her signature and that, once she has signed it, the company may be committed to spend large sums of money. She reads final drafts carefully and takes special pains to verify all dollar amounts included in the text.

As with all computer systems, procedures involve a series of instructions to be followed by people and also programs that establish instructions to be followed by computers. The descriptions above stress the procedures people follow. Specific descriptions of software to support word processing are presented later in this chapter.

## Data (Text)

For any business application, data include the cumulative results of processing, the stored files that can be reused to support continuing operations and as a basis for decisions. In the word processing area, data files play a special role. In the drafting of documents, executives and managers rely heavily on previous texts, which are treated as precedents. To illustrate, a user who receives and decides to accept a sales proposal cites the original, basic document in creating a response. In creating new proposals, users can rely heavily on the content of previous documents that have been used successfully.

In the past, users have had to rely on files of paper documents for this purpose. Each reuse of information presented a need to retype the text completely, then to proofread and correct drafts. With computer files to store and protect text, the ability to find and reuse documents or portions of documents is enhanced greatly. In effect, computers store the text files that represent the cumulative experiences and successes of an organization.

The value of data files is different in the word processing area from the values of files that contain financial and statistical information. But the values can be just as important in the ongoing management of a business.

## Equipment

Word processing is implemented on a computer system with the aid of special software. Equipment itself requires no special or unique features to support word processing applications. The one essential, today, is a random access storage capability. Early word processing equipment used tape and other serial devices for storage. When diskettes became available, the other approaches fell rapidly into disuse.

It is possible to support word processing service on a large computer that serves hundreds of users at on-line (directly connected) terminals. It also is possible to do word processing on a microcomputer that serves just one user. Many word processing systems are implemented on local area networks that interconnect a series of microcomputers and storage devices.

Like all systems, word processing combines the people, procedures, data, and equipment subsystems to produce desired results. Word processing systems, like all computer information systems, have helped to solve problems associated both with volumes of work to be done and the support capabilities that make the work of people more effective.

## Word Processing Functions

Word processing capabilities can be implemented through use of a wide variety of off-the-shelf packages. These packages contain sets of diskettes, storage devices recorded with application programs. Also included is a manual that provides sets of procedures to be followed by computer users. (These descriptions apply to packages that run on microcomputers. Arrangements are similar, though more complex, for larger computers.) Until these word processing tools are loaded into memory, the microcomputer is an undirected collection of machinery.

Use of many word processing packages begins with selections made from choices offered on menus. This menu display supports a popular word processing package, WordStar 2000.

```
C:\WS2000
              O P E N I N G   M E N U – 1 of 2

    Edit / create              Print              Get help

    Remove                     Copy                 Quit


    Directory / drive          Key glossary

    Move / rename              Typewriter mode

    Spelling correction        Format design

        Press a highlighted letter or Spacebar for more choices.
```

Scores of different functions are used to implement word processing systems. These functions have different names and are applied through varying techniques by individual application packages. However, there are common functions that must be supported by all software packages. These are described below within the context of a few, basic, generic groups:

- Creating text files
- Editing text files
- Formatting and printing documents.

## Creating Text Files

Document development through word processing begins with use of software functions that create files and capture text. The user establishes a file to hold text, actually enters or captures the text, and records the files for storage and future use.

As just one example of the power of word processing for creating documents, the content of this book was written on microcomputer keyboards, saved through a series of editing operations, then converted electronically into the type you are reading. The software commands used to capture text and establish files are reviewed below.

■ **Create a File.**  Under most word processing systems, the first step is to establish a file on a storage disk. This provides a place to record your work for future use. You do this by establishing a name that your software will use to set up and maintain a disk file for the document you are creating.

■ **Enter.**  Keying text on a microcomputer is similar to typing, except that word processing software provides more advanced tools. One of the most powerful of these tools is *word wrap.* When your entries reach the end of a line, the computer ''wraps'' the text to the beginning of the next line automatically.

   All entries, of course, are displayed on a screen for continuing review. Any errors can be fixed as part of the entry process simply by covering up the errors with correct entries.

■ **Save.**  A *save* records the captured text on a storage unit such as a diskette. Without a saving operation, you may lose your work.

   Some word processing software packages have automatic saving features. Any time you start work on a new page or quit work on a file, saving is automatic. Other packages require user action. At the very least, every user should be aware of the need to save text files so that they can be retrieved at any time for review, revision, and/or printing.

■ **Case Example: Creating Text Files.**  The functions described above are basic, or primitive, steps used in capturing text and creating files from which drafts and finished documents can be developed. To illustrate how some of these functions are applied in actual business situations, consider the procedures followed by Vera and Roxanne in generating correspondence involving purchases of aircraft screws, bolts, nuts, and other fasteners.

   As correspondence originators go, Vera can be considered a sophisticated microcomputer user. When she carries a lap-top computer with her, she creates files and turns diskettes over to Roxanne, along with the letters or other documents, such as specifications or bids, that are part of the same transaction or project.

   If a letter is dictated, Roxanne starts by calling up a menu and entering the file name indicated by Vera. The name is recorded in the directory stored on disk so that the file can be retrieved at any time. In entering text, Roxanne starts by keying exactly the dictation provided by Vera. If blank spaces are left for names or part numbers, Roxanne enters a notation within text to remind herself that additional information is needed. Roxanne does this by entering two asterisks (**) within the text. Then, she can find the symbols and provide the missing information in the course of formatting and printing drafts.

## Editing Text Files

Revision or editing of text can take place at any time. You can change and revise as you enter text. Or, you can retrieve a stored document for later editing. Editing is performed with a series of specific functions or commands, described below.

Document origination is both convenient and efficient when laptop computers are used during business trips or at homes of business managers.

■ **Retrieve.** To retrieve a previously stored document, you refer to the name that you gave the file when it was created. In some instances, this is done by entering a command on a blank screen. Software packages that take this approach are called *command driven*. Another approach involves the use of function selection *menus*. A menu is a display that lets the user know what features or services are available. The user then makes a selection through a keyboard entry and the system responds.

■ **Control Cursor.** An initial requirement as you begin to edit is to get the *cursor* to the point on the screen where additions or changes are to be made. A cursor is, in effect, an electronic place marker that usually takes the form of a blinking line or block. Each keyboard entry is made at the cursor position. Keys also are provided to move the cursor to the point where entries or corrections are to be made.

Speed and convenience in the selection of menu options and in movement of a cursor can be achieved through use of a mouse.

Some word processing systems use a *mouse* or *track ball* for cursor movement. A mouse is a device with a roller built into a small casing. Moving the mouse across a desk surface moves the cursor rapidly in a corresponding direction. A track ball has the roller exposed for manipulation with the user's hand.

■ **Scroll.**   A typical display screen presents up to 24 lines of text. As more text is captured, lines disappear over the top of the screen. To review the content of documents, you require a way to move text up and down so that you can get to the full content. This kind of text movement is called *scrolling*. All word processing systems provide some method for scrolling.

■ **Delete or Backspace.**   Text changes often require that some letters or words be removed. One way to remove text already displayed on a screen is with the BACKSPACE key. Each time this key is depressed, the cursor moves one space to the left and the character to the left is removed. Most microcomputers also have a DELETE key that can be used for removal of unwanted text.

■ **Insert.**   Editing changes often require the insertion of new text. These can be letters within existing words or words to be added. One of the great benefits of word processing systems lies in the ability to *insert* new words, sentences, or even paragraphs within existing text. An INSERT key is provided to activate this capability.

■ **Move and Copy.**   Under traditional document preparation, ''cut and paste'' methods are used to rearrange text. That is, the document is cut and the portions are rearranged and pasted in place with mending tape. With word processing software, cut-and-paste operations are carried out electronically. A *move* function identifies a block of text in one portion of a document and places it elsewhere. Another option, *copy*, reproduces an existing segment of text elsewhere in the document, but leaves the original text in its established place.

■ **Search and Replace.** You can identify a word or group of characters that you want to find within a document and have the computer *search* for them. The computer examines the text character by character and stops when it finds your target text. You also can instruct the computer to *replace* identified text portions with new text items. For example, if you have misspelled a word at several points in a document, you can instruct the computer to find the misspelled words and replace them with corrections.

■ **Check Spelling.**   Many word processing systems provide a capability for finding misspelled words or typographical errors. The spelling program traces through a document and tries to match each word with an entry in a dictionary that is part of the software. Words that are not matched in the dictionary are highlighted for user reference. If words are misspelled, corrections can be made. If the word is correct but not included in the dictionary, the user can enter a command that adds the term to the dictionary so that it will be recognized next time it is used.

The spell checking capability of a word processing system is demonstrated in this screen display. The computer has identified a word, 'unecessary,' with a spelling that is not matched in its dictionary. The system has recommended a correctly spelled word as a replacement. The change will be made following a response by the user.

```
          CASE.WS2        Pg 1    Ln 32 Col 21 (2.00")    Insert Horiz
·  Add to dictionary            Correct all occurrences      · Get help ·
·  Ignore                       Next suggestion
·  Type correction              Previous suggestion          ·  Escape  ·
                    Press Return to correct as suggested.
     Suspect word:   unecessary
       Suggestion:   unnecessary

          Trouble shooter
          Handle more  detail for agents, in  order to improve produc-
          tion
          Should keep up the changes in training manuals
          Keep agents informed
          Develop helps for agents on in house computer

          OFFICE MGR.:
          Track activities of all parties in office
          Try to keep moral up
          Help agents with problem transactions when possible
          Keep unecessary distractions from broker
          Hold sales meetings once a week
          Arrange all  staff  development  opportunities  that  office
```

■ **Check for Synonyms.** If a word is used frequently in text or if a writer wants to find a substitute word, some word processing packages make a thesaurus, or set of synonyms, available. This can be a valuable tool in adding interest to a written document.

■ **Case Example: Editing Text Files.** In an operation like the one implemented by Vera and Roxanne, capturing and editing text becomes part of a continuous procedure. One reason is that much of the content of a typical letter comes from files stored on disks at Roxanne's desk. To illustrate, Vera provides only the name and company of the person to receive a letter. Roxanne retrieves the full name and address from a customer name-and-address library stored on disk.

Each time changes are made, Roxanne executes a save function to be sure that the stored file is updated and that her work is protected. When a working draft has been developed, Roxanne uses a copy function to record the text on a second, or *backup*, disk. The backup is used if the original is damaged. As a protection, one copy of each file is kept conveniently at Roxanne's desk. The backup copy is placed in a safe for protection before she leaves the office every evening.

This screen display shows a typical output control capability for a word processing program. The user indicates the name of the file to be printed and the system shows the output options and default selections that will be applied if the user does not change them. The user can alter any of the selections displayed through keyboard inputs.

```
    B:\                                                Print  CASE.WS2
                          D E C I S I O N S
ÖåàààààààààààààààààààààààààààààààààààààààààààààààààààààÔààààààààààç
· Press Return to accept current answer, or                       ·
· type new answer over old and press Return.           ·^Get help ·
·                                                      ·           ·
·    Press ^V to view all answers.                     ·  Escape   ·
·    Press ^Q to accept all answers.                   ·           ·
âàààààààààààààààààààààààààààààààààààààààààààààààààààààêàààààààààà1
                  ^G means hold down Ctrl key and press G.


Begin printing on what page?                            1
Stop printing after what page? (L for LAST)             L
Print how many copies?                                  1
Pause between pages for paper change? (Y/N)             N
Obey page formatting commands? (Y/N)                    Y
Print and continue working? (Y/N)                       N
Send document to Printer or to Disk file? (P/D)         P
Prepare the printer and press Return.
```

## Formatting and Printing Documents

Under word processing systems, *formatting* refers to the entry of instructions that determine the width, length, spacing, style and other appearance factors for finished text. Under some systems, format specifications are entered into instruction screens or tables and the actual text display is not affected; only the appearance of the printed document is controlled. Under other systems, the appearance of the display reflects the format of the final output. This method is referred to as "WYSIWYG" (what you see is what you get). In either case, the set of options available tends to be standard, as indicated in an accompanying table.

■ **Case Example: Formatting and Printing Text Files.**   A major advantage of word processing over traditional typing is that documents can be formatted and printed after the text has been captured and edited. By comparison, when

The formatting and printing functions generic to word processing application packages are identified and described in this table.

| FUNCTION | FORMATTING OR PRINTING ACTIVITY |
|---|---|
| SET MARGINS | ESTABLISH WIDTH OF MARGINS (RIGHT/LEFT POSITION). |
| SET PAGE LENGTH | DETERMINE THE UP AND DOWN POSITION ON PAGE. |
| LINE SPACING | CONTROL THE NUMBER OF LINES PER VERTICAL INCH. |
| CHARACTER SPACING | CONTROL THE WIDTH OF CHARACTERS. |
| TABULATION | CAUSES CURSOR TO SKIP TO PREDETERMINED STOPS AWAY FROM THE LEFT MARGIN. |
| PAGINATION | AUTO PAGE BREAKS AND NUMBERING. |
| CENTERING | TEXT HEADINGS ARE CENTERED ON PAGE. |
| UNDERSCORE | TEXT IS UNDERLINED. |
| BOLD FACE | TEXT IS PRINTED DARKER THAN OTHER PORTION OF TEXT. |
| SPECIAL FONTS | CHARACTERS ARE PRINTED IN DIFFERENT STYLES AND FORMS. |
| SUPERSCRIPT | CHARACTERS ARE PRINTED ABOVE THE NORMAL TEXT LINE. |
| SUBSCRIPT | CHARACTERS ARE PRINTED BELOW THE NORMAL TEXT LINE. |

a document is to be typewritten, decisions about margins, positions of text on a page, and other appearance factors have to be made in advance.

To produce purchasing correspondence at High Flying Aircraft, formatting and printing decisions are put off until after the text has been reviewed and approved. Managers within the company understand that these decisions can be made later and have confidence that Roxanne will follow the company's style guidelines. Because formatting decisions are put off until just before final documents are produced, Vera and Roxanne can use double-spaced drafts for

**Impact**

## How to Select or Adapt to a Word Processing Package

Many millions of people use word processing packages to produce documents on microcomputers. For each person, the computer and software combine as a personal tool. Therefore, personal likes and dislikes control the selection and use of word processing systems. Your word processing system will be different from anyone else's because it reflects your outlook.

You already may be one of the millions of word processing users. If not, there is a good chance you will have to adapt to or select a word processing package in the near future.

In considering a word processing package, be aware that the decision is important and that a process approach can help you to make the best choice for your situation. So, the first thing to do is to define the requirements for word processing on your job. These preferences become the statement of need that establishes guidelines for your decision.

For example, if you are producing business letters, the fact that a software package has the ability to handle footnotes probably is of no interest. The same may be true for a capability to perform arithmetic or an ability to operate in column formats within a word processing package. In checking features and prices for packages, you may find that sophisticated capabilities lead to higher prices. If your needs are simple, it may be best to buy a basic, inexpensive package. On the other hand, if advanced features have potential value, you should be aware of the shortcomings of the low-cost packages. This line of thinking helps you to identify and rate the usefulness of candidate application packages.

Your next step is to compare the identified packages with the requirements you have identified. Ideally, you will narrow the field to two or three packages. At that point, you can evaluate trade-offs. That is, you should compare the value of each package in your working situation with its cost.

In making your decision, identify the kinds of jobs you want to process. Then, assemble a series of sample documents and ask to process these jobs under two or more different packages. Your software supplier should be able to provide this capability. Remember that a software package is a tool—one you will have to use. Pick the tool that feels best for you.

If you are employed in an organization that already has standardized on a software tool, you may not have a choice. If this is the case, somebody else already has gone through the selection process. You will do well to understand the job and the features of the package that lend themselves to the job. Even if the package you are given isn't your own favorite, it will help to understand why it was chosen and how you can use it to best advantage.

all but the final version of a document. This makes it easy for reviewers to write in comments and to suggest changes.

When a document is ready for final printing, Roxanne considers the amount of text to be generated and figures out how it will fit onto the page or pages to be used. She has considerable flexibility in these decisions. She can change the width of text lines, character width of the text, and the line spacing to be used. In considering the content of a message, Roxanne can print portions of the text in indented or centered mode, underscore key words, use boldface or italics in printing, and add spaces within text for emphasis.

For example, purchasing letters usually include a "subject line" that identifies the job for which commitments are being made. Roxanne usually centers this line on the page and underscores the name and/or number of the project. Key words often are printed in boldface type. Roxanne also uses the superscripting or subscripting features of her word processing package to enter mathematical equations that may be included in specifications.

In many instances, Roxanne prepares two or more versions of a final document to see which is most readable and attractive.

The situation at High Flying Aircraft is both typical and unique. Vera and Roxanne have worked out their own system that has increased effectiveness and efficiency for their specific jobs. However, they have achieved these benefits through use of general-purpose software packages like those available to you and millions of other users. Even though application packages are purchased "off the shelf" and used by many people, each application has unique requirements and challenges. Each user individualizes the methods for applying a package and the benefits derived from its use.

## Chapter Summary

- Word processing software improves the ability of a business to handle written communication functions.
- Types of documents processed with the aid of word processing software include letters, memos, requests for proposal, proposals, price lists, technical reports, and contracts.
- Word processing software helps business organizations to increase efficiency, improve effectiveness, and achieve greater productivity.
- Word processing systems serve almost all people involved in creating correspondence or other business documents.
- Procedures for word processing can be illustrated by the steps in document development: create a message, capture text, produce a draft, review and edit each draft, and approve and distribute the final document.

- Word processing systems are supported by text files created and maintained by computers. Many word processing files are kept on diskettes that can be stored conveniently on desk tops or in the same file folders as the documents themselves.
- Equipment that supports word processing is the same as for any other computer application.
- The functions supported by word processing software fall into three categories: creating text files, editing text files, and formatting and printing documents.

## Questions for Review

1. Why are appearance and accuracy important for business letters?
2. What are requests for proposal and what demands do they place upon businesses that receive them?
3. How can computers and word processing software increase efficiency in creation of business documents?
4. What is a mail/merge capability within a word processing package and how does it work?
5. How does word processing contribute to the effectiveness of document preparation within a business organization?
6. How is productivity of an organization enhanced through use of word processing techniques?
7. How is the process of document creation broken down under word processing procedures and what are the advantages of separating this job into a series of separate steps?
8. Define the term ''draft'' and explain how word processing techniques enhance document drafting.
9. Identify and describe the steps associated with creating a text file and storing it on a magnetic medium.
10. Identify and describe the steps associated with editing a text file and producing a finished document.

## Questions for Thought

1. Word processing separates keying and printing of documents. What special requirements does this separation of functions create in terms of training computer operators and information users?

2. What is the special role of software within a word processing system?

3. What are the advantages and possible disadvantages of the ability to separate the creation of text files and the formatting of text for printing?

4. What contributions to productivity and quality of finished documents come from the ability to edit and change text files without disturbing the parts of the files that are to remain unchanged?

5. What special precautions should be taken in selecting equipment and software and in training users of a new word processing system?

## Terms

| | |
|---|---|
| backup | mouse |
| capture | move |
| command driven | replace |
| copy | save |
| cursor | scroll |
| draft | search |
| format | subscript |
| insert | superscript |
| integrated software | track ball |
| mail/merge | word processing |
| menu | word wrap |

## MINICASE

**Situation:**

You have just started work as a systems advisor in a computer store. A customer asks for help with a problem: The customer works for a medium-sized business that has been using the same word processing package for several years. The customer is concerned because the company that developed his present word processing package has gone out of business. In addition, several executives, on the basis of conversations with friends, have heard of newer packages that, they feel, might enhance efficiency and effectiveness in written communication.

You acquaint the customer with the decision-making process that can be used to select a new package. In discussions about a decision statement, the customer indicates that the main applications in his organization are for letters, memos, and comparatively few short reports. You are told that "fancy" features, such as calculation capabilities, footnoting, or column formatting are not needed.

The customer indicates that, if you can help to select the best package for his job and can provide training to users, he will buy 20 copies of the program you help him select.

### Decision Making: Your Turn

1. From the information you have, identify and describe the problem to be solved or need to be met.
2. Identify alternatives that could be followed to produce best results for the customer's situation.
3. On the basis of the limited information you have: a) Identify additional information you would gather if you were dealing with this problem in a real situation. b) Identify the solution that appears best on the basis of the information that is available and explain your reasons for this selection.
4. What lessons are to be learned from this situation?

## Projects

1. Interview a user of a word processing package. Write a brief report identifying and describing the types of documents generated. Also list and describe the main advantages and disadvantages of the word processing package used by the person you interview.
2. Examine magazine articles and/or brochures available through a computer store. Develop a list of the hardware and software you would use to meet your personal word processing needs.
3. If you have learned to use a word processing system, write a one-page report in which you describe the steps you followed to load your program, capture text, edit your report, and produce an output. Deliver the finished document to your instructor.

# Chapter Outline

End-User Perspective

The Point: Electronic Spreadsheets Enhance Numeric Reporting Capabilities

The Need for Electronic Spreadsheets
*Spreadsheet Content Requirements, Electronic Spreadsheets: Reporting Capabilities, Case Example: Spreadsheets for Decisions*

Spreadsheet Systems
*People, Data, Procedures, Equipment, Case Example: Spreadsheet Design*

Spreadsheet Functions
*Format, Edit, Compute, Move and Copy, Save and Retrieve, Print, Erase, Macros*

Putting Spreadsheets to Work

Chapter Summary

Questions for Review

Questions for Thought

Terms

Minicase

Projects

## CHAPTER 5

# Electronic Spreadsheets

## Briefing Memo

TO:      Information Users
FROM:   T. Rohm, W. Stewart

Electronic spreadsheet software has a special significance for the current period, which some are calling a "computer revolution." Electronic spreadsheet software has done more than any other application to get managers and executives involved in "hands-on" use of computers.

As discussed in this chapter, the reason for the special impact of spreadsheet software is that managers and executives have been responsible for spreadsheet preparation for decades. Under manual methods, spreadsheet preparation was a tedious, time-consuming part of a manager's job. With electronic spreadsheet tools, the work has been simplified. Even more important, managers have been able to enhance their analysis and decision-making skills with electronic tools. Electronic spreadsheets have a potential impact on your own future. This chapter describes some ways in which spreadsheet software can help to enhance your own productivity.

## End-User Perspective

Dan Bricklin was a student in Harvard University's Master of Business Administration (MBA) program some years ago. Like most graduate business students, and like the great majority of business managers, Dan was loaded with assignments that required preparation of spreadsheets. A *spreadsheet* gets its name from the fact that it is produced on a wide sheet of paper that is divided into column (vertical) and row (horizontal) positions for presentation of information. The columns generally represent time periods while the rows represent information categories, such as income, payroll expense, rent, etc. In business, a spreadsheet represents a "snapshot" of the status of a business organization. This picture can reflect past conditions, the current status, or projections toward the future.

For many decades, right up to the late 1970s, spreadsheets represented one of the drudgeries of management. Like millions of managers before him, Dan Bricklin labored on wide, ruled pads into which individual descriptions and numeric values had to be written. At Harvard Business School, Bricklin was faced with numerous assignments that involved preparation of spreadsheets for budgets, financial reports, and other case situations. One of the drudgeries of spreadsheet preparation involved computation. Values in columns and rows had to be totaled on hand calculators and the results entered by hand. Percentages had to be calculated and entered individually. All this work had to be checked and rechecked manually. Then, to add to the time and tedium of this work, individual business problems often had to be reflected in multiple spreadsheet reports, perhaps a dozen or more, to display alternate results of operations or forecasts.

Dan Bricklin saw the minute details of spreadsheet preparation as wasteful, a problem. He did not have to resign himself to bearing the problem as generations of managers before him had done. Dan was a pioneering user of then-new microcomputers. He devised a program that enabled him to harness the power of the computer to capture data, process information changes, compute values automatically, and produce neat, legible electronic spreadsheets—all in a fraction of the time required for manual preparation. Dan not only made life easier for himself as a student but he also launched a software market that met needs of many managers by enhancing their productivity and effectiveness. In the process, Bricklin launched a product that has enjoyed hundreds of millions of dollars in sales. Dan's student project went on to become VisiCalc, the first electronic spreadsheet package for use on microcomputers.

## The Point: Electronic Spreadsheets Enhance Numeric Reporting Capabilities

Dan Bricklin certainly gained practical knowledge and experience as part of his graduate business school training. His situation reflects some important common denominators that have led to the wide acceptance and use of computers in business. Dan recognized, as many other managers and computer specialists have done, that business operations share many common problems that can benefit from shared solutions. The main basis for software application packages lies in the identification and solution of common problems.

In particular, Dan Bricklin made it possible to improve numeric reporting responsibilities in business. His invention automated the computation required to complete spreadsheets and also simplified the work of modifying data items within spreadsheets.

## The Need for Electronic Spreadsheets

In the case of spreadsheet preparation, the advantages for users center around capabilities to eliminate the handwriting of detailed lists of numbers. Look at the accompanying illustration that shows a handwritten spreadsheet. Now picture that many millions of these had to be prepared each year by managers and financial employees at all levels in business. Consider the aggravations that can be encountered. Suppose you are an employee in the marketing department of a large company. You are asked to prepare a budget for the coming year. You are told to take this year's figures and allow for across-the-board sales increases of 11 percent and increases in marketing department expenses of 7.5 percent.

Spreadsheets have been used, for many years, to document and report on budgets and financial status. Before electronic spreadsheet software was introduced, most spreadsheets had to be prepared under labor-intensive, error-prone manual methods. An example of a manually prepared spreadsheet is shown here.

| | | YEAR 1 | YEAR 2 | YEAR 3 | YEAR 4 | |
|---|---|---|---|---|---|---|
| INCOME | | | | | | |
| | Direct Sales | 260000 | 305000 | 355000 | 400500 | |
| | Mail-Order Sales | 80000 | 92000 | 111600 | 120000 | |
| | TOTAL | 340000 | 397000 | 466600 | 520500 | |
| | | | | | | |
| EXPENSES | | | | | | |
| | Personnel | 130000 | 140000 | 160000 | 190000 | |
| | Advertising | 11000 | 12400 | 15000 | 20700 | |
| | Supplies | 15200 | 17700 | 18400 | 24300 | |
| | Rent/Utilities | 17000 | 18200 | 20000 | 22200 | |
| | TOTAL | 173200 | 188300 | 213400 | 257200 | |
| | | | | | | |
| EQUITY | | 35000 | 43000 | 50500 | 60000 | |

INCOME/EXPENSE SUMMARY

Assume your spreadsheet has 40 line-items, or rows, and that there are 13 columns, one for each month and one for year-end. This means you have to perform 12 calculations for each of 40 entries, then develop sums for each 40-item column and every 12-column row. The result of each of these computations has to be entered in an exact row-column position.

After the work is done, you are complimented on a good job and your department head passes along the spreadsheet you have prepared. The next day, you are called in again and told that top management wants to see the results that could be expected if sales increased 12.5 percent and marketing expenses grew by 8.75 percent. This cycle continues. Projections for sales and expenses may be run for 10 or 12 different sets of figures.

Welcome to the world of budgeting and financial planning. Detailed analyses and forecasts of this type are regular occurrences. They are the alternatives that top managers look at in making decisions on facilities, materials, advertising, and hiring. Spreadsheet reporting has been around since the days when business correspondence was handwritten by scribes. From this situation, understand that electronic spreadsheet software has delivered the same kinds of benefits in the area of financial documentation and reporting as word processing has done for correspondence and other textual documents.

## Spreadsheet Content Requirements

Business organizations frequently are thought of as teams. The basic idea is that success in business requires everyone in the organization to work together, in coordination. When this kind of analogy is applied, the role of the operating

Reports and graphs generated by spreadsheet software are used as the basis for management review and decision making.

head of a company is comparable to that of a coach. Carrying this image a step further, the role of electronic spreadsheets can be compared with the purpose and value of scorecards or scoreboards in sports. A spreadsheet report is a tool for performance and status evaluation.

The need for accuracy is supercritical in the business scoreboards presented on spreadsheets. Managers set plans and make commitments on the basis of financial information presented on spreadsheets. Banks rely on these figures as a basis for lending money. Customers use the same information to judge the reliability of prospective suppliers. Spreadsheets prepared by hand are subject to the same kinds of errors as any other manual functions. It is difficult and costly to build accuracy and validity checks into manual procedures that match the quality and reliability of those applied routinely by electronic spreadsheet packages.

In addition to saving time and money while producing more readable, attractive documents, electronic spreadsheet software delivers another advantage: The results are inherently more reliable than handwritten spreadsheets.

Within this same context, spreadsheets that set up budgets or future operating plans are like matchups in lineups or game plans for athletic teams. A baseball manager might want to start left-handed batters against a right-handed pitcher. A business manager might want to be able to reassign manufacturing facilities if a given product enjoys strong sales.

This is a reproduction of a working screen with a spreadsheet under development. The headings and labels represent type entries. The data items are numeric or dollar data types. The subtotal and total rows contain formula entries that will control computations. In the entry area at the bottom, left, a formula has been entered for computation of the value in cell F16.

|  | A | B | C | D | E | F |
|---|---|---|---|---|---|---|
| | | | | | | May |
| 1 | INCOME | January | February | March | April | |
| 2 | Income #1 | $7,000.00 | $8,000.00 | $6,000.00 | $3,000.00 | $7,000.00 |
| 3 | Income #2 | $5,000.00 | $6,000.00 | $5,000.00 | $9,000.00 | $7,000.00 |
| 4 | ---------- | | | | | |
| 5 | Subtotal | +B2+B3 | +C2+C3 | $11,000.00 | $12,000.00 | $14,000.00 |
| 6 | ========== | | | | | |
| 7 | EXPENSES | | | | | |
| 8 | Payroll | $5,000.00 | $5,000.00 | $5,000.00 | $5,000.00 | $5,000.00 |
| 9 | Rent | $2,750.00 | $2,750.00 | $2,750.00 | $2,750.00 | $2,750.00 |
| 10 | Utilities | $400.00 | $400.00 | $400.00 | $400.00 | $400.00 |
| 11 | Phone | $267.00 | $267.00 | $267.00 | $267.00 | $267.00 |
| 12 | Materials | $3,000.00 | $3,000.00 | $3,000.00 | $3,000.00 | $3,000.00 |
| 13 | ---------- | | | | | |
| 14 | Subtotal | $11,417.00 | $11,417.00 | $11,417.00 | $11,417.00 | $11,417.00 |
| 15 | ========== | | | | | |
| 16 | TOTAL | +B5-B14 | +C5-C14 | ($417.00) | $583.00 | $2,583.00 |
| 17 | | | | | | |
| 18 | | | | | | |
| 19 | | | | | | |
| 20 | | | | | | |

```
F16    (C2) +F5-F14

    1help 2edit 3name 4abs 5goto 6window 7data 8table 9recalculate 0graph
    386K                              17:28                              READY
```

In business, most managers from department levels upward have responsibilities to prepare and live with spreadsheet reports. This alone explains why electronic spreadsheet software packages are top sellers for microcomputer use, close behind word processing. This also explains why it is important for users to be aware of the features and capabilities of spreadsheet software packages.

An accompanying illustration presents a microcomputer screen display of a spreadsheet that is partially completed. This illustration includes identifications for the key parts of a typical electronic spreadsheet. Components of this type are included in most spreadsheet packages, though formats and descriptive names may vary among individual packages.

■ **Columns and Rows.** A *column*, which is labeled in the accompanying illustration, is a vertical arrangement of positions that provides spaces for a specific number of characters. A column is identified with a label at the top of the spreadsheet, right under the heading. A label also is used to identify the content of each *row* within the spreadsheet. Row labels identify the nature or function of entries that follow from left to right, such as income, payroll, rent, etc.

■ **Cells.** Data items (or calculation formulas) are entered at points where columns and rows intersect. These entry positions are called *cells*. For example, figures on the income row would be entered in the columns designed for each individual month. Entries in cells can be either data items or formulas for computations. The accompanying illustration includes entries of headings, labels, data values, and formulas.

■ **Data Items.** Note first that the example spreadsheet contains different kinds of data items. Some entries contain descriptions rather than numbers that can be used in computations. Numeric and symbolic entries have other purposes, described below. In general, three types of data items are entered into the body of a spreadsheet:

- *Text* entries are descriptions that include letters, numbers, and symbols. These data items cannot be computed.
- *Numeric* entries can be computed. Numeric entries within a spreadsheet can be used as a basis for computations, with results entered into other spreadsheet positions, as designated by the user.
- *Formulas* determine the computations to be performed and the data items to which the arithmetic functions are to be applied.

On command from the user, the spreadsheet program performs a computation for each formula that has been included. The functions available are standard: addition, subtraction, multiplication, and division. The software finds the values in the identified cells, performs the indicated calculation, and enters the result in the cell that contains the formula.

Storage provisions for a typical spreadsheet package make it possible to retain the basic formulas and to set up separate displays and printed reports showing the computed values. In this way, adjustments in formulas or in data items can lead to development of entirely new versions of a spreadsheet—quickly and conveniently. A typical spreadsheet program can complete hundreds of computations in a few seconds.

## Electronic Spreadsheets: Reporting Capabilities

Recall that the information within a spreadsheet combines to present a picture of the status of the business unit or organization involved. Since the information in a spreadsheet represents its organization, this type of report also is called a *model*. That is, through information, a spreadsheet reflects, or models, the condition and status of its organization.

A number of the entries made by the user into a display format for a spreadsheet serve to clarify meaning for information users. These entries label data content of the spreadsheet and also instruct the software about the processing to be applied. Format entries provided by users of spreadsheet software include the following:

**Headings and Labels.**  Since a spreadsheet is a report that needs to communicate information, most spreadsheet packages provide a capability for entry of one or two *heading* lines. These are entered at the top of a spreadsheet format to identify the report name, its content, and date of preparation. Any information the user wants to include can be entered.

A *label* identifies the information entered within columns and rows of a spreadsheet.

- *Currency* entries are numeric and can be computed. Currency entries automatically establish two decimal positions for the recording of dollars and cents amounts.
- *Percentage* entries identify positions into which percentages are to be entered through computations involving identified data items included within the same spreadsheet.
- *Date* entries are used to specify the way dates are to be formatted within spreadsheets. Typically, users will enter a formatting notation such as MM/DD/YY to indicate that date entries are to be sequenced according to month, day, and year.

## Case Example: Spreadsheets for Decisions

Think back to the situation of Electronics, Inc., introduced in Chapter 2. The company is operating 11 dispersed distribution centers and is thinking of consolidating operations to save money and improve controls over customer services. The description in Chapter 2 indicates that managers study the situation and determine that more than $10 million in annual savings can be realized by closing down satellite distribution points and concentrating distribution services in or near the home office facilities.

This spreadsheet rounds out the picture of the decision-making situation under consideration at Electronics, Inc. The spreadsheet shows total distribution figures for the current year and totals that would be incurred under the projected, centralized system. Then, the differences are computed both in dollars and as percentages.

```
        A       B       C       D       E       F       G       H
 1                     CONSOLIDATED DISTRIBUTION--ANNUAL FIGURES
 2                          (In Millions of Dollars)
 3
 4             Center  Center  Center  Center  Center  Center   TOTAL
 5               #1      #2      #3      #4      #5      #6
 6      -----------------------------------------------------------------
 7      Revenue $27,000 $23,564 $37,896 $57,893 $108,784 $56,789 $321,926
 8      Cost    $21,675 $17,098 $26,987 $53,142 $90,846  $50,413 $260,161
 9      ----------------------------------------------------------------
10      Gross
11        Profit $5,325  $6,466 $10,909 $14,751 $17,938  $6,376  $61,765
12
13      Tax     $2,396  $2,910  $4,909  $6,638  $8,072   $2,869  $27,794
14      ================================================================
15      Net
16        Profit $2,929  $3,555  $6,000  $8,113  $9,866   $3,507  $33,971
17
18
19
20
A17

1help 2edit 3name 4abs 5goto 6window 7data 8table 9recalculate 0graph
386K                              17:29                              READY
```

This spreadsheet demonstrates the role of information about current operations in the decision to be made by Electronics, Inc., management. This is a model of a report for the current year. The report presents and compares figures for profits and costs for each distribution center and for the company's distribution operations as a whole.

```
        A         B         C         D         E       F       G
 1           CONSOLIDATED DISTRIBUTED--PROJECTIONS
 2                (IN MILLIONS OF DOLLARS)
 3
 4           PRESENT   PROJECTED DIFFERENCE      %
 5
 6      ---------------------------------------------------------
 7      Revenue $321,926  $523,897  $201,971    159.39%
 8      Cost    $260,161  $401,547  $141,386    184.01%
 9      ---------------------------------------------------------
10      Gross
11        Profit $61,765  $122,350   $60,585    101.95%
12
13      Tax     $27,794   $55,058    $27,263    101.95%
14      =========================================================
15      Net
16        Profit $33,971  $67,293    $33,322    101.95%
17
18
19
20
 B5

1help 2edit 3name 4abs 5goto 6window 7data 8table 9recalculate 0graph
386K                              17:30                              READY
```

This type of information can be developed by using electronic spreadsheet techniques to model existing and proposed operations. Consider a spreadsheet report like the one in the accompanying illustration. It is headed CONSOLIDATED DISTRIBUTION—ANNUAL FIGURES. The column labels identify the six warehouses and a total. The row labels identify sales and key expense items involved in operation of a distribution center. The consolidated report shows revenues and costs for each distribution center and for the company as a whole. The completed report models the annual financial results of current distribution operations within Electronics, Inc.

For comparison, management could call for preparation of a second spreadsheet model, which could resemble the second of the accompanying illustrations. This spreadsheet is similar to the first. But there are fewer columns. Note that the TOTAL column for the first spreadsheet has been carried over to this new one. Here, it is labeled PRESENT. Additional columns are labeled PROJECTED, DIFFERENCE, and %. The cells in these columns will contain figures projected for a single, central distribution center. The DIFFERENCE column will be derived by subtracting PROJECTED values from PRESENT amounts. Percentages will be derived by dividing PROJECTED values by PRESENT amounts. Overall differences are derived by totalling the entries in all amount columns.

As discussed in Chapter 2, other factors will be considered. However, it is obvious that information models like those developed through use of spreadsheet software can provide powerful evidence for reaching management decisions.

## ■ Spreadsheet Systems

Electronic spreadsheet packages are used to implement information systems that deliver required results to users. The implementation of a spreadsheet preparation and reporting effort involves the same basic elements as those in previous chapters: people, data, procedures, and equipment.

## People

The great majority of spreadsheet applications are implemented by users. These users must start with a knowledge of the operations to be modeled and the body of information to be used. Use of microcomputers and spreadsheet software is relatively easy and can be mastered by the average user in a day or a few days. In most instances, managers use spreadsheet software directly. In fact, electronic spreadsheets are credited with doing more than any other single application to involve managers in direct use of computers and terminals. Other spreadsheet package users include accountants, administrative personnel, secretaries, and others who work with financial or statistical data.

## Data

A spreadsheet is a coordinated collection of data that can be drawn from multiple sources. A manager assembling data for a spreadsheet could use some figures derived from other computer applications. Data also may come from outside sources, such as government economic projections, or from management policies that establish sales or profit goals. In addition, managers input some data items in the form of budget figures.

Another aspect of data content can be the graphic images to be derived from spreadsheets. That is, a manager might use spreadsheet software specifically to derive graphic outputs that can be used for analyses or presentations, as discussed in the chapter that follows.

## Procedures

An important attraction of a number of spreadsheet software packages is that they contain built-in instructions for application. Typically, when spreadsheet software is loaded, or "booted," the user is presented with a display that provides a standard format that can be used to generate a report. The same initial display also includes a list of available functions (described below) that can be selected for execution. As appropriate, specification screens are presented when functions are selected. These selections are made on screen displays presented to the user by the software.

During all entries, however, the user sees a visual display of the spreadsheet format on the screen. This is why an understanding of the operations being modeled and the information being used is so critical. A user must be able to define the information elements to be included and to specify the formats to be used.

Another reason for user familiarity with the underlying business processes is that the preparation of an electronic spreadsheet follows essentially the same pattern as for a manually prepared speadsheet. On a manual form, the user has to label the columns and rows and write in the appropriate figures. With electronic spreadsheet software, the principles are the same, except that formats have to be specified through entry procedures followed by the user. User procedures follow a proven series of steps based on the decision making process introduced in Chapter 2 of this text:

- Define the need by laying out a format for the finished spreadsheet and indicating the content of columns and rows.
- Test alternative designs or formats for alternate models to see which best meets user needs.
- Identify sources for and collect data needed to implement the spreadsheet.
- Using test or sample data, test the model to be sure the results meet the stated needs. Review and modify results as necessary, until a workable solution is achieved.

MULTIPLE LAYOUT FORM

| 1. | CHECK NUMBER | CHECK PAYEE | DESCRIPTION | TRANSACTION TYPE | TRANS-ACTION DATE | TRANSACTION AMOUNT | 1 0 1 1 0 1 0 | BITS |

9 9 9 9 | 9 9 9 9 9 9 9 9 9 9 9 9 9 9 9 9 9 9 9 9 | 9 9 9 9 9 9 9 9 9 9 9 9 9 9 9 9 9 9 9 9 9 9 9 | 9 9 9 9 9 9 9 | 9 9 9 9 9 9 9 9 9 9 9 | 9 9 9 9 9 9 9 9
1 2 3 4 | 5 6 7 8 9 10 11 12 13 14 15 16 17 18 19 20 21 22 23 24 | 25 26 27 28 29 30 31 32 33 34 35 36 37 38 39 40 41 42 43 44 45 46 47 48 49 50 51 52 53 54 55 | 56 57 58 59 60 61 | 62 63 64 65 66 67 68 69 70 71 72 | 73 74 75 76 77 78 79 80

2.

BYTE

9 9 9 9 9 9 9 9 9 9 9 9 9 9 9 9 9 9 9 9 9 9 9 9 9 9 9 9 9 9 9 9 9 9 9 9 9 9 9 9 9 9 9 9 9 9 9 9 9 9 9 9 9 9 9 9 9 9 9 9 9 9 9 9 9 9 9 9 9 9 9 9 9 9 9 9 9 9 9 9
1 2 3 4 5 6 7 8 9 10 11 12 13 14 15 16 17 18 19 20 21 22 23 24 25 26 27 28 29 30 31 32 33 34 35 36 37 38 39 40 41 42 43 44 45 46 47 48 49 50 51 52 53 54 55 56 57 58 59 60 61 62 63 64 65 66 67 68 69 70 71 72 73 74 75 76 77 78 79 80

3

This is a record layout that provides part of the procedure documentation for a planned spreadsheet application. The numbers at the bottom of the printed form identify character positions within the records. The ruled lines and printed descriptions identify the fields for a data record. At the far right, the notations identify content as including one eight-bit byte for each position on the layout form.

These procedures demonstrate that part of the success of spreadsheet packages is that the methods involved come naturally to users because they are so close in form and function to manual techniques.

## Equipment

The equipment used for electronic spreadsheet applications is almost always the same as is used for other applications. For example, the same microcomputer may be used for word processing and spreadsheet work simply by loading different programs or by using software packages that integrate multiple applications. Configurations should include enough memory to handle software, plus a working spreadsheet file, a printer, and secondary storage to accommodate both software and user data files.

If an organization uses a local area network under which users are linked to a central computer through terminals, these equipment configurations also can be used for spreadsheet applications by adapting readily available software packages.

If a user requires graphic outputs from a spreadsheet package, special graphics hardware will be needed. These requirements are covered in the chapter that follows.

## Case Example: Spreadsheet Design

In the example involving spreadsheet preparation for Electronics, Inc., a team would be formed to establish specifications for required information. Membership on a committee of this type may vary with company policy and the nature of the problem addressed.

In the Electronics, Inc., case, assume that the original idea came from analyses performed by Audrey Wise, controller of the company. Audrey's duties include general responsibility for monitoring the operations and administration of the entire company. The information systems and data communications functions of the organization report to her. Certainly, Audrey is a logical committee member. In this case, other likely members would be Hyram English, the vice president, finance, and Woodrow Williams, director of distribution.

At the first meeting, Wise asks Yoko Masuo, the company's director of systems services to join the group. Yoko has been assigned to develop the specifications for implementation of the reports. All members of the group are busy people. So they get right down to business. Wise suggests that the report present a composite picture of revenues and costs for operation of present facilities, and a second report for comparison of overall present costs with the results anticipated for alternative distribution schemes. Alternatives to be considered will be consolidation of all distribution in a single facility; operation of fewer, regional facilities; and continuing the existing distribution arrangement. Note that one alternative available for almost any decision situation is to do nothing.

Spreadsheet reports will be used to simulate all of the identified possibilities, including four different combinations of regional warehouses, in spreadsheet models. The magnitude of the job is large enough so that a special effort will be needed to gather relevant data items.

The committee meeting then focuses on what information is available. It is decided that rows on the spreadsheets will be allocated to information items available from current financial and operating reports. For example, sales, payroll, and other financial information will be provided by English. Operational information, such as size of facility and estimates of the size of required new facilities, will come from Williams. All data will be collected by Yoko Masuo, who will deliver spreadsheets to Wise for review at the next committee meeting.

To start a spreadsheet application, qualified managers should know what they want to achieve and what information is needed to model the decision alternatives. Given knowledge and some sophistication on the part of users, spreadsheet software provides a valuable tool.

## Spreadsheet Functions

Each spreadsheet package provides a set of functions that guide and control user operations. These functions are used as commands to direct the creation and implementation of spreadsheet applications.

To set the stage: When you ''boot'' a spreadsheet program, you are presented with a display that includes a *default* layout. If the default, or standard layout for the given package, meets your needs, you can proceed directly with entries. If not, you use the function commands of the software package to define your own layout and build your spreadsheet within your own design, as described below. The operational descriptions below are interspersed with examples of how the commands could be used at Electronics, Inc., to report on current distribution operations. The major functions selected by spreadsheet users include the following:

- Format
- Edit
- Compute
- Move and Copy
- Save and Retrieve
- Print
- Erase
- Macros.

To access any of these functions on most spreadsheet packages, you depress the slash (/) key. This causes the system to display a line of options, or *menu bar,* at the top (or bottom) of the screen. The cursor control keys are used to select the desired option. Pressing the RETURN key delivers the screens or other input tools needed to implement that function.

## Format

The *format* function is used to establish the number and widths of columns within the spreadsheet layout.

To illustrate, suppose Electronics, Inc., management wants a spreadsheet summarizing current operations information for each of its existing distribution centers. Since the spreadsheet will reflect the present distribution situation, the name CURRENT is assigned. The design for the spreadsheet includes six columns, one for each quarter, one for year-end totals, and one (at the left) for labels. For the CURRENT spreadsheet at Electronics, Inc., 13 rows are established. Eleven are to be used for profit (or loss) figures for each of the distribution centers. There is one blank line following the distribution-center entries, then a final line for TOTAL.

## Edit

The *edit* function is used to make or to change entries within the layout for a spreadsheet. Under some packages, a cursor marks the active cell to be affected, though actual entries are made in a special "scratchpad" area at the bottom of the screen. Under most packages, a cursor marks the "active" cell into which entries will be made. The user enters and reviews data items in a scratchpad area at the top or bottom of the screen. When the entry is correct, the RETURN key is pressed and the data item is transferred to its cell location.

The edit function enables the user to indicate the positioning of text (descriptive) within cells—centered, beginning at the left character position, or flush to the rightmost character position. Formulas are placed flush left when they are entered. All numeric entries within spreadsheet cells are right-justified, or aligned to the rightmost column.

Under the Electronics, Inc., operation, the heading and labels would be entered first. When a spreadsheet reaches this stage of development, with column headings and row labels in position and with a layout established, it sometimes is called a *template*. A template is a working guide. In preparation of spreadsheets, a template guides entry of data items or formulas into specific cells.

Once the template is established, entries are made into cells that correspond with rows for warehouse records and columns for quarterly periods. Totals at the bottom row and the rightmost columns will be developed by entering formulas for computation. These formulas will apply to ranges of cells that take in complete columns or rows, as demonstrated in the accompanying illustration.

## Compute

The *compute* function causes the system to carry out all of the arithmetic described in formulas within a spreadsheet. Basic arithmetic functions are specified through use of standard symbols: + for plus, - for minus, * for multiply, and / for divide. In addition, a number of special functions can be invoked through entry of an @ symbol with an accompanying instruction. For exam-

This is a screen display that will generate a spreadsheet for the report on the CURRENT situation at Electronics, Inc.

|   | A | B | C | D | E | F |
|---|---|---|---|---|---|---|
| 1 | | | | ELECTRONIC, INC. | | |
| 2 | | | | (IN MILLIONS OF DOLLARS) | | |
| 3 | | | | | | |
| 4 | CURRENT | QUARTER 1 | QUARTER 2 | QUARTER 3 | QUARTER 4 | YEAR END |
| 5 | | | | | | TOTAL |
| 6 | | | | | | |
| 7 | Revenue | $75,890 | $90,875 | $89,712 | $65,449 | $321,926 |
| 8 | Cost | | | | | |
| 9 | Payroll | $31,780 | $38,055 | $37,455 | $26,879 | $134,169 |
| 10 | Rent | $3,087 | $3,087 | $3,087 | $3,087 | $12,348 |
| 11 | Utilities | $2,543 | $2,543 | $2,543 | $2,543 | $10,172 |
| 12 | Phone | $89 | $103 | $38 | $78 | $368 |
| 13 | Materials | $16,789 | $21,769 | $19,723 | $14,690 | $72,971 |
| 14 | Insurance | $7,654 | $7,654 | $7,654 | $7,654 | $30,616 |
| 15 | Medical | $250 | $250 | $250 | $250 | $1,000 |
| 16 | Dental | $56 | $56 | $56 | $56 | $224 |
| 17 | | | | | | |
| 18 | TOTAL | $13,642 | $17,358 | $18,846 | $10,212 | $60,058 |
| 19 | | | | | | |
| 20 | | | | | | |

A1

1help 2edit 3name 4abs 5goto 6window 7data 8table 9recalculate 0graph

384K                              17:30                              READY

ple, the formula @SUM tells the system to add the values in the range of cells that are given. Under most spreadsheet packages, the compute function is invoked routinely each time the RETURN key is depressed.

## Move and Copy

Columns, rows, or ranges of cells are relocated under control of the *move* function. That is, the content of the identified cells is written into new locations and removed from old positions. The *copy* function can be applied to columns, rows, or ranges of cells. The system reproduces the values copied into another set of cells. The original content is left in place during a copy operation.

In the Electronics, Inc., case, application formulas for the totaling operations could be entered once, then copied into all of the cells to be summed.

## Save and Retrieve

The *save* function causes the system to store the spreadsheet on disk. To execute this function, the user enters a file name that will identify the spreadsheet on the directory of the disk storage device. The *retrieve* function can be used to recall a spreadsheet in the form in which it has been saved.

For users, the concept of saving spreadsheets after they are formatted and entries are made can provide flexibility. For example, in the Electronics, Inc., situation, the managers could cause the system to display totals for the entire spreadsheet. These could be checked against financial statements for the company to be sure they are accurate. The spreadsheet file need not be saved until its usefulness is established.

## Print

The *print* function reproduces the screen display on paper. Thus, the user can reproduce the spreadsheet either with the formulas or the computed values. The user can designate that the entire spreadsheet file be printed or that only specific ranges be output.

## Erase

The user can eliminate columns, rows, or specific ranges of cells. With a series of instructions, the user also can *erase* all content of the spreadsheet.

## Macros

A *macro* accomplishes a number of operations within a single function. A user can apply macro capabilities to capture a complete set of keystrokes for reuse. For example, if a user was assigned to produce a spreadsheet that followed the same layout each week, a template could be captured as a macro and called up to provide a working model for the entries to be completed. Instead of having to repeat the entries of format instructions, headings, and labels each time the job was performed, the macro could be called up with just a few keystrokes.

Some of the macro instructions available under popular spreadsheet application packages are identified and described in this table.

| FUNCTION | PURPOSE OR RESULT |
|---|---|
| **FINANCIAL FUNCTIONS** | |
| NPV | NET PRESENT VALUE. |
| PMT | PAYMENT, GIVEN PRINCIPAL, INTEREST, AND TERMS. |
| PV | PREVENT VALUE, GIVEN PAYMENT, INTEREST, AND TERMS. |
| **MATHEMATICAL FUNCTIONS** | |
| EXP | EXPONENTIAL. |
| SQRT | SQUARE ROOT. |
| TAN | TANGENT. |
| **STATISTICAL FUNCTIONS** | |
| AVG | MEAN FOR A RANGE OF GIVEN CELLS. |
| MAX or MIN | MAXIMUM OR MINIMUM FOR A GIVEN RANGE OF CELLS. |
| COUNT | DETERMINE NUMBER OF ITEMS IN A LIST. |

Most spreadsheets offer a number of additional functions. Some of these are identified and their function outlined on the accompanying table.

## Putting Spreadsheets to Work

Use of spreadsheets to represent existing status or projected results of decisions sometimes is called ''*What if?*'' simulation. In effect, spreadsheets are used to preview results of decisions. When multiple alternatives are evaluated, managers pose ''*What if?*'' questions to reflect many possible variables. The ''*What if?*'' questions might reflect anticipated changes in economic situations, actions of competitors, changes in interest rates, and many other variables.

The Electronics, Inc., situation is a prime example of the ''*What if?*'' ap-

**Impact**

## How to Select a Spreadsheet Package

In selecting a spreadsheet package, remember that you are choosing a tool. As a tool, the software should fit the job for which it will be used. Buying too much capacity in a package could be like buying an eight-pound sledge hammer to drive nails. The tool is cumbersome and much of the energy required for its use is wasted. Similarly, you can buy a spreadsheet package with capacities for 256 columns and 19,000 rows of data. If you need a maximum of 110 columns and 160 rows, you could be buying more tool than you need. You may be wasting money. You also may find you are wasting time working through software features or capacities that you don't need for your specific job.

Selecting any major piece of software represents a commitment, both in the money to be spent and the capabilities you will gain. Therefore, you should apply a process approach to help you get the best package—in terms of capabilities for your job and value for your money. As a selection starting point, recognize that there are two general conditions that apply to use of electronic spreadsheet software:

- Some packages are used in multiple departments or throughout an organization. If this is the case, compatibility between user systems may be essential. Therefore, standardization of equipment and software throughout the organization probably is a necessity.

- Some packages serve only individuals or departments. If this is the case, the in-dividual user may be free to select software according to individual preferences.

If you are free to make your own choice, use the decision-making procedure you have learned. Define your needs, then look for the closest match between what you want and what available packages can provide. The key to picking the best package lies in developing the most complete set of requirements. Some questions to address:

- How many columns of data items do you need and how wide should each be?

- How many rows of data will you require?

- What groupings will you need in setting up ranges for computation and manipulation of data within your spreadsheets?

- What computation capabilities are provided for inclusion in your formulas? Are these adequate and can you use them productively? Misunderstandings about computation functions lead to too many spreadsheets that include errors.

- Do you need graphics outputs from spreadsheet data and can the packages you review meet your needs?

As you consider these features, think about the reporting you will do and the decisions you will make on the basis of your spreadsheet applications. Make sure the spreadsheet you choose will meet the ultimate test of on-the-job usefulness.

proach to management decision making. In effect, the entire decision-making process is applied to answer the question: "What if we close all our distribution centers and ship everything by air out of a giant facility at the home office?" As happens in real life, one question leads to another. Other questions that could be addressed include:

• "What if some customers are upset by the change?"
• "What if we get a bad winter in New England and experience weather delays?"
• "What if we continue to lose money on certain distribution centers?"

For each of these "What if?" questions, there is another, implied question for which the answer holds the decision key: "How will overall profits be affected?"

Each assumption can lead to changes in the values included in a spreadsheet. Under "What if?" simulation, values or formulas are changed to reflect the results of an assumption. For example, if interest rates rise, management might assume that profits would decrease slightly, that customers would be slower in paying bills, and that overall sales might decline. Content of spreadsheet cells can be modified to reflect the assumed results and new evaluations can be made by generating new outputs from spreadsheet files.

Aside from the decison support applications like those shown for Electronics, Inc., electronic spreadsheet software has a wide range of other uses. One common and relatively simple use is for personal budgeting. To prepare a personal budget, you forecast income and allocate money to essential and optional expense items. Use of spreadsheets brings your financial requirements into the open. Funds are allocated to necessary expenses such as rent, food, car payments, or other commitments before any money is set aside for optional items such as entertainment.

For a major purchase involving land, buildings, or equipment, companies can use spreadsheets to test different interest rates and payment schedules to develop the most favorable amortization schedule. Amortization schedules establish sequences of payments to cover the amount of a loan, the interest payments, and any special costs (insurance, taxes, etc.).

For some major purchases, there may be options between leasing the equipment or making an outright purchase. Spreadsheets can be used to project costs and to determine the most favorable arrangement.

Manufacturing schedules and working time for employees also can be projected and evaluated through use of spreadsheet software.

Numeric reporting is an age-old requirement of business management. Meeting this requirement has become easier and reports have become more valuable following introduction of electronic spreadsheet application packages. You can expect to benefit from these capabilities in the future for applications that may range from personal budgeting to job-related management responsibilities.

## Chapter Summary

- Spreadsheets are used in most businesses for reporting financial and statistical information, and for budgeting.

- Electronic spreadsheet software applies computers to jobs that used to be tedious and time consuming. With computers, information users become more productive, efficient, and effective.

- Spreadsheets are organized into columns (vertical) and rows (horizontal). Points at which columns and rows intersect are called cells. User entries are made into individual cells through use of spreadsheet software.

- Types of entries determine whether data items are descriptive or whether they can be used in computations. Entries can be text, numeric, or formulas.

- Headings and labels are applied to identify content of spreadsheets. Headings are at the top of a report or above specific columns. Headings that identify the kinds of information reported in a spreadsheet include currency, percentage, and date. Labels identify individual rows.

- Most electronic spreadsheets are prepared directly by end users.

- Data included in spreadsheets come from multiple sources, including other applications, research, or estimates entered by managers.

- Procedures required to produce electronic spreadsheets are largely self-documented within programs. Procedures followed by users include definition of needs, design, data collection, and execution.

- Electronic spreadsheet software can be implemented on almost any microcomputer.

- Functions used in producing electronic spreadsheets include format, edit, sum or compute, move, copy, save, retrieve, print, insert, protect, erase, and a number of macros.

- A major technique for application of spreadsheets is to pretest decision alternatives. Managers ask ''What if?'' questions that are answered by modeling results of assumed conditions in spreadsheets. Spreadsheets become a decision-making tool. Application areas include budgeting, income and expense projections, decisions on whether to lease or purchase equipment, and setting manufacturing plans.

## Questions for Review

1. What are the main advantages of using electronic spreadsheet software, as compared with manual methods?

2. What are the main applications for spreadsheet software in business?

3. Describe the positions of and relationships among columns, rows, and cells within electronic spreadsheets.

4. What are the purposes of and relationships among data entries for text, numeric, and formula items?

5. What are headings and labels and how are they used within electronic spreadsheets?

6. What steps are followed and what results are produced in each step within procedures for electronic spreadsheet development?

7. What are the main data sources for spreadsheets and what roles are played by each?

8. What are defaults within spreadsheet sofware packages and what purpose do they serve?

9. What specifications are established through use of the format function within electronic spreadsheet software?

10. What steps are followed to save and retrieve spreadsheet files?

## Questions for Thought

1. What problems are solved and what benefits are realized through use of electronic spreadsheet software in business organizations?

2. How do spreadsheets applications in business resemble the use of scorecards and statistical records in sports?

3. How would you go about using electronic spreadsheet software to establish a personal budget?

4. In what sequence would the following spreadsheet functions be used and what results would be produced at each step: sum, print, edit, format, save?

5. How could spreadsheets be used to reach a decision about which of two sites to choose for a manufacturing plant?

## Terms

| | |
|---|---|
| cell | currency |
| column | date |
| compute | default |
| copy | edit |

| | |
|---|---|
| erase | percentage |
| format | print |
| formula | retrieve |
| heading | row |
| label | save |
| macro | spreadsheet |
| menu bar | sum |
| model | template |
| move | text |
| numeric | What if? |

## MINICASE

**Situation:**

Carol is a college sophomore who has been elected president of the organization of student volunteers for community service work. An immediate challenge is to devise fund-raising projects to support the organization's activities. A first step is to consider whether it is feasible to repeat a successful program that was introduced the previous year. The previous project involved producing and selling a coupon book that offered promotional discounts for purchases at businesses located near the campus.

Carol starts by looking at information on last year's project. A book with approximately 100 coupons was sold for $5. Some 1,500 copies were sold by 30 participating students.

Next, Carol looks at current factors with which she must deal. She learns that the cost of printing will increase by 20 percent. Also, it turns out that only 25 people will be available to sell the book this year. Her committee chairperson feels the price of the book should be raised. Further, the chairperson suggests the organization consider charging merchants for advertising in the coupon book. In the past, there has been no charge to the merchants.

As a guide in reaching these decisions, Carol decides to model the situation on a series of spreadsheets. She prepares the following spreadsheet framework, leaving blanks to be used for "What if?" simulation.

**Decision Making: Your Turn**

1. From the information you have, identify and describe the problem to be solved.

2. Identify alternatives that could be followed to avoid or solve the problem.

3. On the basis of the limited information you have: a) Identify additional information you would gather if you were dealing with this problem in a real situation. b) Identify the solution that appears best on the basis of the information that is available and explain your reasons for this selection.

4. What lessons are to be learned from this situation?

## Projects

1. Visit a computer store or review ads in personal computer magazines you can find in your school library. Summarize the functions provided and costs of at least three electronic spreadsheet packages.

2. In your school's computer lab, obtain a copy of a spreadsheet package and develop a template for preparation of a personal budget. Set up rows for income, revenue from a student loan, and total available. Set up expense accounts for tuition, books, rent, food, entertainment, miscellaneous, and total expenses. Also set up a row for entry of the difference between income and expenses. Set up six additional columns for monthly entries and a seventh column for totals. Complete data entries and sum the spreadsheet. If you don't have access to a computer, complete this project manually.

3. Develop a template for a spreadsheet to be applied in solving any other problem you identify. Begin by writing out a problem definition. Identify the items that are to be used as column and row labels. Sketch the format of your template roughly on paper. Then develop your template on a microcomputer and print out the format. When you are satisfied with the design, add data. If appropriate, alter the data to address ''What if?'' situations.

# Chapter Outline

## CHAPTER 6

# Computer Graphics and Desktop Publishing

## Briefing Memo

TO:      Information Users
FROM:  T. Rohm, W. Stewart

Many information users find it easier to visualize information in graphic form than to derive meaning from pages full of words or numbers. Recently, tools have been developed that allow people to use computers to present graphic outputs.

This chapter provides an opportunity for you to review the principles and applications of graphics software. Presentations are designed to build your understanding of how graphics packages fit into your needs as a computer information system user. Applications discussed include ways in which you might use graphics both for information analysis and for presentations to audiences. Techniques you can use to combine words and pictures to achieve a high level of professionalism in documentation are described in a section of this chapter that deals with desktop publishing.

## End-User Perspective

"This is one of the best decision-making tools for students that I've ever seen," Dean Willoughby said. 'It certainly beats trying to walk a student through mountains of statistics during a guidance review. Congratulations on the excellent work, Julia. Where did these charts come from?"

Julia Hozie smiled modestly. 'I was just trying to make it easier for students to digest this information and reach decisions about their college majors and choices of careers," said Julia, who headed the college's guidance office.

Julia went on to explain that the graphic slides and charts that the dean admired were developed on a microcomputer in her department. "We created two simple statistical spreadsheets," she said. One spreadsheet contained information on enrollments in the college, by major. The other spreadsheet contained statistics on annual job openings according to classifications of the U. S. Bureau of Labor Statistics. Side by side, the charts compared student academic commitments with corresponding job opportunities for graduates.

"With these materials," Julia said, "we can bring students face-to-face with realities while there is still time to do some planning for their academic experiences. The idea is that we couldn't expect them to develop a realistic picture of their prospects and challenges by poring through perhaps 25 or 30 pages of statistical tables. Statistical information is much easier for many people to understand if it is presented in pictures. Now, students can relate their educational decisions easily to the probabilities for career success."

## The Point: Computer Graphics
## Supports Decision Making

In the scenario above, Julia was applying a well-know principle: "One picture is worth a thousand words." In this case, one graphic output is worth dozens of statistical compilations.

As is true for all applications of information, the situation and needs of the user should determine the form of presentation. Julia recognized that most students entering college lack the experience required to deal with extensive sets of career and economic statistics. She understood that, by simplifying the presentation of the information, students would improve their understanding. The net result that Julia was after: Better, more realistic decisions about courses of study and careers.

The same principles apply for all information users, as is borne out by the discussions and examples in the remainder of this chapter.

Clarity of meaning is enhanced when detailed information can be simplified and presented as graphic images. Graphics software packages are able to generate images that interpret massive amounts of data.

## ■ The Need for Computer Graphics

Business managers and other information users at all organizational levels deal with large volumes of text and statistical data as part of their working routines. Deriving meaning from mountains of data can be difficult and time consuming—and can cloud decision making. Even statistical summaries don't paint clear pictures of complex situations. Most people find it easier to summarize complexities pictorially, through easy-to-understand graphics.

A number of computer hardware and software tools are available to enhance communication through graphics, and also to improve decision-making skills by presenting alternatives clearly. Graphic presentations represent meaning—clearly, quickly, and dramatically. They can lead to a better understanding of comparative benefits and adverse consequences of decision alternatives. Better decisions can result.

## Graphics: Enhancing Communication

Day in and day out, people must make decisions. Computer graphics enhance communication in several important ways:

- Graphics outputs reduce the bulk of data presented and make the information more understandable.
- Comparisons are more apparent. Relationships among data values are easier to understand and evaluate.
- Appearances are more professional when data are presented graphically than when statistical tables are provided.

Consider a typical business situation: Brightway, Inc., a manufacturer of electrical appliances, wants to sell its new product line to a large retail chain. Sam Isaacs, the marketing manager at Brightway, understands that his sales presentations have to prove that his products can deliver results. He has spent many years in the retail business himself and, in the past, has been bored to distraction by manufacturers' presentations that stress technical features or designs of products. Sam knows that chain managers want information about how consumers react to products.

In preparation for the sales presentation, Sam arranges for several of his company's salespeople to visit a number of outlets of the chain and gather information on the competitive items currently displayed. Then, he gathers information on sales of the main competitive products for a number of key markets served by the chain. From this review, Sam recognizes that presentations on total sales would not enhance his company's image because some competitors produce more products than Brightway. Therefore, Brightway will do better to compete on a product-by-product basis.

On the basis of his information review, Sam decides to develop a select number of graphic displays to show how his products stack up against certain competitive products now sold by the chain. He elects to use graphs that present comparisons of numbers of units sold through lines, or bars, of different lengths. This approach, he feels, reduces the volume of information customers must review, shows the comparisons he wants to make to best advantage, and also enhances Brightway's image of professionalism. Sam recognizes that the management group at the chain will want to look at specific pricing and marketing statistics. He prepares a series of text and numeric printouts to be left with chain executives. But he plans to base his personal presentation on the graphs that show favorable sales comparisons for his products.

Graphics software makes it possible for managers to review outputs on displays and to interact with computers to develop the images and meanings that meet their needs.

## Graphics: Enhancing Decision Making

Decisions are based upon the evaluations and understanding of alternatives by the decision maker. If a complex situation is represented in masses of information, detail can cloud clarity. With graphic presentations that clarify meaning and reduce bulk, the decision maker gets a clear picture of the alternatives and their consequences. Decisions are based on realistic projections of results, not on guesswork derived from immersion in detail. With clear pictures of their situations to work from, decision makers function more effectively, in less time. Graphics shape the information they must consider to the realities of the problems they must solve or needs they must meet.

## ■ Putting Graphics to Work in Business

The applications for computer graphics in business organizations vary widely with the personal styles of users and their responsibilities. The presentations below review some of the areas of business operation and management in which use of computer graphics has proven most effective.

## Analytic Graphics

Graphic outputs summarize complexities and relate information elements to one another for easy comparison and analysis. The ability to reduce volumes of statistics to simple graphs and to compare alternatives through pictorial review can be a powerful tool for decision making. Analysis is one of the primary applications for computer graphics.

The most common application for analytic graphics is to illustrate presentations derived from data captured in electronic spreadsheets. For example, a spreadsheet program may be used to develop a report with hundreds of lines of detail on income, expense, and earnings statistics for a company. A user of a spreadsheet program can enter instructions that will cause the software to generate a graphic summary of the statistical data through bars printed in different patterns. The bars are presented alongside a scale that shows dollar values. Lengths of the bars represent dollar values and eliminate the need for detailed study of hundreds of lines of detail.

## Presentation Graphics

A major requirement for graphics materials in business centers around the need to present information to business audiences in an understandable, persuasive form. Ideas and information must be presented clearly. Also, the simplicity and attractiveness of graphics, as compared with masses of statistics, helps to promote a professional image for the presenter. By simplifying the message, graphics enhances communication.

Communication with business audiences can be written or oral. Written presentations generally are in the form of printed reports or publications. Oral presentations are at meetings and can include briefings of decision makers, potential customers, suppliers, fellow employees, or trainees who are learning about new jobs or procedures. Computer graphics can be a valuable tool for both types of presentation requirements.

**Reports and Publications.**  Solid pages of text or statistics can cause communication bottlenecks, particularly when information must be absorbed and applied by busy people. Graphics adds clarity to communication and also attracts and holds reader attention. Communication is far more effective when text and numeric listings are interspersed with graphics.

Until recently, it was difficult to enhance the content and appearance of computer-generated reports with graphics. Most people lack the skills and experience to prepare professional graphics themselves, and also lack budgets to hire artists for this work.

Recently introduced software products have made it easier both to develop graphics from numeric information and to integrate the resulting illustrations into text or statistical documents. Users can generate graphics from spreadsheets or with tools that help to develop original drawings. Files containing these illustrations then can be included in documents created through use of word processing or spreadsheet packages, or both. As a result, relation-

SpreadSheet File: 87BUDGET

SuperSellers
1987 Budget Analysis

| ACCOUNT | PROJECTED | ACTUAL | % |
|---|---|---|---|
| INCOME | | | |
| Advertising Sales | 2000000 | 2529986 | 126.5 |
| Advertising Svcs | 800000 | 594607 | 74.3 |
| Public Relations | 950000 | 806815 | 84.9 |
| Consulting | 1000000 | 1219031 | 121.9 |
| Other Income | 850000 | 733775 | 86.3 |
| TOTAL INCOME | 5600000 | 5884214 | 105.1 |
| EXPENSES | | | |
| Equipment/Furn. | 750000 | 549486 | 73.3 |
| Rent | 50000 | 50000 | 100.0 |
| Advertising Space | 1500000 | 1219145 | 81.3 |
| Advertising Time | 2300000 | 2426385 | 105.5 |
| Supplies | 100000 | 43932 | 43.9 |
| Salary | 1400000 | 1065168 | 76.1 |
| Other Expenses | 75000 | 72038 | 96.1 |
| TOTAL EXPENSE | 6175000 | 5426154 | 87.9 |
| PROFIT | -575000 | 458060 | -79.7 |

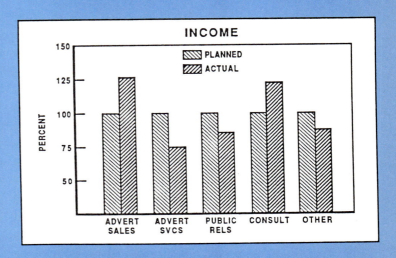

These illustrations show a traditional financial statement (top) represented graphically (bottom) to make the figures more meaningful to users. The graphic presentation uses a bar graph to represent the income figures in the printed report.

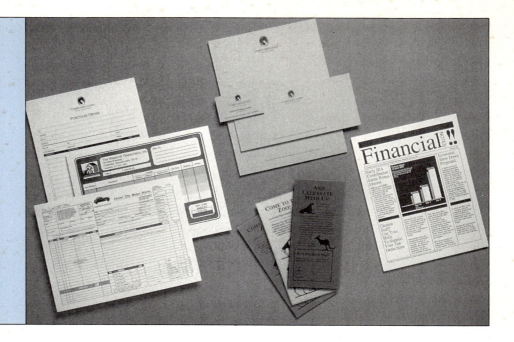

Business reports, forms, and publications like these can be generated on microcomputers through use of desktop publishing software.

ships can be established between text or statistical presentations and the graphics that enhance their meaning.

**Business Meetings and Sales Presentations.** Special communication challenges are experienced by people assigned to make ''stand-up'' presentations before management or other decision-making audiences. Conveying information effectively at oral presentations is one of the most difficult challenges in the world of business.

When presentations are written, people can review statistics or look at pictures. When someone is speaking, graphic images can provide an information base on which to focus audience attention.

Generally, the most effective presentations use simple graphics to demonstrate the point a speaker is making. A problem in the past has been that the costs of manual preparation of first-class illustrations and media such as slides can be high. Since many presentation graphics are used only for a single meeting or a few sessions, it may be hard to justify large expenses. With computer graphics capabilities, quality presentation materials can be produced at minimal, affordable costs. The speaker who uses computer graphics enhances his or her own image of professionalism, achieves an important goal of presentation brevity, and helps to keep expenses in line. An important consideration is that saving time at meetings can deliver savings that more than offset costs of producing superior graphics that achieve necessary understanding in minimum amounts of time.

In summary, computer graphics provides a set of tools that can clarify the meaning of information and provide a solid basis for analysis and decision making. These benefits account for the fact that sales of graphics software packages have grown rapidly. To build upon your understanding of the benefits computer graphics software, the specific parts of graphics systems and their functions are covered in the presentations below.

## Computer Graphics Systems

Computer graphics software generates images by assigning numeric values to points on a computer screen or positions on a printed output. The method for handling data differs significantly from the types of applications covered in earlier chapters. Therefore, there are some corresponding differences in the elements that make up computer graphics applications. These are covered in the

### People

Anyone willing to invest the time and effort needed to understand the process of converting data to images and the command structure of special software packages can generate professional-looking graphics. Graphics packages are easy to use. But they do require that users apply themselves to master different principles and techniques.

Use of laser printers in conjunction with desktop publishing software makes it possible to generate publication-quality and presentation-quality outputs.

Graphics software provides a mechanism for implementing the translations necessary for effective communication. Executives and managers can use graphics software capabilities to clarify meaning of information for themselves, then do a better job of communicating their ideas to subordinates. Users at all levels can establish meaning from their own perspective to information they apply to understand their responsibilities and perform their jobs.

Computer professionals realize new challenges and can broaden the impact of the services they render by harnessing the power of computer graphics software.

## Equipment

Equipment that supports computer graphics represents a major difference from applications such as word processing or electronic spreadsheets. These differences exist at every stage of the processing cycle: input, processing, output, and storage.

■ **Input Equipment.**   For some applications, input is derived from files created under control of other software packages. For example, spreadsheet programs make it possible for users to direct preparation of graphic outputs through simple keyboard entries. However, many graphics applications involve use of special input devices that can include a mouse, track ball, scanner, video camera, light pen, or graphics tablet.

*Mouse.*   A mouse is a small device placed on a desk top alongside a computer work station. When the user rolls the mouse on a flat surface, a corresponding cursor movement is displayed on the screen. This movement can be used to position the cursor quickly on a pictorial menu used for selection of graphics elements or functions. The mouse also can be used to provide access to submenus, or *pull-down menus.* When a function is selected from a menu at the top of the screen, a *submenu,* or listing of further choices, is displayed below the main menu. The mouse is used to move the cursor to the desired function. Buttons on the mouse activate the selection of services.

*Track Ball.*   A track ball operates on the same general principle as a mouse, except that the ball is at the top of a stationary device. The user rotates the ball to move the cursor. Buttons are provided for user control of menu selection and for entry of processing commands.

*Scanner.*   A scanner "reads" input information from images that are printed or drawn on paper. An electronic beam moves back and forth across a sheet of paper. The light beam senses light and dark spots. These values are converted to graphic information that forms computer-generated images. With scanners, computers have the ability to accept pictures as inputs, rather than being limited to character sets generated from keyboards.

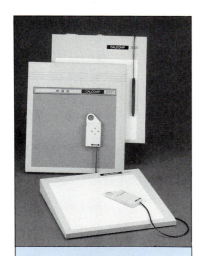

Graphics tablets can be used for direct input of data in pictorial form.

*Video Camera.*   A television camera is another way of transferring images directly into computers for processing. The principle is similar to that of the scanner. In a video camera, an electronic beam scans a picture formed on the face of an image tube. The light and dark (or color) values sensed by the scanning beam are processed as graphic input signals by a computer.

*Light Pen.*   A light pen also is known as a *light-sensing stylus.* It is an instrument that senses a bright cursor generated by the computer on the display screen. A user establishes contact between the light source and the pen-like device. Then, the user writes or draws on the face of the display screen. The computer accepts these drawn lines as input. The image created by the user is stored and processed as graphic information.

*Graphics Tablet.*   A graphics tablet is an alternate method of accepting input in the form of written or drawn images. Instead of writing on the face of a display tube, the user writes with a pointed instrument, also called a stylus, on a flat metal surface, called a tablet. Beneath the surface of the tablet are sensors that identify the positions over which the stylus is moved. These sensors generate signals that provide graphic input to a computer.

■ **Processing Equipment.**   Processing equipment that supports graphics applications requires large memory capacities. As an example, a microcomputer that handles graphics software generally is equipped with 1 MB (megabyte) of memory, sometimes more. By comparison, word processing can be handled comfortably with a memory of 256 K. A memory of 640 K is considered large for a word processing application.

Computer graphics systems require special processors that generate and interpret images—in monochrome or color. Microcomputers that handle graphics processing generally require installation of a special circuit board. The graphics hardware added to a microcomputer for graphics applications generally is called a *co-processor.*

■ **Output Equipment.**   Output devices used to deliver graphic images can include displays, dot matrix printers, plotters, film recorders, or video tape. Outputs can be in a single color (monochrome) or in full color.

*Monitors.*   A monitor is a screen display that shows computer outputs. It is best that computers used for graphics processing have *high-resolution monitors.* These are video displays that present images at a level of detail that is finer than those typically used for word processing applications. The higher image resolution makes it possible to show a greater level of detail for drawn images or for characters. Special monitors also are needed for systems with color graphics capabilities.

*Dot Matrix Printers.*   Dot matrix printers can provide graphics outputs in a form that is good enough for evaluation, or possibly for informal reports, but not of quality sufficient for formal presentation.

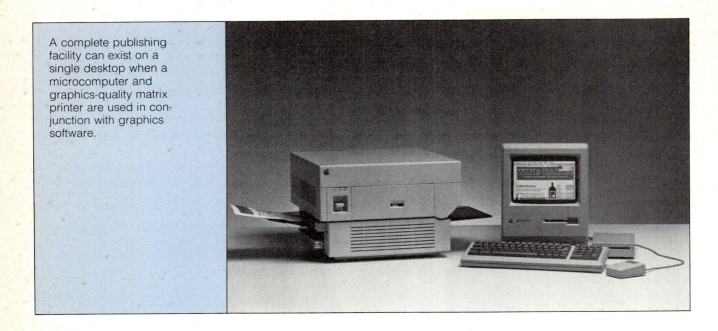

A complete publishing facility can exist on a single desktop when a microcomputer and graphics-quality matrix printer are used in conjunction with graphics software.

*Plotters.*    Plotters are output devices that draw, rather than print, output images. A plotter uses one or more pen-like stylus devices that are driven by the computer to trace images on paper. On plotters, each stylus contains a writing pen. For multiple-colored outputs, a separate stylus draws each color.

*Film Recorders or Videotape.*    Some graphics outputs must be used to create printing plates or slides for projection at presentation sessions. To meet these requirements, output units are available that can record computer-generated images on film or videotape.

Additional information on input and output devices is presented in Chapter 13, which contains an overall review of input and output hardware.

■ **Storage Equipment.**    The discussion of processing equipment above indicates that high memory capacities are needed because graphics imaging involves high volumes of data. This requirement carries forward into the storage area. High storage volumes are necessary for any graphics applications. A typical microcomputer used for graphics has a 10 or 20 MB hard disk; many have more. Both the software and the outputs require extensive storage capabilities. Therefore, even with a 20 MB hard disk, users generally find that it is necessary to download files to floppies to provide enough storage to keep a system operating.

## Procedures

To support computer graphics, special software capabilities and special manual processing routines are necessary. The need to think about formation of images, in turn, means that computer graphics users must follow a special sequence of steps to process information and develop effective graphics. The challenge is to understand the data to be presented, the audience that is to receive the presentation, and the desired impact upon that audience. These factors form the basis for the design of graphics presentations. The steps for achieving effective graphics presentations include:

- Create graphs
- Enter data
- Evaluate results.

■ **Create Graphs.**  To control the functions of a computer for image generation, the user must begin with an image in mind. To create a bar chart from a spreadsheet package, for example, you would start by examining the data within the spreadsheet. You would decide what meaning you wanted to convey from the spreadsheet entries and identify the type of graph and labels that convey the ideas to be presented.

■ **Enter Data.**  The next step is to format a spreadsheet that corresponds with the graphic results you want to generate. Data items are entered into spreadsheet cells to establish the values that will be used in creating the graphic image you want.

■ **Evaluate Results.**  To get a picture that shows the ideas or information you want to convey, you may have to repeat the input and output sequence several times. That's one of the beauties of computer graphics. You can see your results quickly and can adjust your activities to produce the effects you seek. The major outputs that can be generated through use of these procedures are described below in the discussion on the data component of graphics systems.

## Data

Graphics systems create, store, and present data as images or as sets of values that will generate images. Three formats are applied most frequently by computer graphics software:

- Pie charts
- Bar graphs
- Line graphs.

■ **Pie Charts.**  The *pie chart* gets its name from the fact that it usually is shown as a round circle divided into slices that resemble portions of a pie. Most pie charts show values of slices as percentages of a whole entity. For a company or special project, for instance, a pie chart may show the allocation of expenses to different areas, such as salaries, materials, rent, etc.

**Bar Graphs.** A *bar graph* presents information in terms of comparative lengths of lines, as measured on a *scale,* or *grid,* that is included in the graphic. The scale or grid generally is a series of lines or indicators marked along the sides and bottom of an image area to represent horizontal and vertical axes. The scales show such measurable elements as time and quantities. For example, a set of scales might show amounts of expenses along the side of a bar graph and time periods along the bottom. Bars of different lengths indicate the values of the items reported. For example, income can be compared with expenses and profits. Also, results or values for different time periods can be compared.

**Line Graphs.** *Line graph* presentations are used largely to show trends in business situations. The values represented on a line graph are indicated by points on a grid. Then, to show trends, the points are connected with lines. If multiple trends are to be compared, lines of different colors or patterns can be used.

A scale at the bottom of the graph indicates time periods. A scale at the side indicates business volumes. Points are placed on the grid to indicate volumes for time periods. Lines that connect the points show patterns of business results.

The three graphic output formats described above are available with most spreadsheet packages. The format you choose should reflect the points you want to make. Bar graphs compare size, pie charts relate parts to a whole, and line graphs show trends. Through menus, the user generally can select the type of illustration desired. The finished graphics can be used on their own, incorporated in reports produced through use of word processing software, or included in professional-looking publications created through desktop publishing, described below.

## Desktop Publishing: Combining Graphics With Text

The earlier description of computer graphics applications identifies a need to mix text and graphics content in reports and publications. A major tool for integrating text and graphics into the same document is available through software packages known as *desktop publishing.* The term desktop publishing dramatizes computer type formatting and graphics capabilities by pointing out that, literally, an entire publishing operation can be set up on a single desk or table. As information continues to proliferate, desktop publishing meets a growing need among business organizations, reflected in the fact that this segment of the computer industry has become a billion-dollar business.

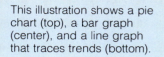

This illustration shows a pie chart (top), a bar graph (center), and a line graph that traces trends (bottom).

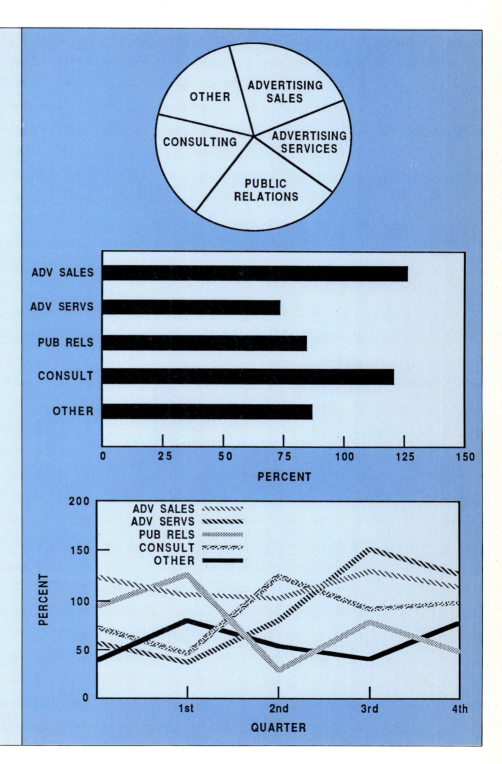

**Impact**

# How to Select a Graphics Package

Unlike software packages that enable users to implement complete applications, as is the case with word processor and electronic spreadsheet software, graphics application packages tend to be designed for special purposes. In the area of word processing, for example, you generally can meet all your needs with a single package. If you have extensive requirements in computer graphics, by contrast, you might need a half dozen packaged programs—possibly even more.

From a purchaser's eye view, it is a good idea to divide graphics packages into two broad categories. First, there are packages that accept data inputs and generate corresponding graphics. In this category, some graphics packages are included within spreadsheet software and are able to produce pie charts, bar graphs, or line graphs to reflect spreadsheet data content. Other generator-type packages enable users to enter numeric values and use the software to produce corresponding graphics.

The second category enables the user to create graphics directly, without conversions from numeric inputs. Within this group, there are two major subcategories. One is for drafting, the other for drawing. Drafting packages provide users with libraries of shapes that can be combined under control of menus to form finished diagrams or charts. Drawing packages enable the user to add drawn lines of any form or shape through use of drawing instruments. Menus provide a basis for controlling the kinds of lines and the patterns or textures to be included in drawings.

To select a graphics package:

- Define the outputs you seek. It is a good idea to prepare rough drawings of the kinds of outputs you need. Use these as guidelines to see which package makes it easiest for you to produce the results you want.

- If you want to generate graphics from spreadsheets or numeric inputs, prepare sets of input data and check to see how each package you consider handles your job. Check to see what you have to do to control placement of graphics elements and use of space on an output document.

- If you consider drafting or drawing programs, identify outputs that resemble those you want to generate and find out how they can be created under control of each package you consider. There are many variations in technique and capability among graphics packages.

- Find out what hardware features are needed to use each software package.

- Find out what output devices can be driven by each software package. There are many hardware-software incompatibilities in the area of graphics outputs.

- Find out if you need or can profit from the use of an "integrator" or "switcher" software package. These packages make it possible to move back and forth among multiple packages and to mix outputs to form composite images.

Answers to these questions should help you to identify the package that fits best into your job requirements. Once you have narrowed the choice to a few possible products, you can select the individual product that gives you the best value for your money.

A desktop publishing system includes a microcomputer with graphics capabilities, special software that converts text to typeset images, graphics software, *page-makeup software,* and a *laser printer* with graphics output capabilities. A desktop publishing system also requires that people take the time to learn use of these special tools.

A user starts, typically, with a word processing system used to capture and format text. The text files are "imported" to a typesetting program. Then the text is formatted into any of a variety of typefaces and formats to create a document with professional printing quality. A typeface implements a special style or format for a set of characters. Each separate typeface is called a *font.* Dozens of different fonts may be selected by users for formatting of text for professional appearance. Actual publications are assembled through page-makeup software that enables the user to position type and graphic illustrations on a screen display that previews the appearance of a printed page.

When the page elements are assembled, the document is generated on a laser printer. Most laser printers use processes similar to those of office copiers. An image is recorded on a light-sensitive drum. In the case of a laser printer, the images are formed by a beam of intense (laser) light passed over the surface of a drum to recreate the image patterns. The resulting laser printer output is of high enough quality for use as an image master for printing newsletters, magazines, letters or other business documents, and books. Along with computer graphics, desktop publishing represents an explosive growth area for use of microcomputers.

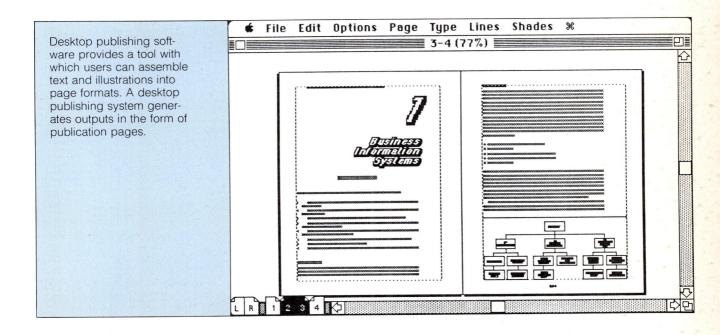

Desktop publishing software provides a tool with which users can assemble text and illustrations into page formats. A desktop publishing system generates outputs in the form of publication pages.

Professional-quality publications can be created through use of typesetting and graphics capabilities of desktop publishing software.

Pictorial content is a normal, vital part of human communication and response patterns. People are exposed to graphic images in everyday activities. Words and numbers are used to communicate information largely because the creation of graphic images traditionally has been a problem—technologically and in terms of expense. Computers are in the process of bringing communication tools into closer coordination with the way people think. Graphics tools are in the forefront of this trend. In many situations, graphics deliver benefits far in excess of their costs.

## Chapter Summary

- Computer graphics assist communication of information by reducing complex textual or statistical documents to easily understood images. Graphics presentations also improve capabilities to show relationships and/or comparisons among information items. With these capabilities, computer graphics outputs are important tools for decision makers.

- Application areas for computer graphics include information analysis, presentations before groups, and illustration of textual documents or publications.

- Computer graphics simplify presentations of information for users, but present special challenges for computer professionals who must select and/or develop special software and hardware tools to convert numeric values into images.

- Computer graphics systems can utilize a number of special input devices, including the mouse, track ball, scanner, video camera, light pen, and graphics tablet.

- Computers used for graphics applications require a special graphics board. High-speed processing, large memories, and extensive storage capabilities also are needed.

- Output devices required to support computer graphics can include high-resolution monitors, dot matrix printers, plotters, and film or videotape recorders.

- Procedures for computer graphics systems include special imaging software and manual procedures for design, graphic input, and revision of images.

- Within graphics systems, data assumes image-type formats, such as pie charts, bar graphs, and line graphs.

- Graphics and text can be brought together in professional-looking products through use of desktop publishing software packages.

## Questions for Review

1. How do computer graphics systems promote communication?
2. How do computer graphics outputs assist decision makers?
3. Why do graphics outputs enhance capabilities for evaluating and comparing data as compared with textual or statistical reports?
4. What are the benefits of computer graphics for group presentations?
5. What is a mouse and why does this device often play an important role in implementing computer graphics systems?

6. What methods are available for the manual drawing of inputs to computer graphics systems and how are they used?

7. What are pie charts and how do they convey information?

8. What are bar graphs and how do they convey information?

9. What are line graphs and how do they convey information?

10. What is desktop publishing and what role can this methodology play in enhancing communication by and within organizations?

## Questions for Thought

1. How might you use computer generated graphics in your activities as a student?

2. How would analytical and presentation graphics differ in terms of quality, preparation technique, and other factors?

3. How do computer graphics systems differ from those for word processing and electronic spreadsheets?

4. What are some practical applications for desktop publishing systems?

5. In which situations would you use pie charts, bar graphs, and line graphs? How do these graphics data tools compare with one another? What are the special advantages and/or shortcomings of each?

## Terms

| | |
|---|---|
| algorithm | mouse |
| bar graph | page-makeup software |
| co-processor | pie chart |
| desktop publishing | plotter |
| film recorder | pull-down menu |
| font | raster image |
| graphics tablet | scale |
| grid | scanner |
| high-resolution monitor | submenu |
| laser printer | track ball |
| light pen | trend line |
| light-sensing stylus | video camera |
| line graph | videotape |
| monitor | |

# MINICASE

**Situation:**

"Start by telling me what you want to accomplish," Zelda said. She was talking to Hy Settleman, the marketing manager at Flyaway, Inc., an air taxi service. Zelda was an independent microcomputer applications consultant who had helped Flyaway design and install a customer billing system that had been implemented on microcomputers. On one of Zelda's regular visits to the Flyaway office, Hy indicated that he needed help in preparing some dramatic presentation materials.

In response to Zelda's request, Hy explained: "We're adding an eight-passenger executive jet to our fleet. I want a dramatic piece of art that I can use in brochures and at sales presentations. We really have a convincing story. With our new jet, we can just about match commercial fares for business people who want to travel in parties of four to eight. If they are going to a destination within 300 to 800 miles away, our charter fee will be just about the same as business-class travel. If they are going to a meeting and returning the same day, we may even be able to beat commercial fares."

Hy continued: "I think we have a good potential for lining up trips for small groups. What I want is a graphic that shows comparative costs for our service and for airlines that serve a number of different cities in the distance range we are talking about. Once we demonstrate that we are cost-effective, the advantages of charter flying will wipe out the competition. With us, they can go whenever they choose, rather than fitting in with schedules. Also, we can land at small airports that may be closer to their destinations than airlines can. Here are the figures for comparative charges. Can you help me?"

**Decision Making: Your Turn**

1. From the information you have and from Zelda's viewpoint, identify and describe the type of graphic you would develop and the approach you would take to creating the finished product.

2. Identify alternatives that could be followed in devising an effective graphic for Flyaway.

3. On the basis of the limited information you have: a) Identify additional information you would gather if you were dealing with this problem in a real situation. b) Identify the approach

that appears best on the basis of the information that is available and explain your reasons for this selection.

4.  What lessons are to be learned from this situation?

## Projects

1.  Use one or more spreadsheets you developed in completing a project for Chapter 5. From these outputs, either through use of a graphics program or manually if necessary, create at least two graphics images. Your outputs should be one each of a pie chart, a bar graph, or a line graph.

2.  Study two or more computer graphics and/or personal computer magazines. Assume you want to establish capabilities for generating graphics from spreadsheets. Describe the results you want to achieve and identify the software packages and hardware components you would need. Assume you have a basic microcomputer configuration available.

3.  Bring in an advertisement that stresses both graphics and text in their content. Write a critique identifying what you believe to be the strengths and weaknesses of the graphic and verbal presentations. Base your critique on the audiences targeted by the ad.

# BUSINESS COMPUTER GRAPHICS

## Persuasive Power at Your Fingertips

A picture is worth a thousand words, but why? Some experts believe that there are fundamental differences between the way the human brain processes words and the way it processes pictures. Words are processed one at a time. Visual images, on the other hand, seem to be processes in parallel. Many separate brain circuits processed different parts of the visual image simultaneously. Consequently, humans are able to assimilate more data graphically than they can reading words or tables of data.

*"Not only can graphics applications save corporate time and money, but they are also another step toward converting data processing into a strategic and competitive weapon."*

Alan Paller, AUI Data Graphics

## ▥ WHY GRAPHICS?

Every picture tells a story, but some pictures tell it better than others. Hence, the art of computer graphics — the professional polish of sharp, lively images that allow your audience to focus on the important aspects of your presentation.

Computer Graphics has quickly become one of the fastest growing fields in the computer applications industry. Why? Several reasons, among them lower hardware and software costs and advances in computer graphics technology.

Another significant reason for the growing demand for and popularity of graphics is that people today are more visually oriented than in the past. Not only are they attracted to colorful graphics; they expect them.

Graphics: Yet another computer application that can offer companies improved sales effectiveness and satisfied customers.

Business graphics would be worthless if they did not satisfy a need. Obviously they do.

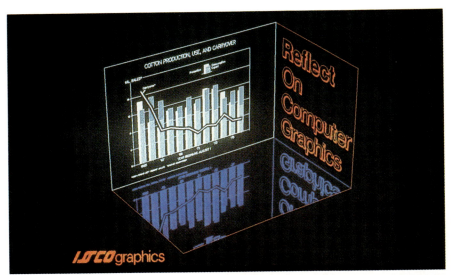

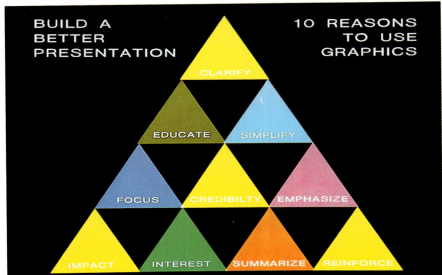

# GRAPHICS: A TREND

Research done by a magazine, Personal Computing, found that almost half of their subscribers already use a microcomputer for presentation graphics. Within the next year, an additional 36% plan to begin using microcomputer graphics.

The amount of dollars spent on computer graphics over the past few years reflects this trend.

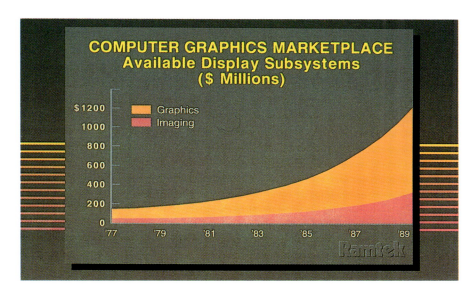

The business graphics marketplace is booming. Graphics hardware and software are becoming more and more sophisticated, providing more options as to how you display information.

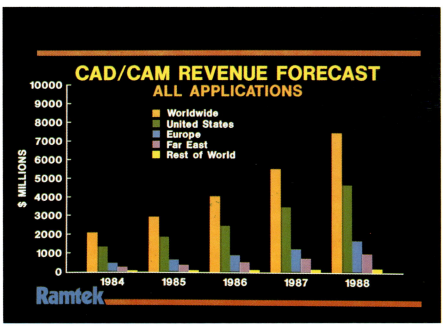

While computer-aided design/-computer-aided manufacturing (CAD/CAM) still represents the largest segment of the computer graphics industry, the emergence of business graphics has helped to move the technology into the commercial sphere.

# ▦ HARDWARE: WHAT'S REQUIRED FOR YOUR MICROCOMPUTER?

The capacity to generate and display graphics is a prerequisite for using presentation software.

Once you have a microcomputer, the minimum hardware includes:

- Monitor (color is best)
- Enough RAM for the program and any special data storage
- Input devices, such as the keyboard or joystick
- Printers, from dot matrix to color plotter
- On-line storage devices
- A graphics board or addition, depending on the microcomputer

Several sources of presentation hardware.

## HARDWARE

**Color Digital Imager**   Bell and Howell, 411 Amapola Ave., Torrance, CA 90501; (213) 320–5700

**Datacom 35**   Photographic Sciences Corp., PO Box 338, Webster, NY 14580; (716) 265–1600

**HI PC Pens Plotters**   Houston Instrument, 8500 Cameron Road, Austin, TX 78753; (800) 531–5205

**HP Graphics Plotters, LaserJet**   Hewlett-Packard Corp., 16399 W. Bernardo Drive, San Diego, CA 92127; (800) 367–4772

**IBM Color Printer, Color Jetprinter**   IBM Corp., PO Box 1328, 1000 N.W. 51 St., Boca Raton, FL 33432; (800) 447–4700

**Matrix PCR**   Matrix Instruments, Inc., 1 Ramland Road, Orangeburg, NY 10962; (914) 365–0190

**Polaroid Palette**   Polaroid Corp., 575 Technology Square, Cambridge, MA 02139; (800) 225–1618

**VideoShow**   General Parametrics Corp., 1250 Ninth St., Berkeley, CA 94710; (800) 556–1234

**Videoscope, Multiscan projectors**   Sony Corp. of America, Sony Drive, Park Ridge, NJ 07656; (201) 930–6432

More and more for less and less. That trend applies to graphics software as well as graphics hardware.

# ▓ SOFTWARE: WHAT'S MOST IMPORTANT?

Once you've had experience developing and using business graphics, you'll become a more critical user. You'll become especially sensitive to the capabilities of graphics software to make your presentations more effective.

**SOFTWARE**

**Chart-Master, Sign-Master, Map-Master**  Decision Resources, Inc., 25 Sylvan Road South, Westport, CT 06880; (203) 222-1974
**ExecuVision, Concorde**  Visual Communications Network, Inc., 238 Main St., Cambridge, MA 02142; (617) 497–4000
**GEM Graph, WordChart**  Digital Research, Inc., 60 Garden Court, PO Box DRI, Monterey, CA 93942; (800) 443–4200
**Graphwriter, Freelance**  Graphic Communications, Inc., 200 Fifth Ave., Waltham, MA 02254; (617) 890–8778
**Harvard Presentation Graphics, PFS:Graph**  Software Publishing Corp., 1901 Landings Drive, Mountain View, CA 94043; (415) 962–8910
**Inset**  American Programmers Guild, Ltd., 12 Mill Plain Road, Danbury, CT 06811; (203) 794–0396
**Microsoft Chart**  Microsoft Corp., 16011 N.E. 36th Way, Box 97017, Redmond WA 98073; (206) 882–8088
**PC Storyboard**  IBM Corp., PO Box 1328 1000, N.W. 51 St., Boca Raton, FL 33432; (800) 447–4700
**Show Partner**  Brightbill-Roberts & Co., 120 E. Washington St., Suite 421, Syracuse, NY 13202; (315) 474–3400

Several sources of presentation software.

Quality and easy of use rank as the most important graphics software attributes, according to users.

## ▥ RUNNING THE SOFTWARE: THE EASY PART

With the appropriate software and hardware, your microcomputer will let you prepare a professional-looking presentation — from start to finish — in one sitting.

No longer does this user have to create an image in his head.

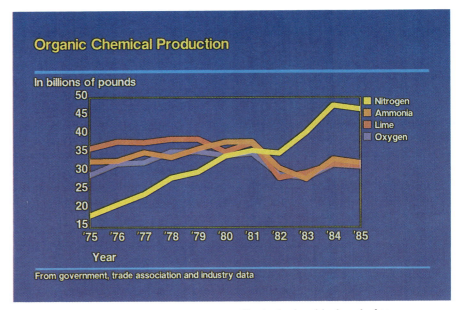

Adding color helps get the point across more effectively than black and white.

This experienced user of business computer graphics says that the process of developing graphics forces him to present his information more succinctly.

Artistic talent isn't a necessary prerequisite, either. Let's say you want to create a graph in Lotus 1-2-3. Basically, these are the steps you would follow:

1. Title your graph and the categories of your data or information
2. Enter your data or information
3. Select the kind of graph you want the program to create
4. Name the data range to be shown on the graph
5. Decide how to use the X and Y axes
6. Choose your colors (if you have a color monitor)....

And poof! The computer does the drawing for you. Often it's that simple.

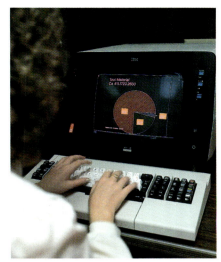

This user doesn't have a printer. She prefers to photograph her graphics while they are displayed on the screen. She uses the resulting prints and slides in visual presentations.

Some spreadsheet programs, such as Lotus, include graphing programs. This integrated feature makes it easy for this user to take information or data directly from his electronic spreadsheet and put it into a graph.

Even though graphs do not supply all the details of the raw data, they make it easier for this user to recognize trends and conditions.

## ▥ APPLYING COLOR FOR IMPACT: HELPFUL HINTS

Andrew Corn, Admaster, Inc., a design and production agency, suggests the following elements of design in creating a presentation:

- Maintain good contrast such as dark text and brightly colored graphics set against a light background.
- Choose appropriate colors — yellow, blue, and green are usually good choices.
- Fill charts with bright, solid colors. They're pleasing to the eye and easy to distinguish.
- Spare the colors, don't spoil the picture. More than five colors in one graphic will overshadow the message.
- Accentuate with color — bright color to emphasize, darker or lighter colors to anchor the remaining pieces.
- Adapt color to your environment. Factors like lighting and audience size should influence your use of color.

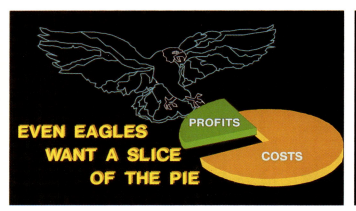

Company logos can be displayed on the screen to help viewers associate a company name with its products.

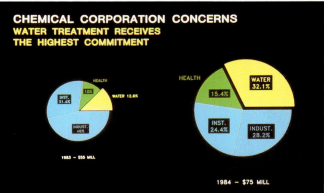

The pie chart is popular and widely used for simple business applications.

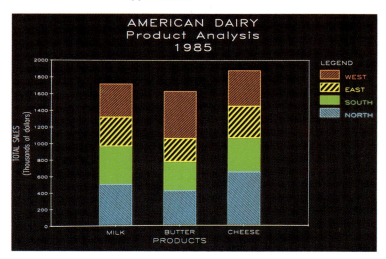

Bar charts are commonly used to illustrate business data.

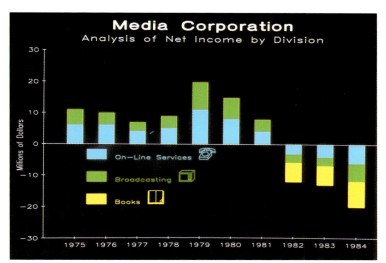

Bar charts may be stacked one on top of the other to summarize the income of several divisions.

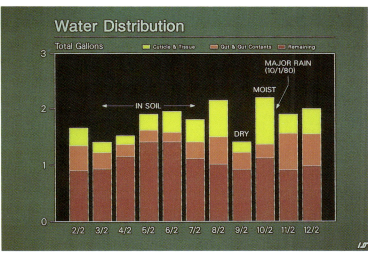

This bar chart illustrates the impact of contrast; that is, the use of light text and of brightly colored graphics set against a dark background.

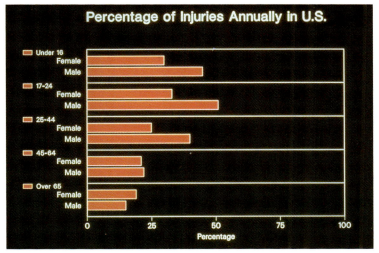

Bar charts can be drawn horizontally or vertically. The selection of this format is useful for a change of pace to get, or retain, the viewer's attention.

## KNOWING WHAT YOU WANT TO SAY: THE CHALLENGE

But slick isn't everything. Once you've learned how, putting your chosen medium to work for you is the easy part.

What makes some graphs effective, valuable, and memorable when so many are unnecessary or misleading? What is your challenge?

Line graphs are excellent for displaying financial and daily, weekly, monthly, quarterly, and yearly data. It is also possible to plot more than a single relationship on the same chart for purposes of comparison.

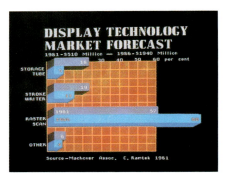

Three-dimensional graphics are far less common than bar graphs or pie charts. Most users aren't willing to spend more for the required hardware and software. But for some users the benefits outweigh the costs.

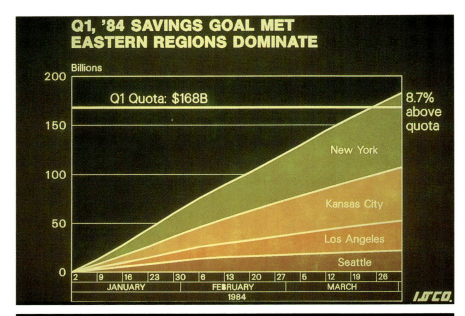

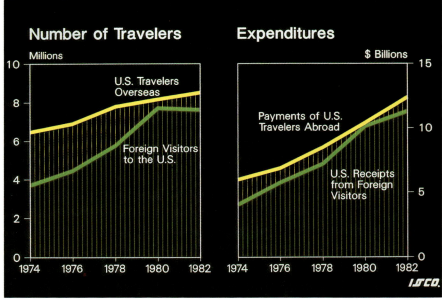

Filling in spaces with color can dramatize and add meaning to the presentation of data.

Above all, it's how well you know your audience and the information you want to communicate.

Computers can generate vast quantities of data, but more data is not necessarily better for your reader. Concepts can confuse and numbers can numb without the instant translation that pictures can relate.

Again, the art of computer graphics is to focus the viewer's attention, to communicate, to persuade.

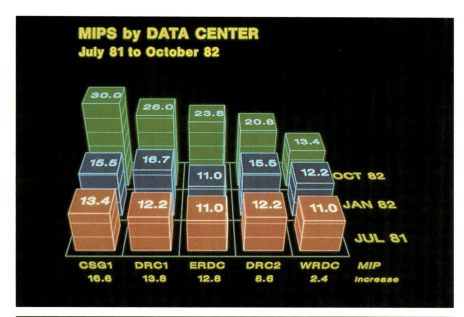

This three-dimensional graphic provides an interesting presentation of a bar chart.

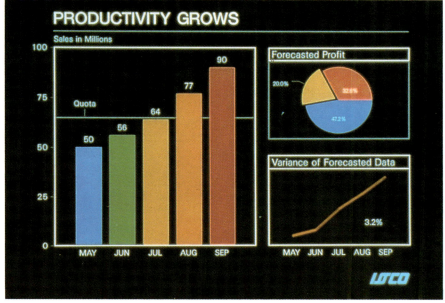

Pie, line, and bar charts may be designed to illustrate the same information. However, bar charts can incorporate the widest range of variables through the use of colors and different shadings.

Using different types of charts in one presentation gives the viewer several perspectives from which to analyze the data.

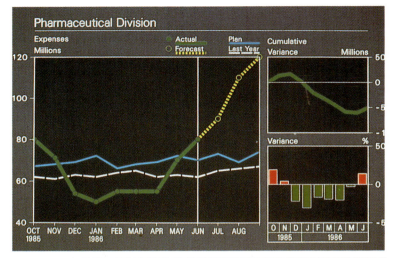

Bar and line charts can be combined to give both the big picture and the detailed picture simultaneously.

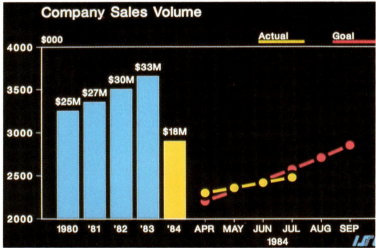

This combination of charts gives managers immediate access to key performance indicators, allowing them to reinforce outstanding performance quickly and to anticipate weak performance before it becomes critical.

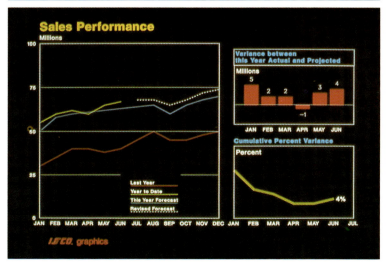

# ⦚ HOW TO BE PERSUASIVE

Microcomputer graphics are a tool for the professional to use in accomplishing business objectives. Common objectives of business graphics are:

- To evaluate past relationships between variables
- To project expected relationships for decision-making
- To monitor ongoing business operations
- To find and demonstrate trends and deviations
- To communicate information to a targeted individual or group
- To sell your ideas — and yourself!

First, what point do you want to make? Answering this question will be your biggest challenge. To do so, you must first gain an understanding of the essential ingredients of a persuasive presentation: your audience and the information you want to communicate.

Once you've answered this question, then and only then are you ready to select the data and graph type that will best illustrate your point.

According to a recent University of Minnesota/3M study, presentations using visual aids were found to be 43% more persuasive than unaided presentations.

Graphics is likely to be the key communication aid of the next decade.

A recent study from the Wharton School of Business demonstrated that those who used graphics in their presentation enjoyed shorter meetings, and that they also achieved consensus quicker than those who did not use graphics.

Commercial art and photography shops offer you an alternative to enlarging an image yourself.

# ▥ TYPICAL BUSINESS APPLICATIONS

The number of applications of computer systems continues to grow.

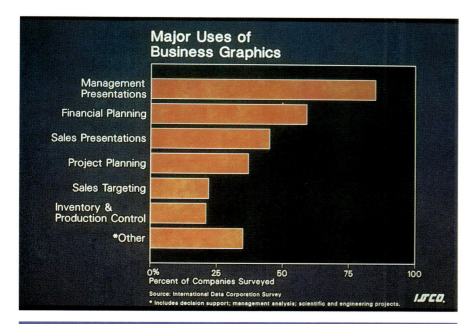

Uses of business computer graphics are not only increasing but spreading into all areas of business. Still, graphics are used primarily for management presentations and summaries.

3M is just one of the many companies that now prepares and delivers "on-call" graphics.

3M has an alternative for users who would rather not, or who can't afford to, purchase a computer system and develop their own graphics: graphics by phone —24 hours a day, seven days a week.

Here's how it works:

1. Choose a format from the more than 100 displayed in their format guide
2. Relay your choice to 3M with a keyboard of any microcomputer that has telephone communication capability
3. Within two days your 35mm slide, overhead transparency, or full color print will arrive.

## WHAT'S AHEAD?

In the midst of the changes, the measure of an effective business graphic remains constant. The important consideration is whether or not actions will result from the graphic, whether decisions will be made on the basis of it.

Computer graphics stands at a crossroads: It can either be supported as a personal tool for presentations or as a strategic resource for decision-making. Many successful organizations have discovered that their strongest approach combines and supports both these aspects of computer graphics.

## QUESTIONS

1. What are two of the many reasons the use of computer graphics is increasing in the business world?
2. What are the minimum hardware requirements for a microcomputer graphics system?
3. Name three attributes of microcomputer graphics considered important by users.
4. Identify three guidelines to be considered in the use of color graphics.
5. Describe three business objectives that can profit from the use of business computer graphics.
6. What are three important considerations in creating presentation graphics?
7. What is the greatest challenge in creating effective computer graphics?

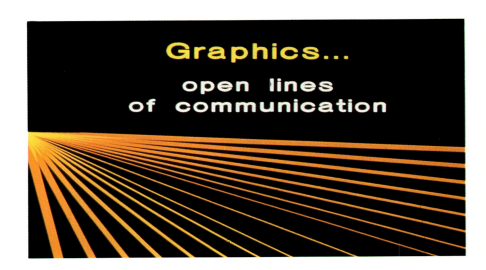

# Chapter Outline

## CHAPTER 7

# Database Management Systems

## Briefing Memo

TO:      Information Users
FROM:   T. Rohm, W. Stewart

Database management system (DBMS) packages provide tools that enable users to take direct control over information resources. With DBMS packages, users have the ability to specify their needs, design systems that store and maintain information resources, and produce meaningful reports when and as they are needed.

You are represented in many databases. The process starts when the event of your birth is recorded and proceeds throughout your school and work experience. The advent of friendly, inexpensive database packages has increased the likelihood that you will become a direct user of database systems. At the very least, your ability to deal with computer professionals about your information needs starts with your understanding of data structures, database management systems, and their applications, discussed in this chapter.

## End-User Perspective

"You've got a problem, Steve," Dean Herman explained. "If you go ahead with the program you have set up, you will be short one of the courses you need to meet graduation requirements."

That was all Steve needed to hear. Frustration and registration had gone together throughout Steve's college career. Now, as he headed into his senior year, things seemed to have eased up. All of the courses he had requested were available. Things actually seemed to go more smoothly with the college's new computer system. There was a terminal at each departmental table. It took no time at all for the staff to check the student database to make sure he was qualified for each course. Confirmations of registration were printed out and handed to him immediately.

"You're lucky this new computer system is in place for your senior year, Steve," the dean said. "In past years, your problem might not have been discovered until mid-semester. By then, it could have been major. You're missing a course in government that you should have had in your sophomore year. This course is required at all state colleges. We can adjust your program right here, at this terminal."

As Dean Herman worked, he explained that the new student database had become valuable to everyone in the college. The previous computer system had grown through piecemeal expansion, as so many computer operations did. There were separate files for a series of applications that had been implemented individually. Course files had been separate from tuition records. Then there had been separate files for faculty teaching assignments. Finally—and this was important in Steve's case—the check to be sure that graduate requirements were met had been handled manually in the counseling office. It had been impossible to perform this time-consuming check at registration.

"The database system makes it possible to integrate references to all of our information sources," Dean Herman said as he handed Steve his amended program. "The database approach opens up a whole new dimension of capabilities for services to students."

## The Point: Information Access Enhances Decision Making

Steve's college had developed an answer to a universal problem: To reach effective, workable decisions, people need access to information. This information must be available at the time and in the place where decisions are reached. Database management system (DBMS) application packages are the tools that enable organizations to manage information as a resource—and to respond to user needs for information access and analysis.

Information access plays a vital role in education, both for administrative and academic activities. Many colleges and universities make computer work stations available to students in libraries, laboratories, and classrooms.

## ■ The Need to Manage Data Resources

The need to access information has been present for business generally. As people and computers have interacted, new outlooks on information and its value have evolved. Managers have recognized that information resources are vital tools for analysis, decision making, and planning. However, in attempting to gather needed information, managers have been frustrated by the fact that resources were spread and, in most instances, unrelated. Information resources tended to be scattered throughout an organization in individual departments or operating functions. Recognition of the need to coordinate and integrate these resources led to application of computers for this purpose, and to the development of *database management system (DBMS)* software.

A *database* is a collection of data integrated according to content and for convenience of access. Collectively, the content of a database contains information that reflects and represents the using organization. For example, a business serves customers. A database within the business would contain information about its customers and the services each customer requires. The database could be used collectively for overall information about customer activity. Or, the same database could be used for references to information about individual customers.

Before the advent of DBMS concepts, computers were paperwork mills. To support their production role, computers built up individual, unrelated files for each application. With recognition of information as a vital end product of computer processing, demands emerged for new tools. Most of the time, effort, and money expended for each application went into designing, developing, and implmenting separate storage files. In the long run, however, this approach fragmented and isolated information resources. In an informational sense, an organization became a series of isolated parts rather than an integrated whole. Over time, creation and maintenance of separate files for applications have led to basic operating inefficiencies.

Today, managers and computer professionals have tools to deal with the problems that arise when multiple applications have to use the same data item. For example, customer name-and-address information may be needed for credit references, billing, promotional mailings, and collection of outstanding bills. If a company has multiple application programs to handle this work, the same data items have to be duplicated in each supporting file. If a customer moves, or if there is new information to add to a record, the change has to be made separately in each of the files. If the change is not made, one or more of the files has incorrect information. Incorrect files are dangerous because they can lead to erroneous actions or invalid decisions—continuous threats when organiza-

Database access is becoming a valuable, often necessary, tool for millions of jobs involving applications that can include sales, service, administration, and decision making at all levels.

tions relied on multiple, fragmented information files. DBMS software provided the capability to integrate information resources and to eliminate this type of problem.

## The Value of DBMS Software in Organizations

DBMS software has become a standard tool for managing information resources. Wide acceptance of DBMS techniques has resulted because of proven value to organizations in three key areas:

- Access
- Legal
- Application development.

**Access.**  Information can have value throughout a business organization. Restricting information access to applications for individual departments could be inefficient and frustrating. For example, the marketing department regards customers as one of a company's greatest assets. Customer information is potentially important for special mailings to promote sales. Under a system of separate applications, customer information is recorded in a billing application file and may be formatted in a way that makes its use for mailing labels difficult, expensive, and/or impossible. When data are stored in separte, unrelated files, they are inaccessable to meet the full needs of users. DBMS software bridges these needs by reducing duplicated data and supporting access to a wide range of data resources.

Massive data-storage capabilities often are necessary to support database applications. Files maintained on disk devices, like those shown, model the operations of the organizations they support.

■ **Legal.** All businesses must maintain files and produce reports to satisfy government regulations. At the very least, payroll, Social Security, injury protection, and unemployment benefits taxes must be withheld from employees and paid to federal and state agencies. Many businesses must report on sales to state and local governments and pay taxes on the basis of reported figures.

Governmental agencies also require that businesses store information on operations for which they report. The information files are subject to review and audit by these agencies. Therefore, information storage and retrieval requirements have a basis in legality, as well as a motivation for access efficiency. DBMS software must be designed to reflect these storage and reporting obligations.

■ **Application Development.** A computer-using organization faces continuing requirements for development and modification of computer applications. Under traditional approaches, major projects were mounted for the development of each individual application. Typically, a large portion, possibly most, of the resources in time and money for any project have gone into defining and developing the information files to support the specific job.

Databases and DBMS software are changing the outlook for application development. A database regards an entire segment of a business—typically supported by many applications—in terms of coordination of required information resources. By coordinating access and eliminating duplications, a database has the potential to support multiple applications.

When a company initiates database development, a major, expensive project is necessary to pull together the information resources. Once a database exists, however, application development becomes far simpler and potentially less expensive. Where individual application projects devote most of their resources to design and creation of files, much of this work is eliminated when an operational database is available. Systems developers build upon the content of existing databases for support of new applications. If needed data items are not available within an existing database, these usually can be added to accommodate new requirements.

An organization that has implemented a database is said to have created a *database environment*. This applies equally for massive systems that support large organizations, for intermediate-size systems, and for tiny systems implemented on microcomputers by individuals. In many respects, the entire information systems field has become or is becoming a database environment.

## Database Building Blocks

Computers, as you know, process data to develop information. Recall the lessons of Chapter 5 about accumulation of data under control of electronic spreadsheet software. Collections of data serve to "model" the organization,

## DATABASE

```
┌─────────────────────────┐
│                         │
│        PERSONNEL        │
│                         │
│ ······················· │
│                         │
│          SALES          │
│                         │
│ ······················· │
│              ·          │
│ PRODUCTS  ·  CUSTOMERS  │
│              ·          │
└─────────────────────────┘
```

A database consists of a series of building blocks—individual files that are organized so that data can be accessed as needed for support of user applications.

department, or group that they represent. The same is true of a database, except on a larger scale. A database can represent segments of an organization or even the organization as a whole. This means, in turn, that data within a database must reflect the organizational and operational patterns of information use within the corresponding organization. Organizations are built around information content that reflects the jobs being done. Thus, for example, customer information is an important information requirement. Other requirements might be information on employees, products, sales, and other areas.

One basic component of a database is an *entity*, defined as any collection of information that is of lasting interest to the organization that can be identified uniquely. Computer professionals and advanced users refer regularly to customer entities, product entities, personnel entities, and so on. In summary, an entity is a distinct, identifiable part of an information model.

Every informational entity, in turn, is described by a number, or series, of related data items, called *attributes*. For example, a customer entity includes data on name, street address, city, state, ZIP code, telephone number, and others. These data items are attributable to the customer entity, of which they are a part.

To *transform* data into information, it is necessary to plan for formats to be followed in organizing, accessing, modifying, and using data and information. As a basis for processing and use, data and information are organized into sets that have different sizes and complexities. The parts of a data organization set include:

- Bit
- Byte
- Data element or field
- Record
- File
- Database.

## Bit

The term *bit* is an abbreviation of Binary DigIT, a value of 0 or 1 in binary arithmetic, on or off within the circuits or magnetic states of computing equipment. A bit does not represent data or information, but is part of a code that does represent units of data.

## Byte

The smallest unit of data that has meaning is the *byte*, which consists of a number of bits organized to represent data. Different computer designs use varying numbers of bits to represent a byte. Existing hardware accommodates six, seven, or eight bits as a single byte, with eight-bit bytes used most widely. Each byte uses a series of 0 and 1 bit values to represent a letter, number, or symbol.

For support of applications, data must be organized, or structured. Building blocks for data structures include bits, bytes, data elements or fields, records, files, and databases.

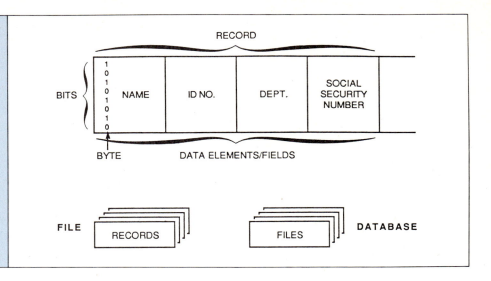

## Data Element or Field

One or more bytes that identify the smallest unit of data suitable for processing is called a *data element*, or *field*. The term *data item* also is used at this level. Within database software, a data element or field is an attribute of an entity.

Examples of single-byte data elements include Y or N to represent yes or no conditions or M and F to represent sex. Examples of longer fields include name, street address, city, state, ZIP code, height, weight, shoe size, and others.

## Record

A *record* is a group of fields that provides information on a specific person, place, thing, or idea. To illustrate, an educational information system would have a record for each student. One vital field in each student record would, of course, be name. Other fields would include identification number, Social Security number, permanent address, school address, telephone number, major, and other items.

## File

A group of related records makes up a *file*. That is, a file reflects a business segment that is modeled through use of information. To illustrate, information systems for a college might have separate files for student master records, classes, faculty, requirements for academic majors, grades, tuition payments, and others. Each file supports one or more specific applications and is separate and independent of other files.

If an application requires only one file for its support, special software tools, called *file handlers*, may be used in place of DBMS software. A file handler is less complex than a DBMS package and can be implemented on computers with less processing and storage capacities than those required for a DBMS.

## Database

A database, for the purposes of computer processing, is a storage capability that encompasses multiple files. Implementation of a database provides the ability to control access to individual records and data items within these multiple files. Because of its breadth of capabilities, a database can support multiple applications. Users or user application programs interact with a database through a special type of software known as a database management system (DBMS).

## ▪ Database Systems

As is true for all information tools, database systems are made up of a series of elements: people, data, procedures, and equipment.

## People

Almost everyone uses databases. You use a database every time you make a telephone call. You became part of a database when you were born, were included in another database when you went to school, and still another when you entered college. If you have seen a doctor or received health care at a hospital, you are included in other databases. As a worker, you will be both a set of information items and a user of one or more databases.

In business organizations, databases provide information support that makes it possible for managers to understand and analyze entire businesses rather than being restricted to limited, sectional reviews.

For computer professionals, database technology has opened new career paths. Information systems departments in many large organizations have created a job title—*database administrator (DBA)*—in recognition that the work of database creation and maintenance represents a full-time profession. This individual serves as a resource to users in designing applications that meet their information needs.

Databases also have become the basis for a growing subindustry that consists of information utility companies. These organizations establish large databases of reference materials that appeal to large groups of users. As one example, the current prices of all securities traded publicly can be accessed through on-line terminals. Qualified securities dealers can execute buy or sell transactions for stocks or bonds through use of this database system. Merchants who use credit cards can get authorizations for customers through terminals that connect to a database for credit card plans. Students, scientists, journalists, and others can do research through database services that contain vast files of newspaper stories, magazine articles, or texts of books.

On-line references to databases support operations such as this warehousing and shipping facility. The orders shown being assembled and shipped in this photo also are generated with support from database inquiry and processing applications.

## Data

The data subsystem within a database system includes a number of requirements:

- Data structures
- Data dictionaries
- Data models.

■ **Data Structures.**    A *data structure* is a plan for organizing data to reflect the records and elements that form each file within a database. To illustrate, consider the data structure for a typical information system within a college or university. A diagram for this system is presented in an accompanying illustration. Note that files are established for STUDENTS, FACULTY, COURSES, CLASSES, and GRADES. Within each file, fields are identified. For example, the CLASSES file has COURSE#, ROOM#, DAY, TIME, and INSTRUCTOR as attributes. Thus, to produce a list of classes for a given student, the computer would find this file and search the STUDENT# field. Then, the system would display or list all classes that show the given student number.

Note that certain attributes appear in more than one file. These fields are used as cross-references among stored data files and are known as *keys*, or *key fields*. A key field is a unique identifier that can be used in instructing a computer to store or access a given record. These keys make it possible to assemble information from a database on command from a user or application program. The connections among records and their uses within database applications are known as *relationships*. A data structure design defines these relationships as a basis for creating the files that will be required to support a system and identify the fields that should be included in each file.

For example, in producing grade reports, the system would derive name and address data from the STUDENTS file, course descriptions from the COURSES file, and grades from the GRADES file. This illustrates how the structure of a database makes it unnecessary to duplicate field content within files that support individual applications. Under database techniques, all data can be made available to a number of application programs.

An important characteristic of a data structure is that it is designed from the viewpoint of the user. A diagram or set of specifications for a data struc-

This illustration reflects the content of a database for an information system modeling a college or university. The files within the database are represented as a series of tabbed cards. Headings along the top of each file card indicate the fields that would establish the record structure within each file. Data records would include entries in columns and rows within the file structures.

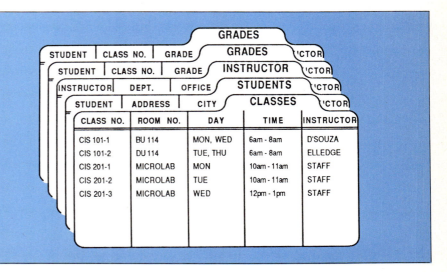

| CLASS NO. | ROOM NO. | DAY | TIME | INSTRUCTOR |
|---|---|---|---|---|
| CIS 101-1 | BU 114 | MON, WED | 6am - 8am | D'SOUZA |
| CIS 101-2 | DU 114 | TUE, THU | 6am - 8am | ELLEDGE |
| CIS 201-1 | MICROLAB | MON | 10am - 11am | STAFF |
| CIS 201-2 | MICROLAB | TUE | 10am - 11am | STAFF |
| CIS 201-3 | MICROLAB | WED | 12pm - 1pm | STAFF |

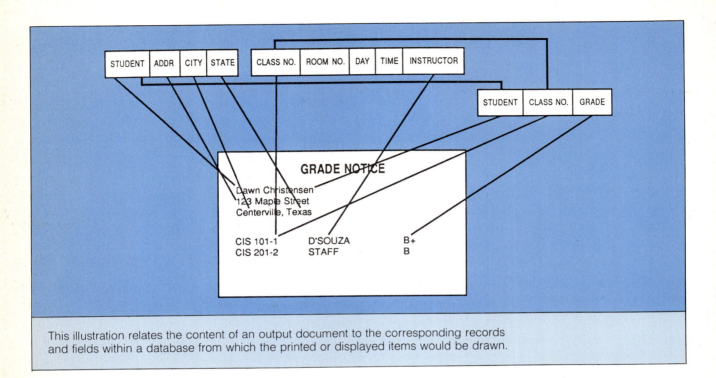

This illustration relates the content of an output document to the corresponding records and fields within a database from which the printed or displayed items would be drawn.

ture reflects the processing that will take place under application programs specified by users. Because of the viewpoint used, a data structure is called a *logical design.*

**Data Dictionary.** When a logical design for a database is completed, descriptions and identifications for data files and the items they include are listed in a *data dictionary.* As its name implies, the data dictionary identifies and defines the data elements that comprise a database. Definitions are in terms of data element names and relationships. For example, customers might represent a data file (relation) with elements (attributes) for name, address, and so on. Relationships would be established so that customer elements could be combined with product elements to create customer invoices. The naming of data elements is important because of the need to avoid duplication and for clear identification.

By establishing relationships among data elements, the dictionary also establishes access paths, or channels followed in retrieving information. As files and fields are established within a database, the DBMS software notes storage locations for each data element. The data dictionary then directs the processing of user references to the content of a database. The dictionary, in effect, becomes an interface that enables the user to avoid technical involvement in the physical storage of data. The user simply references data elements by name and the dictionary provides a basis for data searches.

This is a set of typical data dictionary entries for the CLASS file of a database to support a college or university information system.

```
FILE: CLASS
                NAME        TYPE   SIZE      DESCRIPTION
        FIELDS: CLASS NO.   TEXT    9    CLASS SCHEDULE NO.
                ROOM NO.    TEXT    7    ROOM NO. USING COLLEGE'S CODE
                DAY         TEXT    5    DAY OF WEEK CODE
                TIME        TEXT    5    TIME OF DAY
                INSTR       TEXT   15    LAST NAME, FIRST NAME, M.I.
```

**Data Models.**   A *data model* is a plan for organizing and storing data within a database. Data models within DBMS software function at two levels: For users, the data model implements a *logical design,* or a view of data in terms of application requirements. To implement a DBMS on a computer, data model software generates a *physical design,* or a set of instructions about the storage locations and access techniques to be used in building and using the database.

In terms of its role in the implementation of a database, a data model is the foundation upon which a DBMS is built. Three general types of data models (as well as combinations, or *hybrid models*) are used. These are relational, hierarchical, and network models, described below.

*Relational model.*   A relational model organizes data as a series of interrelated files. A *relation* is a file structure in which records are positioned in rows and fields are placed in columns, in a manner similar to the organization of a spreadsheet file. Multiple relations that can be coordinated for access and information queries form a *relational database.* An accompanying illustration shows a table structure that represents a typical relation. Technical terms sometimes are applied to the organizational parts of a relation: Rows are called *tuples* and columns are called attributes.

DBMS packages that use a relational model establish separate relations to serve as indexes to the data files and attributes. Commands or queries that use the database access data items through use of the index. The use of dedicated index files plays a critical role in providing user and application program service through databases.

In some database systems, the great majority of storage space is dedicated to index files that provide access paths to individual records required by users. The great value of index files lies in the user convenience that is made possible. The user initiates a search through entry of a query command. The software examines its extensive index structures to find the item and to respond to user needs. A relational database may have dozens of files, each with multiple attributes. However, the user with an information need can simply address the desired data element and the software will handle the searching automatically.

Today, relational models are the most popular basis for implementing DBMS software. One reason is that a relational approach is most logical to the average user, who can relate to organization of data into tables containing columns and rows. By comparison, the other types of models used for database software tend to be more technically oriented and complex in their structures. Another reason for the popularity of relational databases is that they can support development of applications on a user-oriented basis. That is, a relational database makes it possible to utilize existing data resources for new applications. It is not necessary to establish special file or access structures to support applications that take advantage of existing databases. The final factor leading to popularity of relational DBMS software is that this model is easiest to implement on a microcomputer, thus opening database potential for millions of users. The other types of models, discussed below, require more complex processing and do not lend themselves as well to capabilities of microcomputers.

An accompanying diagram illustrates the structure and access pattern of a relational database.

*Hierarchical model.* A hierarchical model, also known as a *tree structure*, organizes data for most efficient use of storage space and for most rapid access. However, special conditions must exist to support use of a database that uses a hierarchical model. The word hierarchy suggests a top-down plan of organization.

Each hierarchical database is organized around a top level data entity, called a *root node*. All access functions start at this point. At lower levels, the root node is connected with one or more nodes that contain data items that are attributes of the higher-level nodes. This series of connections is tracked through multiple levels of nodes. At each transition, the higher-level node is called a *parent* and the lower-level node is called a *child*. A root node or parent node may have multiple children, while each child may have only one parent, as diagrammed in an accompanying illustration.

Hierarchical models were used in the first major database systems introduced in the late 1960s for implementation on mainframe computers. Many hierarchical systems remain in use on large systems.

The major advantages of hierarchical organization are that storage space is used efficiently and that access to data is rapid. To benefit from these advantages, however, the user must organize data and access functions so that all entries to the database are through the root node. An airline reservation system often is used to illustrate use of a hierarchical model. To make a reservation or check seat availability, an agent identifies the origin of the trip. To book a flight from Los Angeles to New York for example, the first entry would be Los Angeles. The system would go to the next level, or child node, and identify destinations that can be reached from Los Angeles. When an entry is made for New York, the system moves to the next level of the hierarchy and displays a list of flights and/or connections between these points. The agent then inquires about a specific flight number and is presented with a display of its book-

The top diagram illustrates the structure of a typical relation that might be included in the database of a college or university information system. The data records are aligned horizontally in rows, or tuples. The columns represent individual data items within the records. These items also are known as attributes. The diagram below demonstrates how a relational database serves users. Keyboard-entered queries or instructions are processed through an index file first. Access paths are established to files that contain the needed data elements. Records are assembled and displayed or printed according to user instructions.

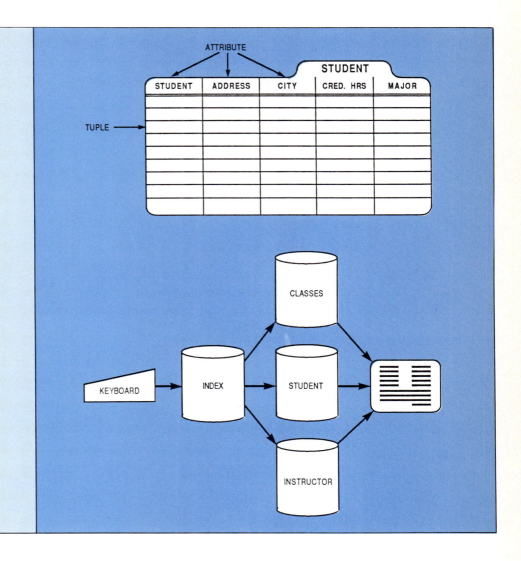

ing status. If a seat is to be booked, the database proceeds to the next-lower node and for entry of passenger identification.

By contrast, some applications do not lend themselves to implementation through hierarchical models. The college information system is an example. There is no single focal point that can serve as a root node. Inquiries may be based on student, faculty member, course, or class schedules. For this kind of system, reference through an index to a relational database would be preferable.

Processing volumes for an application also are a factor in selection of a DBMS on the basis of its data model. An airline reservation system requires fast service for large volumes of transactions. For large airlines, volume alone can mandate use of a hierarchical model. If the organization requires access on the basis of information items other than the content of the root node, separate index tables may be added to the hierarchical structure. This is one form of hybrid model that combines features of relational and hierarchical models.

*Network model.*   The network model applies some of the same principles used in the hierarchical model. However, this design attempts to add flexibility in the processing of inquiries. Under a network design, child nodes can have multiple parents. Also, parent nodes still can have multiple children. There is no single root node. Instead, access operations can begin at any level within a network and can be processed either upward or downward.

   To illustrate, if an airline reservation system used a network model, inquiries could begin with flight number or date, then proceed to a destination. Also, inquiries could involve seat availabilities on specific flights or reservation status of individual passengers. The organization of a network model is depicted in an accompanying illustration.

   DBMS software using the network approach is a little less efficient than a DBMS that uses a hierarchical model. However, this model still makes effective use of computer hardware. Many large systems use network models and a few DBMS products designed for use on microcomputers also follow a network design.

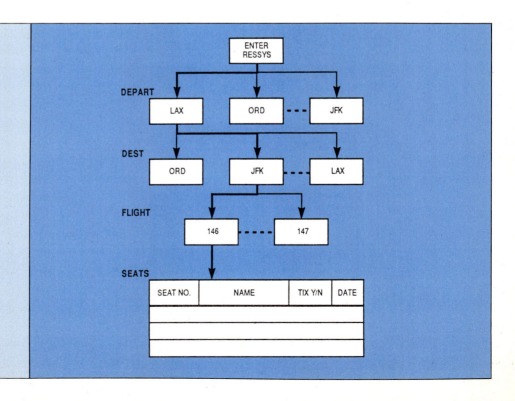

This diagram models the access procedure for a hierarchical database representing an airline reservation system. A user query begins by identifying an origin point for a journey, then seeks a destination point, specific flight, and seat availabilities. An assembled record is displayed for user viewing.

This data access diagram for a network database structure demonstrates that queries can be entered at any level in the system. Access paths can move upward or downward, as necessary to assemble and display required information.

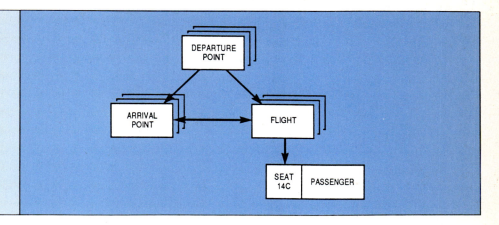

The relational model is by far the most popular for microcomputer users and is thus the basis for further descriptions of databases in this chapter.

## Procedures

The procedures for setting up and using a database are much like those involved in developing a complete system. A problem or need is defined. This definition is translated into a data structure design which, in turn, is used to select the DBMS package on the basis of the most appropriate model. Data structure entries then are made to create a database design.

Once a structure has been created, users typically gather and enter data into the database. Even for a relatively small database, this can be a massive job involving hundreds, even thousands, of hours of work. The creation of a database also is exacting. Each entry must be validated either through multiple key entries or through visual checking and validation. For this reason, most experienced system developers start by loading a database with small amounts of sample data or with only parts of files. Then, the database is tested under realistic conditions to be sure that it meets user needs before the investment is made in full implementation.

The ability of users to process inquiries directly is a major advantage of database methods over separate application files. Inquiry command sets, or *query languages*, provide the tools for direct retrieval of data under instructions from users. In addition, query language commands often are used to enter items into a database and to update or modify content of an existing database.

## Equipment

A special consideration for equipment to support a database centers around storage capacity. For large systems, databases can contain hundreds of thousands, or even millions, of data items. Even on microcomputers, database applications can require large storage capabilities to handle the complex DBMS software and large numbers of data items. Such volumes tend to be inevitable once users understand the capabilities of database systems.

For situations in which use of a database is vital to an organization, some users are installing specialized database machines. These units are included in multiprocessor configurations as specialized devices for maintaining and accessing data.

## DBMS Functions

Functions provided by DBMS software encompass the operations needed to enter data into a database, modify existing records, and produce meaningful outputs in response to user query language commands or application programs. The names given to and the operations performed by functions performed vary among individual DBMS packages. The functions described below are general; counterparts can be found within most DBMS packages. The descriptions below apply to relational databases.

- Create
- Enter
- Edit
- Compute
- List
- Sort
- Select
- Project
- Union or Append
- Join
- Print.

### Create

The *create* function enables the user to establish a name for the database and to set up the disk file to receive its contents. This function requires additional specification entries on the part of the user as compared with the setting up of files under word processing or spreadsheet software. Remember that a database can present large data storage requirements. Therefore, before you create a file, you must think about the size of records and the number of records to be accommodated.

To illustrate the importance of this specification, consider what happens in creating the STUDENTS relation within a college information system. Say current student enrollment is 4,000. The school graduates an average of 700 seniors and admits approximately 1,300 freshmen each year. The designer wants to allow enough space to accommodate all records, including the potential for expansion. Once a database is set up and in use, considerable difficulty can be incurred if the relation becomes overcrowded and the database must be reorganized.

For the STUDENTS database, the designer needs to establish school policies that will govern the creation of new records and the deletion of old ones. For example, assume the school keeps records active for three years after a student drops out—in case there is an application for reentry or for transfer to another college. Also, the school probably keeps records active for some years after a student graduates—so that transcripts can be provided for graduate schools or prospective employers. With such considerations, a student body of 4,000 may present requirements for perhaps 12,000 to 15,000 records.

## Enter

The *enter* function is used for actual entry of data into a relation. The record format serves as a guide. The user or operator makes data entries for each field in every record.

Data entry can be a massive job when a database is set up. In the STUDENTS example, for instance, users would have to assemble records for recent graduates and dropouts as well as for the 4,000 enrolled students. The enter function would be used continuously to add records for newly enrolled students.

## Edit

The *edit* function is used to modify existing records. Typically, the system will display the content of an existing record and permit the user to enter new content for any given field.

## Compute

A usual strategy for databases is to keep source data only in a computer file. Fields that represent computations performed upon other fields are generated as needed, usually for user-requested outputs. This saves storage space and also avoids situations in which obsolete figures are maintained, or in which extra computation steps would be needed each time a record is changed. This capability is implemented through use of the *compute* function.

An example of a computed field in a student record system would be grade point average. This value can be calculated as part of an inquiry function whenever it is needed. To support this service, the user identifies computed-value fields and specifies source data items and arithmetic functions to be performed.

**List**

The *list* function causes the contents of a relation to be displayed on a screen. The function can be used to review information for decision making or to examine records during updating operations.

**Sort**

The *sort* function sequences records in alphabetic, numeric, or combined alphanumeric order. The order can be ascending (from high value to low, Z to A, 9 to 0) or descending (from low to high, A to Z, 0 to 9). Sorting is done according to the content of a key field specified by the user.

Sort functions are applied to support specific applications. For a STUDENTS relation, for example, lists may be desired according to the alphabetic order of last name. On the other hand, an application may require sorting according to numeric order of identification numbers. A single group of records can be arranged quickly to meet the needs of any application.

**Select**

The *select* function enables the user to choose records to support special projects or applications. Selection is on the basis of data content of a specified field. The selected records may be placed into a separate working file for temporary use.

To illustrate, the administration of a college may want to send a notice to all freshmen. The select function could be applied to a grade-level field. As an alternative, the system could be instructed to pick all records for students with 30 or fewer credit hours.

**Project**

The select function chooses full records, or tuples within a relational database. The *project* function selects columns, or attributes, for segregation from its relation. Individual or multiple columns of data can be included.

The project function can be valuable for data analysis. For example, suppose the administration of a college wanted to determine the failure rate for a given course, perhaps freshmen English. Information could be extracted from the GRADES relation. Student identifications could be eliminated from this operation as a privacy protection because, of all of the fields within the target relation, only grade and grade-level attributes are selected. Thus, the projected data has no personal identification.

**Union or Append**

The *union* or *append* function is used to bring together records from two or more relations. The operation can be applied to entire files or to sets of records chosen under a select function. Note that the union function is for records only. To combine columns from different relations, a join function is used.

To illustrate, suppose pre-graduation notices were to be sent to qualified students. Records could be selected from the GRADES file to establish qualification. Then, a project function could be used to create a list of identification numbers for students to receive the notices. This list would be used to select names and addresses from the STUDENTS relation. The selected STUDENTS and GRADES records then could be combined to create a working file for advisors, who could contact the students by mail or personally.

When two complete relations are to be joined, the append name may be used. The append capability would be used in situations for which it is desirable to capture sizable groups of new records and to validate data before including the new records in the system. For example, a college has a large number of new student records to add at the beginning of the school year. It may be desirable to create a working relation for entry of these records. The new file can be validated completely before its records are merged into the main database.

## Join

*Join* brings together columns from different relations. To illustrate, a student grades list could combine names from the STUDENTS relation and class designations and grades from the CLASS file.

## Print

The *print* function causes the system to create a hard-copy output of file content on a printer. One approach is to use the functions described above to assemble a working file for printing. Some DBMS packages have special report functions that enable users to designate output content. The reports are assembled internally by the software.

## ■ Putting DBMS to Work in Business

DBMS software provides a general-purpose information systems tool. DBMS packages can be used to organize data for and support operation of virtually any application. The following are typical examples of business applications of DBMS capabilities.

## Manufacturing

Early DBMS applications in manufacturing involved basic inventory control for parts and products. The database identified each part or product in stock. As parts were ordered, received, and used, corresponding records were updated. With this kind of database, application programs could be programmed to produce messages automatically when stocks were low and parts had to be reordered.

More recently, manufacturing systems have been expanded to incorporate detailed records on work stations throughout a plant and the capacity of each.

These records include tallies of work backlogs at each station. With this information, application programs can develop production schedules for manufacturing jobs. If problems or conflicts in work loads occur, managers can review the database to support decisions about whether to work overtime, hire more people, change schedules, etc.

## Financial

Financial reports represent the status of a company to managers, governmental agencies, banks, and investors. Information contained in financial reports comes from many sources. For instance, all business transactions involving receipt or payments of money impact financial status and must be reflected in the organizations's financial database. The multiple applications for invoicing, collections, purchasing, payments to suppliers, payroll, and other expenses can be related to the same database. The combined applications then are said to constitute an *integrated accounting system*.

## Human Resources

The term *human resources* emphasizes the importance of people—and information about people—to the management of an organization. Through a series of relations, companies can establish and correlate information from employee master files, job descriptions, work performance records, and payroll files.

A database of this type can support routine information processing functions, such as payroll preparation, administration of health care insurance programs, or vacation plans. In addition—and of growing importance—managers can use the same kind of database for plans and decisions on human resources. For example, as job openings occur, searches can be made within the employee master file to find individuals who qualify for promotion.

## Decision Support and Planning

Decisions that establish operating plans and future directions for a company are made on the basis of information in databases that reflect operating experience and financial status. In addition, decision makers can combine information about their own company with analysis from external databases. For example, government census reports can be used to review the availability of labor in areas being considered for new plants. Transportation support facilities also can be referenced from external databases. In addition, a DBMS can be set up to include information on local and state taxes in a number of alternate locations for future plant sites. This type of application is known as a *decision support system*.

These applications demonstrate an important characteristic about the use of databases and DBMS software: A database can and should organize information resources to meet the needs of end users. Database methods integrate data resources for accessibility and efficient use. By supporting access to needed information, databases assist users in analysis, decision making, and planning. Also, once a database is in place, development of new computer applications can be simplified greatly.

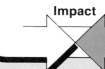

**Impact**

# How to Select a Database Package

To select a database package, the place to start is with your own data. Determine the structure of the data items you want to store and access. Each file, or relation, should be identified. Within each relation, you should identify the entities, or items, you want to store. For each entity, you should establish the type of data to be entered and the size, in number of characters.

As a selection tool, set up a chart, or table. Use one column on the chart for your maximum needs—the relation that demands the greatest capacity in entity size, number of items, and number of records to be stored. Then use the first row of your table to enter descriptions of your needs. Set up additional rows, one for each of several database packages to be considered.

After you enter your needs on the top row, enter the corresponding figures for the capacities of the packages you consider on the rows below. Compare your needs with the capacities—and prices—of the packages. Select the best two or three packages and go on to the next step.

Prepare a similar table for further consideration. Set up a column for each function or inquiry command you feel you should have for your database application. Then set up rows for each of the qualifying packages and note, in each column, whether the capabilities are available. By the time you complete entries on this second chart, you will have identified the package or packages that can handle your application.

To continue your evaluation, ask the following questions about the packages that still are under consideration:

- What user documentation is available and how good is it?
- Is a special training manual and/or a software tutorial available to instruct you and others in the use of the package?
- Can you import electronic spreadsheet files into the database package?
- Can you set up and use the software package on a shared basis, possibly on a local area network?
- Is a report generator available? What are its capabilities? How well do these capabilities match your needs?

When you have settled on a package that appears best, determine whether it will run on the computer you have. Find out if you will need to add to your hardware capabilities to support the package. If you are considering two or more packages, find out about hardware additions (and comparative costs) for each.

Answering these questions will help you to identify the two or three packages that come closest to meeting your needs. Once you have narrowed the field, you can choose the product that gives you the best value for your money.

## Chapter Summary

- As business computer applications proliferated, the files of information accumulated became vital resources for using organizations. The information files have become the basis for analysis and decision making by managers.

- When files were developed to support individual applications, it was difficult to correlate and combine information for decision support. Database concepts provided techniques for relating information from multiple files for coordinated use. When database systems are implemented, it is possible to develop new applications by deriving information from existing data resources.

- In addition to supporting application development, databases also enhance information access and help using organizations to comply with development of reports required by law.

- A database consists of a group of files that represent portions, or functions, of a business. Each collection of data that models a distinct business operation is called an entity. In turn, the data elements that establish an entity are called attributes.

- Data resources are formatted in a series of structures that include, from smallest to largest, bit, byte, data element or field, record, file, and database.

- Use of databases is approaching the universal. The majority of information users rely on databases to meet their needs.

- The data resources within a database need to be organized into structures that relate data elements to corresponding files as a basis for rapid, convenient access. Data structures are defined in a data dictionary that provides the basis for organization and reference to entities and attributes. In turn, data definitions are translated for computer implementation through development of a schema, or plan of organization, for a database.

- Each database is built upon a data model, or structure that organizes data for storage and reference. The three major types of models are relational, hierarchical, and network.

- Procedures for use of a database center around the capabilities of a set of special commands that form a query language. Query languages are used to build, manipulate, and report information from a database.

- Equipment used to support a database needs extensive storage capabilities.

- The functions available through use of a database query language include create, enter, edit, compute, list, sort, select, project, union or append, join, and print.

## Questions for Review

1. How did the development of database software reflect the recognition that information is a vital resource?
2. How does a database improve information access for users?
3. How does a database help an organization to comply with development of reports required by law?
4. How does availability of a database improve an organization's capabilities for application development?
5. What are entities and attributes and what relationships exist between them?
6. What is a byte and what role does it play in representing data for use in a database?
7. What is a field and what is its purpose in representing information?
8. What are records and files and what are the relationships between these two units of data?
9. What is a data dictionary and what purpose does it serve?
10. What are the main features of relational, hierarchical, and network data models?

## Questions for Thought

1. Identify the three data models identified in this chapter and tell which is easiest to design and implement. Why?
2. Describe the steps you would follow and the functions you would use to develop a list of students with grade point averages of 3.5 and above for nomination to an honor society.
3. What databases are you aware of that contain information about you?
4. What are the major advantages of databases over traditional files that support individual applications?
5. What role do index files play within database systems and why are index files important?

## Terms

append                                    bit
attribute                                 byte

| | |
|---|---|
| child | key |
| compute | key field |
| create | list |
| database | logical design |
| database administrator (DBA) | network model |
| database management system (DBMS) | parent |
| data dictionary | physical design |
| data element | print |
| data item | project |
| data model | query language |
| data structure | record |
| decision support system | relation |
| edit | relational database |
| enter | relational model |
| entity | relationship |
| field | root node |
| file | select |
| hierarchical model | sort |
| human resources | transform |
| hybrid model | tree structure |
| integrated accounting system | tuple |
| join | union |

## MINICASE

**Situation:**

You work for a retail store that has its own credit card plan. Management prefers to provide credit for its best customers because interest charges on account balances generaly produce greater profits than the income realized from merchandise sales.

One advantage that results from providing direct credit is the ability to use the customer database for special sales or promotions. Availability of purchasing and credit payment information leads to highly effective use of advertising dollars.

Your store's database includes relations for customer master file, accounts receivable files showing amounts owed by each customer, and a customer credit file. The customer master records include fields that show cumulative purchases for the current year and for the previous year. The accounts receivable file has separate records for each unpaid bill. The credit file shows the credit limit and amount currently owed by each customer.

Management wants to do an advertising mailing to customers who have made purchases totalling more than $300 for the current year and have open credit balances (credit limit minus amount owed) of $400 or more.

### Decision Making: Your Turn

1. From the information you have, identify and describe the problem to be solved.
2. Identify alternatives that could be followed to avoid or solve the problem.
3. On the basis of the limited information you have: a) Identify additional information you would gather if you were dealing with this problem in a real situation. b) Identify the solution that appears best on the basis of the information that is available and explain your reasons for this selection.
4. What lessons are to be learned from this situation?

## Projects

1. Review ads for DBMS packages in a number of computer magazines. Compare the features of at least three packages for implementation of the retail store customer credit application described in the Minicase above. Identify which package seems best suited for the job and explain why.
2. Check want ads in your local newspaper for management or information systems positions that include database responsibilities. Write a summary of values that you can see for an understanding of database principles and functions by a sophisticated end user.
3. You decide to use a relational database package to build a personal telephone directory. Define a data structure, prepare a data dictionary, and describe the steps you would follow to implement this system.

# Chapter Outline

Briefing Memo

End-User Perspective

The Point: Data Communications, Window to a
World of Information

The Need for Data Communications

Data Communications Systems
*People, Data, Equipment, Procedures*

Putting Data Communications to Work in Business
*Local Area Network (LAN), Electronic Mail, Bulletin
Boards and Information Utilities*

Chapter Summary

Questions for Review

Questions for Thought

Terms

Minicase

Projects

CHAPTER **8**

# Data Communications Systems

## Briefing Memo

TO:     Information Users
FROM:  T. Rohm, W. Stewart

Communication among computers represents a growth area. Eventually, experts believe, computers will require more communications facilities and services than will all of the conversations among people. As a user of computer information systems, you will almost surely be a user of data communications services.

In this chapter, you visit the exciting area where computers meet communications networks. In the process, you gain the knowledge you will need as an effective user of the independent technology that connects computers to a worldwide network of communications circuits. Business organizations have led the way in blending the technologies and terminologies of the communications and computer fields. Now it's your turn to do the same. The content of this chapter is your starting point.

## End-User Perspective

"Everything you will need for your spring break can be found and reserved right here, in this handy little machine," Darlene said. Darlene is a travel agent. She was talking to Juan and Joshua, roommates, who had come in to ask about costs and reservations for their spring break.

Darlene pointed to a computer terminal at the side of her desk, explaining that her terminal was linked into an airline reservation system and that the airline system was part of a larger system that included car rental and hotel reservations. Through the hotel systems, Darlene added, she had the ability to arrange for local tours or attractions.

Juan explained that he and Joshua were on a tight budget. Darlene demonstrated that the computer could help them shop for travel bargains. To illustrate, Darlene asked for a screen display on flights between their home town and the destination in which they were interested. Darlene showed that she could look up rates at 12 different hotels in the destination city and find the best bargains. Car-rental information showed that the travelers could save $10 per day by renting from an agency with a location off the airport grounds—as distinct from agencies that had service counters in the airport terminals.

"There was a time," Darlene said, "when I would have had to be on the phone for close to two hours to get the information I just got for you in a few minutes. Communication networks can put the whole world at your fingertips."

## The Point: Data Communications, Window to a World of Information

Juan and Joshua benefited from a simple fact of business life. To compete in many fields, businesses must have data communications capabilities. Modern business organizations use data communications networks as competitive tools. Think of the example of Electronics, Inc., from Chapters 2 and 5. The opportunity to consider consolidation of distribution points could not even have existed without availability of a data communications network to support transmissions of operational information between field locations and a central facility.

## The Need for Data Communications

Businesses have depended on the ability to communicate information for hundreds of years. In the days of the American colonies, the information lifeline took the form of packet ships from England. Later, the railroads played a role in the movement of information, as did the telegraph, teletypewriter, and telephone. Before computers came upon the scene, a standard communications language (ASCII) was in place for use with teletypewriter equipment.

The significance of these developments is that the same code developed initially for teletypewriters is now the internal machine code for most microcomputers. In retrospect, it is safe to say that microcomputers were built at least partly to implement and improve data communications capabilities. Currently, it seems certain that volumes of data communications messages to support business activities ultimately will exceed use of telephone networks for voice communication.

Clearly, data communications and information processing activities are linked closely for many business organizations. Therefore, a knowledge of data communications functions and capabilities surely will enhance your knowledge base and effectiveness as a user of information services.

## Data Communications Systems

The overall parts of a data communications system fall within the same broad categories as for other systems. However, further breakdowns are appropriate because separate technologies are used in communication and computing systems. To reflect these needs, the discussions that follow cover the four basic parts of systems:

- People
- Data
- Equipment
- Procedures.

## People

Anyone who uses a computer or benefits from computer-generated information can profit from data communications capabilities. Some examples:

- You are reading one result of data communications services right now. The text of this book was written and edited on microcomputers, then transmitted over telephone lines for computerized typesetting.
- As another example, businesspeople talk to one another over computer connections in much the same way as they do over telephone lines—except that computers are quieter.
- Salespeople transmit orders and market information from portable computers to company headquarters.
- Computer professionals extend the scope of capabilities and services through data communications. For example, a technician can monitor

Data communications networks enable key information users to keep track of transactions and conditions on a national or international basis.

and overcome functional problems in a distant system through use of on-line diagnostic programs.

- Managers keep track of national and international operations and implement plans through access to massive databases that reflect conditions in widespread areas of concern and responsibility.

**Data**

Data resources acquire new dimensions and values when data communications capabilities are included in a computer information system. The entire concept of database reference and maintenance is tied to data communications capabilities. That is, a database would be of little or limited value if users did not have convenient access. With data communications capabilities available, database access can be made available at points ranging from offices next door to facilities situated around the world.

As the flexibility of data communications has increased and costs have come down, entire new segments of the computer industry have evolved. These organizations are said to provide "value added" services. That is, they store data and provide subscription services to persons or organizations that access the services. The value added services charge fees for access to data resources. This industry segment is described further in later sections of this chapter.

**Equipment**

Data communications capabilities make it just as feasible for a manager to reach decisions on operations 3,000 miles away as it is to deal with operations in the next room. With data communications, managers receive information that enables them to evaluate and deal with widespread situations on a knowledgeable basis. To achieve this business monitoring capability, a data communications system must incorporate three distinct classes of equipment:

- Signal carriers
- Sending/receiving devices
- Networks.

**Signal Carriers.**   Any point that can send and receive signals over wires or through the air can function as a data communications site. Data communications uses a wide range of *signal carriers,* including public telephone networks or other circuits that can deliver electrical tones and digital signals over distances. These carriers make it possible to link one or more computers of any size or type for exchange of information or computer programs. A sampling of common data communications signal carriers is identified and discussed below.

*Simplex Lines.*   A simplex line consists of a single strand of wire that handles transmissions in only one direction at a time. This type of carrier also is known as a *telegraphic line* because this is the type of connection over which telegraph operators used to transmit Morse code. In terms of data communications, simplex lines have severe limitations. As indicated, transmission is in one direction at a time. To communicate in the other direction, it is necessary for people at each end of a circuit to reset switches that adapt the line for transmission in the other direction. Also, speed of transmission is limited and signals are subject to more interruption and errors than with other methods. Simplex lines were introduced during the days when information was transmitted among telegraphers via Morse code. In the computer era, their use is limited to slow speed transmissions in remote areas, and in situations where it is satisfactory to transmit in only one direction at a time.

*Duplex Lines.*   Duplex means double. A duplex line consists of a pair of circuits that connect two or more communicating points. With a duplex connection, both parties can send or receive simultaneously. A less expensive version of duplex service is known as *half-duplex.* This service is a step up from simplex transmission but is not of the same caliber as full duplex. Communication takes place in one direction at a time. But once a transmitting station has completed a message, either party can claim the line and transmit data or text.

The most common form of duplex carrier is your telephone system. Each telephone instrument is connected to a pair of wires that, in turn, are connected to transmission lines and to other instruments with the same capabilities. As compared with simplex service, duplex transmission is many times faster, and

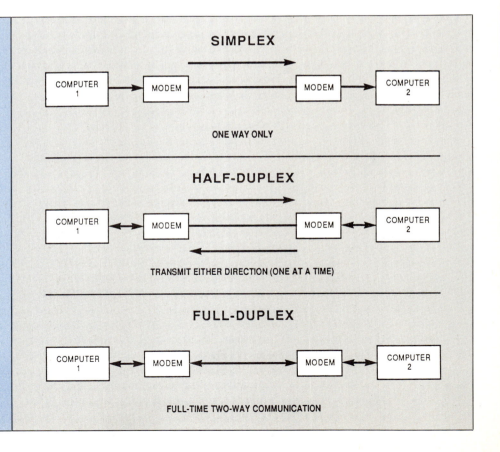

Data communications can be implemented through different types of circuits, which carry varying costs and provide a range of capacities. As shown in these diagrams, a simplex circuit supports only one-way data transmission. A half-duplex circuit provides a two-way capability, but in only one direction at a time. A full-duplex circuit provides full-time, two-way capabilities.

**SIMPLEX**

COMPUTER 1 → MODEM → MODEM → COMPUTER 2

ONE WAY ONLY

**HALF-DUPLEX**

COMPUTER 1 ↔ MODEM ↔ MODEM ↔ COMPUTER 2

TRANSMIT EITHER DIRECTION (ONE AT A TIME)

**FULL-DUPLEX**

COMPUTER 1 ↔ MODEM ↔ MODEM ↔ COMPUTER 2

FULL-TIME TWO-WAY COMMUNICATION

also far more accurate and reliable. The factors of transmission speed and accuracy are covered in discussions below. Duplex lines of the public telephone system are the most commonly used carriers for support of data communications by microcomputers.

To transmit the text of this book to the typesetter, an editor uses software that causes the microcomputer to dial the telephone number of the typesetting machine. A tone signals that the connection has been made and pressing a single key causes transmission of a complete file, consisting of one or more chapters.

In many business organizations, branch offices use this same approach to transmit orders to warehouses or sales departments. Many insurance companies have systems that permit agents to call in over telephone lines for rate quotations and commitments on policies. A restaurant chain receives operating data from all of its locations through telephone calls by microcomputers. Multiple transactions, from bank deposits to restocking of food supplies, are handled through processing of these messages.

*Broadband and Coaxial Lines.*   Services implemented with broadband or coaxial lines provide higher capacities and greater levels of accuracy and reliability than duplex lines. These carriers provide greater capacity because they simply have more lines open. Broadband service, for example, might consist of two, four, or even eight ''pairs'' of carriers. The service is formed by assigning more lines within a public telecommunications network to a data transmission channel. Coaxial service uses a specially assigned, or dedicated, cable of the type usually used for television signals. Coaxial cables contain special wrapping, or shielding, material to protect transmission lines from electronic interference, or *noise.*

One option that provides greater capacity in some broadband carriers is that signals can be transmitted in *parallel*, rather than in *serial* mode, as is necessary with simplex or duplex lines. In parallel transmission, each line carries a separate bit of data concurrently with transmissions in other lines. Thus, a four-pair line can carry eight bits, or a full byte at a time. An eight-pair line can carry two bytes at a time, and so on. By comparison, simplex or duplex carriers are limited to serial transmissions in which bytes must be broken down and sent one bit at a time, to be reassembled into byte code formats at the receiving end.

Because of the large volumes of data that must be transmitted, broadband services are necessary when large computer systems communicate directly. In one system operated by an international electronics corporation, for example, computers in Texas, Iowa, and Europe are linked by broadband services implemented through satellites. If one of the computers has a backlog of work, the software implements *load sharing* capabilities. That is, jobs are shifted to systems that have capacity available. Thus, a job entered in Texas might be processed partly there, partly in Europe, and partly in Iowa. The user has no indication—nor any concern—with what facility is used. The concern, rather, is that all work is done in a minimum of time and is delivered according to specifications, to people who need the information.

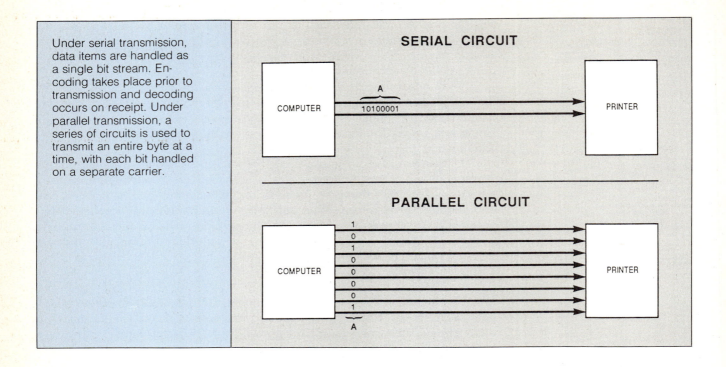

Under serial transmission, data items are handled as a single bit stream. Encoding takes place prior to transmission and decoding occurs on receipt. Under parallel transmission, a series of circuits is used to transmit an entire byte at a time, with each bit handled on a separate carrier.

*Radio and Microwave Transmission.* Radio and microwave carriers utilize signals that are radiated through the air rather than along strands of wire. Radio signals have comparatively low frequencies, or signal-generation rates, and provide comparatively low transmission capacities. Microwaves have higher frequencies, which means that thousands of additional carrier waves are generated each second. This makes for higher capacities. A limitation on microwave systems is that transmissions must be made in a direct, straight line, known as a *line-of-sight* range. This limits distances between sending and receiving points because the earth, which is round, limits the range of the signals. Therefore, microwave services require send/receive relay points approximately 90 miles apart.

*Laser Beams.* A laser is a single-wavelength, or "coherent," beam of light with enough intensity to carry digital communication signals. This capability makes laser beams, which travel through the air, ideal direct links between large computers or for other high-capacity jobs such as television signals. In these applications, laser transmissions eliminate the need to construct transmission lines. Yet, laser transmission provides high capacity with great reliability. Laser transmission, like microwave signals, has line-of-sight limitations. At this time, most laser carriers operate over short distances.

*Fiber-Optic Lines.* Continuous strands of glass are used to carry fiber-optic signals. The glass carriers transmit streams of light that can be turned off and on at rapid rates to carry digital signals. These signals are capable of transmitting either voice or data transmissions. Fiber optics carriers are being added to public telephone networks to provide service of improved quality and capacity. A single strand of glass can carry more signals than a large, broadband cable made from wires.

*Satellites.*    Use of orbiting satellites for communication, in effect, represents a breakthrough for microwave transmission techniques. Microwave signals are beamed to satellites in stationary orbits 20,000-plus miles above the earth. The satellites reflect and relay the signals back to earth stations. Satellite facilities can provide carriers that range from duplex circuits to massive broadband connections.

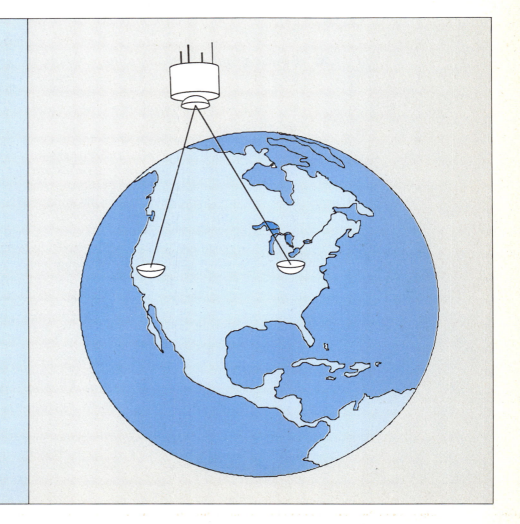

Satellite transmission beams signals from ground stations to satellites in stationary orbit. The signals are reflected back to earth, where they are decoded and relayed by ground stations.

*Dial-Up Service.*   This term means simply that transmission takes place through public telephone networks and that access is through dialing from one number to another.

*Dedicated Lines.*   A dedicated line is a point-to-point communication carrier that is assigned to one user only. Dedicated lines can be secured by leasing facilities from a public telephone carrier or by establishing connections through special installation. During the time when a line is leased to a using organization, the telephone company may not transmit public messages over this channel. Local area networks (LANs) usually include dedicated lines built by their using organizations.

To summarize: Just as computers are collections of equipment assembled to meet users' needs, so also is the communication field a virtual infinity of choices for transmitting conversation and/or data from point to point or among multiple users. Speeds, complexities, and volumes are available in wide variations, all with trade-offs of costs against capacities.

■ **Sending/Receiving Devices.**   Devices that fall within this category perform a specialized service: They generate and receive the signals that move over carrier circuits like those described above. In general, *sending and receiving devices* are classified according to the type of signal handled or signal generating capabilities.

One major breakdown separates *analog* and *digital* devices. Analog signals are continuous tones or electrical-current values. Examples include musical instruments, sirens, or the human voice, all of which transmit signals on the basis of continuous sound patterns. Radio and voice telephone systems use analog transmission. Digital devices transmit and receive through a series of start-stop pulses that can correspond with the binary formats of information for computer use. Digital signals also can carry voices or reproduce music, as is done on compact discs. In general, digital devices provide higher quality performance than analog devices because they are less subject to electronic interference, or noise.

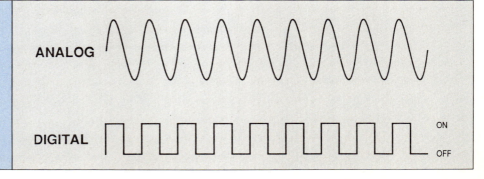

Analog and digital signals are represented by different wave forms. An analog signal is a series of cycles. A digital signal is a series of stop-start pulses.

ANALOG

DIGITAL

ON

OFF

Another factor in the classification of transmission devices centers around applications. Some units generate and receive signals transmitted over communication carriers. Others are internal to computers or are used for direct links between computers and external devices. The devices covered in the discussions below include modems, communications ports and interfaces, and internal communication links within computers.

*Modem.*    The term modem is an abbreviation of the functions, MOdulate-DEModulate. Modems are used to send digital signals over analog telephone circuits. To handle the pulses of digital codes, analog signals must be modulated, or converted from one signal type to another. This process, performed by the sending modem, applies different volumes, or amplitudes, to 0 and 1 binary values. At the receiving end, a modem converts the analog signals back into digital codes for computer use.

Even though some modems are built into computers, these devices are not part of computer processing. The modem function accepts output from or provides input to a computer and monitors transmission over telecommunications channels. As you deal with data communications capabilities to enhance user services for microcomputers, you probably will encounter the term *RS232 port*, or *COM 1 port*. This is the standard interface between microcomputers and any communication devices. The port itself is a plug at the back of your microcomputer with a standard plug into which you can fit modems, printers, or direct links to other microcomputers.

An external modem, placed under the telephone in the foreground, is linked through a Touch-Tone telephone to a typesetting computer. This modem was used to receive text transmitted from a microcomputer to set the type for this book.

Modems function as communications interfaces for computers. For transmission, digital signals from computers are converted to analog signals that are carried over communication channels. At the receiving end, a modem translates analog signals back into digital formats for use by computers.

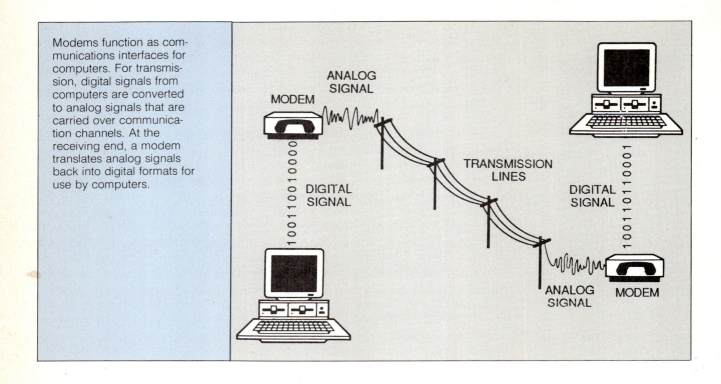

MODEM
ANALOG SIGNAL
DIGITAL SIGNAL
1 0 0 1 1 0 0 1 0 0 0 0
TRANSMISSION LINES
DIGITAL SIGNAL
1 0 0 1 1 0 1 1 0 0 0 1
ANALOG SIGNAL
MODEM

A modem user gains access, literally, to a world of information. This capability is illustrated by the example at the beginning of this chapter. Individuals interested in making travel plans can open a whole world of travel, hotel, and activity information through a terminal on the desk of a local travel agent.

Hooking up travel agencies does not change the basic design or capabilities of existing reservation systems. Data communications links extend those capabilities to users at widespread geographic locations.

*Communications Ports and Interfaces.* Recall that a computer is a collection of devices connected to provide coordinated operation. This means that a computer processor needs a basic ability to communicate within its own connected devices. A *port* is an element of a computer system that accepts direct, high-speed transmissions from related devices. Each port represents a *channel* through which a computer communicates with its supporting devices.

Within the computer, or within a connecting device, communication *interfaces* are needed. The job of an interface is to establish communication capability between a device and the computer. This processing is needed because individual devices operate at different processing speeds and/or communication rates. One example is the use of interfaces between microcomputers and the printers to which outputs are delivered. The computer operates at much faster speeds than the printer. Therefore, the interface to a printer includes a *buffer* that stores data output by the computer until the printer is ready.

■ **Networks.**  In the communication field, a *network* represents a system designed to make the process of communication efficient and cost-effective. Networks are linked communication devices configured to support the interchange of data.

A bank with multiple branches is a good example of how a data communications network supports business operations. Within a bank's branch office, each teller may have a terminal. Terminals also are provided for officers of the branch. The branch also may have one or more automatic teller machine (ATM) units at which customers can process their own transactions. All of these terminals need access to a central computer that maintains the bank's master account records.

To help meet this need, special devices are interposed between user terminals and the communication lines to central computers. These units are known as *multiplexors*, a term that describes the ability to consolidate multiple inputs into a single stream of data communications messages. The multiplexor accepts partial messages from terminals and assembles them for transmission to a central computer. Then, messages from the computer to terminals are consolidated at the multiplexor for delivery to users. Interconnected devices that handle data communications in this way are called networks. The discussion that follows covers three major types of networks used in data communications.

*Ring.*  To get the idea of a *ring network,* think about the connections used by many Christmas tree lights. The sockets are connected in series. Current moves from one bulb to another, in order. If one bulb burns out, the circuit is broken and all the lights go out. Following the same principle, a ring network usually is pictured as a circular string of connected data communications stations, called *nodes.* Any message entered into the network travels to all points in the network. If one node is out of order, the network is down—unless provisions are made for switching around nodes that are not in use.

Disadvantages of ring networks lie in the limitations upon service. Private or confidential messages cannot be safeguarded, since all stations have access to each message. Also, it can be slow and cumbersome to send—and to have to sort through—all messages at each node.

For the proper application, however, ring networks can be advantageous. For example, suppose it was necessary for all parties on a network to receive all messages. As one illustration, a news agency sends stories over computerized transmission networks. All subscribers are entitled to see all of the transmissions. In a fast food restaurant, orders taken at service counters are printed out in the kitchen and recorded on a terminal that will store and forward operating information to headquarters. In a distribution business, a network might be used to record customer orders and to deliver copies of those orders to warehouse locations where they are to be filled. The same information also could be recorded for processing on a central computer system.

*Bus.*  To picture the principle of a *bus network,* think of a railroad. A railroad has lines that spread out from central terminals. Along the lines are stations at which people or packages can get on or off the trains.

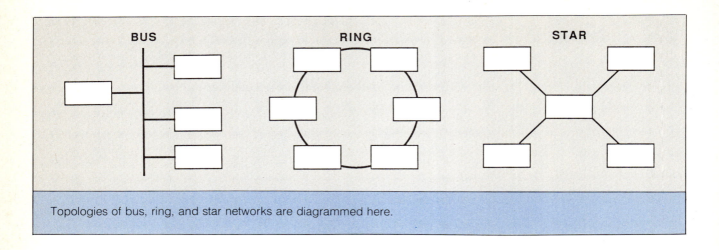

Topologies of bus, ring, and star networks are diagrammed here.

A *bus* is a communication channel onto which communication nodes can be linked. The nodes in a bus network are like stations on a railroad system. A bus can be local or long distance. For example, most of the storage drives and printers in a computer center are linked to the main processor through bus channels. A bank might use a bus approach, with lines running out from the central computer to branches or groups of branches. The terminals within individual branches are linked to nodes that consist of minicomputers with *message concentrator* capabilities. This linkage is similar to that among the stations, switches, and track lines of a railroad. When messages are returned from a central computer, they are stored at the node and transmitted serially to the user terminals.

An advantage of a bus configuration, or network *topology,* is that it permits each node to communicate directly and independently with any other node. This is possible because each node has a known, or addressable, location on a bus. Thus, a bus tends to be more flexible than a ring network. With a bus, a central computer can control its own communication traffic. The central computer can call, or *poll,* individual nodes to check for waiting messages and to lock out inactive nodes while it is in the process of communicating with a selected point. This feature can be a disadvantage in that network monitoring occupies considerable amounts of computer time. Because of this, a bus also tends to be more expensive to install and operate than a ring network.

*Star.*    A *star network* gets its name from its appearance on a configuration diagram. A central, or master, node receives and processes messages from a number of nodes. Each node is connected directly to the communication controller. Individual nodes may serve a group of local terminals in a satellite network.

Under a star topology, all transmissions, from all nodes, are routed through the central processor, or switch. There is no opportunity to transmit messages directly among nodes.

Star networks can be efficient because all nodes have immediate and direct access to the resources of a central facility. A potential disadvantage is that the communication system has ''all its eggs in one basket.'' If the central switch goes down, all users are out of business. For this reason, large star networks often have two computers at their hub. One computer can do batch work while the other handles communication. If the communication switch goes down, the batch system takes over its work load.

*Hybrid Networks.*   Many networks, of all sizes and scopes, use combinations of topologies. For example, a large bank may set up a star network to serve branches in a given city or area. The controllers of the star systems then can be part of a bus network linked into a central computer. In summary, networks are configured to the jobs to be done and the volumes of communication traffic to be handled.

## Procedures

Separate procedures apply to two different concepts of data communications:

- Communication protocols
- Operational.

**Communication Protocols.**   Data communications are possible largely because equipment and software designs establish compatibility between devices that are essentially incompatible. Telecommunication and data communications are controlled by devices and code structures with different formats, standards, and operating speeds. That is, the code structures required for internal processing within a computer are different from those used to transmit and receive data within the telecommunications industry.

To make communication possible, there must be sets of rules and standards for translations between languages that are essentially foreign to one another. In the United States, the standard language for data communications, identified earlier, is ASCII. Many computers use another coding language, EBCDIC. In addition, the International Standards Organization, which is particularly strong among European nations, supports a standard known as OSI (Open Systems Interconnection). The rules and standards that make these varying code formats compatible are known as *protocols*. The discussion that follows highlights some of the principles and rules of data communications protocols.

*Transmission Rates.*   Obviously, for communication to take place, speed of transmission must be the same for sending and receiving devices. It also is obvious that some standards are necessary; it would not be acceptable for each organization to select its own speed without regard to others. For this reason, the communications and computer industries have settled on a series of standard speeds. Most devices are made to operate at one of these rates. Some devices have switches or software capabilities to select from among available standards for transmission.

The standard measure of transmission speed is the *baud*, taken from the name of Louis Baudot, the Frenchman who invented the automatic telegraph. One baud is equal approximately to one bit per second of transmission speed. Common transmission rates include 300, 1,200, 2,400, 4,800, and 9,600 baud. Most microcomputers that use dial-up service operate at 300, 1,200, or 2,400 baud. Transfer rates between microcomputers and their disk drives usually are at 9,600 baud. Late-model microcomputers can function at even higher rates; 9,600-baud is becoming a standard option. Large-scale computers can move data at rates of more than 1 million baud.

Usually, there is a direct relationship between transmission speed and cost of service. The higher the speed, the greater the cost will be. Trade-offs also involve the time required for transmissions and the volume of data to be moved. To put these trade-offs into perspective, consider that a microcomputer transmitting at 1,200 baud moves a page of text in approximately 15 seconds. A complete book the size of this text can be transmitted via dial-up telephone service in a total elapsed time of two to three hours. The line costs for transmission are measured in pennies per minute.

By contrast, think of the needs of an airline reservation system. Customers waiting for reservations expect immediacy. Turnaround time for a complete transaction, from entry of an inquiry to a response displayed at a terminal should be two to five seconds. This kind of service cannot be supported at 1,200 baud. A high-volume system needs greater capacity.

*Synchronous Transmission.*   To achieve the highest quality and greatest speeds in data transmission, the sending and receiving devices should operate at the same speeds and should be able to validate messages on a byte-by-byte basis. This capability is known as synchronous transmission. As indicated, an advantage is that quality can be assured through synchronous transmission. A potential disadvantage is that, if a computer is involved directly, it may be inefficient to limit its operating speed for synchronization with a slower device such as a terminal or disk drive. Synchronous operations often are handled by special communication controllers that are designed specifically for this type of service.

*Asynchronous transmission.*   The opposite of synchronous transmission is asynchronous transmission. In this operating mode, communication devices can operate at different speeds. To accommodate the differences, the devices usually contain buffers that hold data received at high speeds for convenient processing by slower devices.

Asynchronous protocols are used between microcomputers and their output devices. Say you have a printer that operates at a rate of 200 characters per second. The output port of your microcomputer can generate signals at up to 9,600 baud, or almost five times the rate at which printing can be performed. To coordinate these devices, either the computer or the printer, and sometimes

Data communications capabilities play key roles in such applications as hotel reservation and registration systems (left) and police dispatching (right).

both, have buffers that store the equivalent of several lines of output. The printer is driven by the buffer. In between the operations required to load the buffer, the computer can do other processing.

*Start/stop codes.*   In any function connected with computer information processing, accuracy and reliability are vital. Each byte of data received over a communication line can be checked, under some protocols, to be sure it represents a valid character format. Since most data communications between computers and external devices is serial, transmissions are manipulated to coordinate the encoding and decoding of message units.

One way to do this is to have the originating modem add bits to a character during transmission. *Start bits* are added at the beginning of a byte and *stop bits* are placed at the end. These added bits, in effect, serve as place marks to help the modems keep track of the content of data received as bit streams.

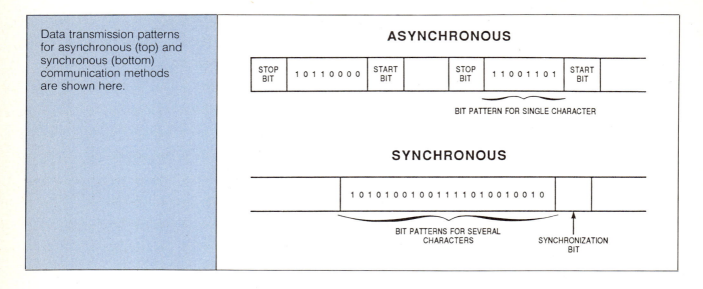

Data transmission patterns for asynchronous (top) and synchronous (bottom) communication methods are shown here.

**ASYNCHRONOUS**

| STOP BIT | 1 0 1 1 0 0 0 0 | START BIT | | STOP BIT | 1 1 0 0 1 1 0 1 | START BIT | |

BIT PATTERN FOR SINGLE CHARACTER

**SYNCHRONOUS**

1 0 1 0 1 0 0 1 0 0 1 1 1 1 0 1 0 0 1 0 0 1 0

BIT PATTERNS FOR SEVERAL CHARACTERS

SYNCHRONIZATION BIT

*Handshaking.*   Some method is necessary by which sending and receiving devices can acknowledge one another and acknowledge that messages are sent and received. Handshaking methods can be as simple as regular, dialed telephone calls during which people set manual switches on their respective devices. At the higher end of this spectrum, automatic answering and monitoring devices can validate each character transmitted. Under some systems, a receiver can cause a sender to retransmit portions of messages to validate accuracy.

Communication protocols can be complex and highly technical—as well as representing key cost factors in network configuration. End users should be aware of the level of quality needed by a communications link and should know enough about their own needs and the options available to deal with technicians who can meet user-stated needs.

■   **Operational.**   Separate sets of services and standards are required to accommodate end users. As in almost everything else associated with computer systems, recent emphasis has been on making services user friendly. Some of the tools encountered by users of computer systems with communication capabilities are described below.

*Communication software.*   For some years, advertisements for communication software have stressed "smart" capabilities. A *smart modem* actually is a combination of hardware and software features that lead a user through the process of data communications.

Smart modems designed for microcomputers are by far the most popular types of communication software. Generally, a modem is installed on a circuit board within the microcomputer and is attached to a communication port that sends and receives serial signals. The software is loaded from a diskette and generates menu displays. The user chooses desired services through menu selections and initiates service through keyboard entries.

## Insight

## How to Select a Data Communications Package

In considering your needs and in selecting a data communications package, remember that you are dealing with two separate, related technologies. The special needs of each of the technologies—communications and computing—must be considered. You need a coordinated system that deals with both requirements.

When you buy a data communications package, you must install both hardware and software components. Further, these components must be compatible in terms of both the computer system and the communications link to be used. Factors to consider in package evaluation include speed, transmission mode, data format, protocol, and operating characteristics.

Transmission speed, the rate at which data are sent and received, usually is measured in baud, roughly equivalent to bits per second (bps). For microcomputers, available packages have transmission rates ranging from 300 to 9,600 baud. In general, costs of packages increase with baud rates. Also, the prospect and potential loss of data through electrical interference on lines increases at higher baud rates. Often, a decision to transmit at higher speeds leads to extra line costs to assure needed signal quality. The most common rates selected by microcomputer users are 1,200 and 2,400 baud. Some modems have fixed rates for transmission and receiving. On others, baud rates can be varied, either through use of switches or through software entries. One factor in selection of transmission speed lies in the volume of data that you want to transmit. Another factor is the rate established for the

stations to which you want to transmit. The sending and receiving stations must operate at the same speeds.

Transmission modes are synchronous or asynchronous. Both sender and receiver must be set for the same mode. Most microcomputers operate in asynchronous serial mode. Formats and protocols have settled into a *de facto* standard, established by Hayes Microcomputer Products. Hayes introduced the first successful and widely accepted modem for microcomputer use. The great majority of manufacturers in this field have elected to build products compatible with Hayes standards. For microcomputer users, it is a safe practice to insist that any package proposed for data communications be Hayes compatible.

Most microcomputer users communicate over telephone lines. Therefore, important considerations in package selection lie in ease of connection between the computer and the telephone network. Also, most software packages now available provide capabilities to dial numbers from a directory maintained on a stored file. A communications package also should be able to answer and prepare itself to receive transmissions automatically, without user intervention. These features make for convenience of use.

As with any other tool for computer use, you should start your procedure for selecting a data communications package by determining what you want to do, then check packages to find the one that meets your needs best—at the most reasonable price.

To send a chapter of this book to the typesetter, the editor starts by indicating that a transmission (rather than a receiving) operation is to be performed. The name of the file to be transmitted is entered into a menu. Then, the typesetter's code is entered; this causes the computer to look up the telephone number in its directory and to dial that number automatically. The typesetter's computer answers the telephone automatically and emits a tone indicating it is ready to receive the transmission. At this point, the editor presses the RETURN key and the transmission is handled automatically.

## Putting Data Communications to Work in Business

Packaging has taken place in the data communications area—just as it has in software—and has been reflected in the development of general-purpose hardware. In the communications area, general-purpose application programs often must be combined with the hardware elements required to make computers work. For example, software houses that produce communication packages also must provide circuit boards and modems that generate the needed signals, since modems are not normally included in microcomputers.

**Local Area Network (LAN)**

As its name implies, a local area network (LAN) connects a series of terminals located in close proximity to one another. Typically, all nodes of a LAN are within a company's office building, on the same floor or a few floors of a high-rise building, or possibly in adjoining structures. In general, a LAN is limited to transmissions over a few hundred yards.

Under common usage that has evolved, a node for a LAN is known as a "work station." There are office work stations, transaction processing work stations, and executive work stations. Almost invariably, a work station includes a microcomputer supported by standard software packages like those described in earlier chapters. Options can include choices of memory size, storage capacity, and inclusion of printing devices.

A LAN might be interconnected with a large-scale computer. This can permit users to download programs and/or information from a large-system database or to upload information from an individual work station to the organizational database. Due to the popularity of LAN installations, standard signal carrying and plug-in circuit equipment has gained strong market inroads. That is, suppliers are offering complete interconnection packages that include cables and connectors for easy installation in office situations. Two LAN network products that have gained wide acceptance are Ethernet, developed by Xerox Corporation and Digital Equipment Corporation, and Token Ring, from IBM.

A local area network links
work stations and facilities
that are adapted to the
specific needs of users.

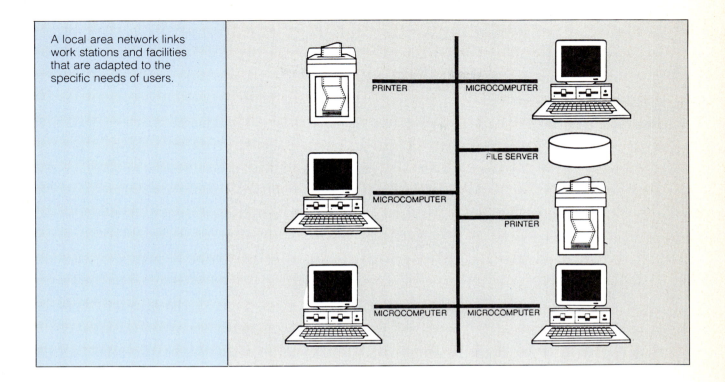

## Electronic Mail

Once a data communications network exists, it can be relatively easy to realize savings in time, and possibly money, by replacing paper documents with files delivered by *electronic mail.* The idea is simple: Each user has a storage area identified for his or her use. Any user can address a document for the storage address of any other user, or for identified groups of users. The document is created on a screen in much the same way as with a word processing system. However, instead of printing and forwarding the document through external or company mail, the originator enters instructions for delivery to one or more electronic mailboxes.

Periodically, users check their mailboxes by querying the system to see if they have correspondence waiting. Messages can be displayed on the screen of the recipient's work station. The receiving person can store a message locally, print out a hard copy, or release the message once the information has been noted.

An obvious advantage of electronic mail lies in the immediacy of delivery. Another advantage can be actual cost savings through reductions in the need to create, package, and transport physical documents. The main disadvantage is that people are used to generating and filing paper. It takes training and some discipline to get people used to checking electronic mail systems and treating electronic messages with the same seriousness as paper documents.

## Bulletin Boards and Information Utilities

As described earlier, information requirements often exceed the capacities of individual companies. A portion of the computer industry has been established to provide such reference or information exchange services. One type of service, a *bulletin board,* involves exchanges of information items or messages among people with common interests. For example, a manufacturing company might use bulletin board-capabilities to provide general information or advice for its customers. Users of the service call in periodically to check notices posted on the electronic bulletin board—electronic mail messages available to all users.

Large bodies of information are stored and made available for reference by suppliers classifed as *information utilities* or *teletext* services. These organizations assemble large libraries of information in databases. Examples include the entire content of newspapers or news information services, stock quotations, the text of encyclopedias, airline schedules, dating services, and others. A user can search index files established by these services and can call up and read items of special interest.

Data communications capabilities can open new horizons of access to information sources for all computer users. This capability alone can serve to make an understanding of data communications principles and operations worthwhile for users. In addition, however, the close relationships among data communications and computer technologies can serve to make users with a knowledge of data communications more efficient in use of their computing resources.

## Chapter Summary

- Modern business organizations use data communication networks as competitive tools. Through data communications, businesses can reach out to serve customers or to improve operations in distant locations.
- Through data communications, people can gain access to more information, stored in more locations, than would be possible if computer use were confined to direct access at central locations.
- Data availability takes on worldwide proportions in scope and variety through use of data communications.
- Special equipment required to support data communications includes signal carriers, sending/receiving devices, and networks.
- Communication carriers include simplex lines, half-duplex lines, duplex lines, broadband and coaxial lines, radio and microwave transmission, laser beams, fiber-optics lines, satellites, and dedicated lines.

- Sending and receiving devices that support data communications include modems, communication ports and interfaces, and internal communication links.

- Networks are configured in a number of topologies, including ring, star, bus, and hybrid.

- Procedures for data communications systems include separate considerations for protocols (rules for sending and receiving data) and operational requirements.

- Protocols deal with transmission rates, synchronous transmission, asynchronous transmission, start/stop codes, and handshaking.

- Operational requirements center around special data communications software and modems that generate and receive signals.

- Local area networks (LANs) serve users who work within a short distance of one another.

- Electronic mail systems use computer storage and data communications capabilities to deliver messages electronically, eliminating the time delays of mail services. In many instances, electronic mail is less expensive than the handling involved in conventional mail delivery.

- Bulletin boards are, in effect, public implementations of electronic mail services. Authorized users can call in and scan messages for services or information that may be of interest.

## Questions for Review

1. What is networking and how does networking differ from direct, point-to-point communication with a modem through dial-up service?

2. Identify and draw diagrams of the three different types of data communications network topologies.

3. Describe the capabilities of simplex and duplex lines and compare the two types of carriers.

4. How do transmission speeds differ for different types of carriers? Which speeds are considered low and which are considered to be high speeds?

5. What are the differences between dial-up and dedicated-line service?

6. Compare the data communications features of analog and digital signal carriers.

7. What is electronic mail and what needs does this type of service meet?

8. How can bulletin board services be applied to research projects undertaken by students?

9. What is an information utility and what services does it perform?

10. What benefits can result from linking microcomputer work stations and mainframe computers within a local area network?

## Questions for Thought

1. Before on-line reservation systems were introduced, airlines were able to sell only 90 percent of their seats prior to flights. With computerized reservation systems, all seats can be sold. What benefits do airlines realize from the use of data communications capabilities through this feature of reservation system operations?

2. Imagine that you work for a small company that is interested in establishing a communication link to a supplier organization for direct ordering. Use the decision-making approach described in Chapter 2 and referenced elsewhere to answer the following question: What would be a suitable problem statement that could start application of the decision-making process?

3. On-line, interactive applications provide a level of service that appears as though the entire computer is at the disposal of each individual user. What are the benefits from giving users this impression? How does an interactive system achieve this result?

4. What are the comparative advantages and disadvantages of the star, bus, and ring networks?

5. How does the ability to upload information from a microcomputer work station to a mainframe and to download database content for use by an executive, contribute to the effectiveness of decision making in business?

## Terms

analog

asynchronous transmission

baud

broadband line

buffer

bulletin board

bus

bus network

channel

coaxial line

COM 1 port

communications interface

communications port

dedicated line

dial-up service

digital

duplex line

electronic mail

fiber-optics line

half-duplex line

handshaking

hybrid network

information utility

laser beam

line-of-sight transmission

load sharing

message concentrator

microwave transmission

| | |
|---|---|
| modem | sending/receiving device |
| multiplexor | serial transmission |
| nanosecond | signal carrier |
| network | simplex line |
| node | smart modem |
| noise | star network |
| parallel transmission | start bit |
| poll | start/stop code |
| port | stop bit |
| protocol | synchronous transmission |
| radio transmission | telegraphic line |
| ring network | teletext |
| RS232 port | topology |
| satellite | transmission rate |

## MINICASE

**Situation:**

Interstate Insurance is a regional company specializing in group health insurance. Marketing is done through 10 regional offices, each of which has between 10 and 30 agents. Each agent calls in an activity report to the regional office every day. These reports are expected to cover between 15 and 30 client contacts by each agent, every day. Reports are consolidated in the regions and forwarded daily to the home office. All reports are prepared manually. Under the existing system, the home office does not have access to the detail call reports of agents. Relaying the information on the telephone takes about a half-hour for each regional office.

Interstate's accounting firm has noted the high telephone bills and has suggested that management consider setting up a data communications capability that would make it possible to capture information on microcomputers in the branches. The data then would be transmitted directly and automatically to the home office computer. The company president, Barry Koffman, authorizes the accounting firm to perform a study and design a computerized system.

**Decision Making: Your Turn**

1. From the information you have and from Barry Koffman's viewpoint, identify and describe the problem to be solved or need to be met and its related benefits.

2. Identify alternatives that could be followed to produce best results for Interstate's need.

3. On the basis of the limited information you have: a) Identify additional information you would gather if you were dealing with this problem in a real situation. b) Identify the solution that appears best on the basis of the information that is available and explain your reasons for this selection.

4. What lessons are to be learned from this situation?

## Projects

1. Through a computer store and/or computer publications, find a list of bulletin boards that you could access through a microcomputer and modem. Find out what kinds of information or services are available through each.

2. Arrange a call to a bulletin board service. Prepare a brief report on the procedures followed and describe the information accessed. What did you learn from the experience?

3. Find a person who has access to an information utility. You may have to offer to pay a small charge to cover a demonstration call. If possible, ask the person to call the utility and show you the directory of services displayed. Report on what you observed and learned.

4. Call your local telephone company. Determine the data communications services available and ask about the best way to assure transmission quality. Discuss your findings.

5. Refer to computer magazines for information about local area network capabilities. Prepare a one-page summary comparing features of at least two different types of local area networks.

# Hardware and Software: Concepts and Applications

Unit III provides an inside view of the hardware and software of computer systems. As Unit III is organized from the user's perspective, coverage in Chapter 9 begins with a presentation on the role of different kinds of software systems. Chapter 10 looks at how data are organized and stored on tape and disk. Different types of processing hardware are presented in Chapter 11. Finally, Chapter 12 explores the different techniques and hardware for input and output operations.

# Chapter Outline

# 9

# Software Systems

## Briefing Memo

TO:     Information Users
FROM:  T. Rohm, W. Stewart

The usefulness of computers depends on the availability of software. Without software between you and the hardware, the computer would be useless. With effective software tools, the computer has become a major force in modern society.

In this chapter, you will learn what happens inside the black box that is a computer system. Specifically, this chapter identifies and explains the functions and relationships among multiple levels and types of software that you require to support your use of computer systems. Included are operating systems that control operation of the computer itself, programming languages used to write application programs, and application software that serves you directly.

## End-User Perspective

"I'm sorry you have been disappointed." Melinda was sincere as she finished hearing the customer's complaint. The man seemed frustrated almost to the point of tears. He explained that he had spent almost $3,000 for a microcomputer and several software packages. He said he had been told that all he had to do was plug in his computer and he could start to produce business documents.

"The salesman said all I had to do was to follow some simple instructions," he continued. "When I opened the manuals, I was lost, totally lost!"

Melinda was working at a computer exposition for her company, a computer manufacturer. She rarely heard this kind of complaint. She had given too many classes herself at which she had stressed that prospective computer users have to understand what a computer system is and what it does. Melinda used an explanation she had heard during her own schooling:

"This is not like turning on a TV set," Melinda said, "you have to learn how the computer works, what problems you want to solve, and what results you expect the computer to deliver for you."

Melinda explained that information doesn't come out of thin air. A user has to assemble data and load software programs before the data can be processed and useful information can be developed. She appreciated the relief she saw on the man's face when she explained that the company sponsors a series of classes for people who want to take hold of computers and information processing concepts. She invited him to the next session and assured him that the computer would become a valuable tool—once he learned what it was for and how it worked.

## The Point: Software is Your Connection to Computer Hardware

This incident demonstrates that you need a general understanding of what goes on inside the computer so that you can improve your effectiveness as an information user.

A good place to begin your own review of computer software and hardware is to take stock of what you already have learned from this book. You started with a general overview of what computers are and what they can do. Then you reviewed the major computer applications, along with the common features and functions of the software packages that support those applications.

At this point, you are on the outside of the computer and are about to look inside. In this and the three chapters that follow, you will build your understanding of the software and hardware that support your activities as a computer user. First, this chapter will examine the multiple levels and types of software needed to put a modern computer to work.

## The Need for Software

When computers were first applied to business applications in 1951, only a small group of technicians controlled the actual use of computers. There was no such thing as a user. Everyone without special technical training was excluded. Back then, programs were written in binary code, or machine language, represented by a series of 0 and 1 notations. But that was only part of the problem. Early machines didn't have the processing, memory, or storage capacity to handle entire applications. Rather, programs covered individual tasks, or *runs*, on the computer. For example, to process a payroll, there would be different runs to consolidate data for employees, to compute gross pay, to compute individual deductions, to figure net pay, and to write checks. The computer had to be set up and programs had to be loaded separately for each run.

Through the years, it took billions of dollars of investments in software to make computers friendly to users. Along the way, a series of major breakthroughs occurred.

People discovered quickly that writing programs in binary notation was not practical. From this rudimentary beginning, computer scientists devised a technique under which human programmers could work in alphabetic characters and digital numbers they could understand. These sets of codes were referred to as *assembly languages*. When assembly-level instructions were entered into a computer, they were translated into binary code by special programs called *assemblers*.

By today's standards, these early programs were crude and cumbersome. The programmer had to write a separate assembly-language instruction for each operation to be performed by the computer. But a principle had been established: It was better for people to work in codes they could understand than to have to master the language of a computer.

A next important step, clearly a major breakthrough, came in 1956 with introduction of the FORTRAN language, developed by IBM. FORTRAN is an abbreviation for FORmula TRANslator. The idea: Scientists and engineers could write instructions for the computer in mathematical notation, the language of their professions. A special program, called a *compiler*, would convert these instructions to machine code. A major new dimension of FORTRAN was that multiple machine-language instructions were generated for each command

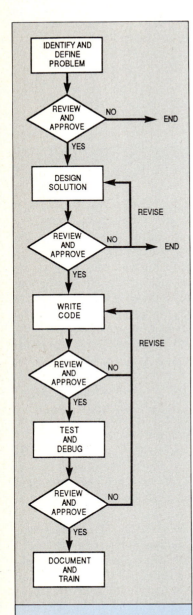

This flow diagram traces the systems development life cycle and shows the relationships among the steps in the systems development process.

written by a person. The power of the computer was being harnessed to make programmers more productive as programmers.

Business programming moved a giant step forward when the COBOL (COmmon Business Oriented Language) compiler was released in 1960 after years of development under guidance of the Department of Defense. When the Defense Department mandated that all of its suppliers use this language, a *de facto* standard was created and, as a direct result, millions of people pursued careers in application programming.

At this point, however, programming and computer operation were still very much job-oriented. The computer had to be set up especially for each run of every program. Only one program could be run at any time, and it had to be processed from start to completion. Also, the processor had to operate in sequence. A record was input, processed, then output, one step at a time. Since computer hardware could handle input, processing, and output functions simultaneously, this meant that two-thirds of a computer's capacity was idle during each operating cycle.

A major increase in productivity came when software was created that overlapped processing functions. When a first record was moved forward for processing, a second record was input. When the first record was output, the second was processed and a third was input. Processing functions became continuous and computers became more productive. A concept had been proven under which one set of software controlled operation of the computer while another controlled processing of data.

A series of refinements followed that led to the concept of the *operating system,* a set of programs that oversees the setup and use of the computer, including the application of programming language software and user applications. Operating system software free the user from concerns with the technical aspects of computer operation and makes it possible for people to concentrate on productivity and/or problem solving.

Today, layers of software are positioned between the user and the internal hardware of a computer. A user works through a *friendly* application package which, in turn, calls upon an operating system to run the computer and to perform the "housekeeping" associated with generating and storing information. In most systems, sets of programs are included as part of the computer hardware. These programs, known as *firmware,* are stored on chips within the computer and provide routines used to prepare the system for service when a computer is turned on initially. Another layer of software encompasses the language translators, or programming software packages, that support application program development.

The remainder of this chapter reviews and describes the software support that stands ready to serve you. Therefore, the discussions are presented from a user's perspective, starting with application packages and proceeding inward to examine the features of *system software,* the programs devoted to operation and control of computer equipment.

# Software Meets User: Application Packages

An application package solves a problem shared by multiple users, who form a market for that product. The major families of application packages—word processing, electronic spreadsheets, graphics, and database management systems—are covered in the four previous chapters. Application packages provide a familiar ground from which you can begin to explore the software and hardware elements of what is known as *computer architecture.*

The architecture of a computer takes in all of the elements that combine to input, process, output, and store data. Both hardware and software are elements of computer architecture. The presentations that follow examine the computer architecture of application processing.

## Applications: Entry Points to Features of Computer Architecture

Architecture, any architecture, is a design for a structure. The design combines principles and materials to provide an environment that supports a defined type of activity. A house provides a place in which people can live and pursue personal activities. An office is a place to work, as is a factory. Architects devise plans to help achieve these end results.

The architecture for computer systems aligns the resources that make computers useful: computing machinery, software, and work station configurations. For a user, an application package is an entry way for access to a larger structure devised by computer architects, and for an understanding of how application packages are created and how they function.

## Building and Supporting Application Packages

The application program you use is part of a complex structure that results from skillful integration of program design, programming languages, operating system software, and computer equipment. Consider this structure:

- The diskette you use to load your packaged program is written in a programming language. Many packages, particularly early products, were written in assembly languages that could make efficient use of computer capabilities that still were limited. Through the years, there has been a transition into higher-level, or compiler, languages. The principle: The capabilities of some programming languages underlie the application programs you use.

- The application package, regardless of the language in which it is written, must interact continuously with and rely on support from the operating system that controls operation of your computer. Every time you make keyboard entries, store data, or print outputs, elements of the operating system are called into use.

- Ultimately, the computer itself must be configured to support your work. The user selects the memory size, storage units, and printers or other output units that determine hardware capabilities. This hardware configuration, in turn, must be communicated to the operating system—and must meet the performance requirements of your application package.

Consider these architectural interrelationships. The application package is the point at which the end user encounters the elements of computer architecture. Inside this entry, the next architectural element you encounter is the programming language in which your package is written.

## Programming Languages

A programming language, like any language, is built upon a set of terms, or basic vocabulary. The vocabulary of a programming language is called an *instruction set*, a set of specific commands that follow strict usage rules, known as *syntax*. Programs are written by people who master the vocabulary and syntax of a programming language and have a basic knowledge of how computers process data and generate information. The language program translates these human-developed instructions, called *source code*, and produces machine-language commands, called *object code*.

### Compilers and Intepreters

A language program follows one of two approaches in accepting source code and producing object code. One type of program, called a compiler, produces and stores object code. Compilation is done before the program is used for production work. The object program becomes the user's application program.

The other approach is used by programs called *interpreters*. Programs written in interpreter languages are stored and used in their source code versions. Transaction takes place at the time of execution. When a program is run, the programming language, which must be present in computer memory, translates one instruction at a time and turns it over to the operating system for execution.

In general, interpreters are slower and more costly to use than compilers. Slowness stems from the need to translate instructions while a program is running. Costs result from the need to provide enough memory to handle the programming language, which must be present before applications can be run.

### Application Programming Languages

The makeup of the instruction set determines the kinds of applications that can be developed through use of any given programming language. Most computers are general-purpose devices. Programs equip computers to do specific jobs. The special need of business programs is to assemble files and to access large stores of information. Most business-oriented languages are described as *procedural*. That is, the programs written in these languages follow processing sequences designed to produce known results under specific application conditions. Some major programming languages and language trends are described below.

■ **FORTRAN.**   The purpose of programming languages is to provide capabilities that make it possible to communicate with computers in terms that people can understand. *FORTRAN* is designed to ease communication for certain types of people, those who make extensive use of mathematics in their professions.

■ **COBOL.**   As indicated earlier, *COBOL* stands for COmmon Business Oriented Language. Its strengths include the ability to manipulate large amounts of data and to build and manage information files. Originally, COBOL was designed chiefly for handling batch applications. Recent updates add flexibility for interactive services.

■ **BASIC.**   This language's name stands for Beginner's All-purpose Instruction Code. As the full name suggests, *BASIC* was originated as a language for neophytes. It was designed to ease the process of teaching students to use computers. Development was by two professors at Dartmouth College, Thomas Kurtz and John Kemeny. Largely because of its relative simplicity, and also because it was designed for interactive use, BASIC became the most popular language for microcomputers, which were introduced about a decade after BASIC.

■ **Pascal.**   This program gets its name from the young Frenchman who developed one of the first mechanical calculators and devised some of the concepts that have been carried forward for machine processing of data. The *Pascal* language was developed by Nickalaus Wirth of the Federal Institute of Technology, Zurich, Switzerland. Pascal has been popular among computer scientists as a teaching language and has found wide use for microcomputer systems. A strong attraction of this language is that it follows modern concepts for program development, known as *structured programming*.

■ **Ada.**   This language is named after Lady Ada Augusta Lovelace, a British noblewoman and advanced mathematician who developed programming concepts for implementation on the Babbage calculator. Functionally, *Ada* is regarded as an advanced language that has enlarged upon Pascal and has applied some of the same structured programming principles for use on mainframe computers. Development of Ada has had strong support from the Department of Defense, which has mandated use of this language by many of its own computer facilities and by suppliers.

■ **C.**   The letter *C* stands for Computer language. This language is designed chiefly for computer professionals who make advanced use of microcomputers.

C has a range of capabilities that includes instruction sets at both assembly and compiler levels. Also, C is designed to interact with advanced operating systems that implement networking and data communication capabilities, such as *Unix*, an advanced software package developed by Bell Telephone Laboratories.

■ **RPG (Report Program Generator).**   Program generators, introduced during the 1960s, open an entirely different approach to application development from coding methods like those described above. Under generator programs, users describe data, files, and functions through use of standard forms, called *parameter sheets*. Rather than coding, these entries represent sets of specifications that are used to generate programs directly. *RPG* is one version of a generator language developed for use with IBM computers. Generators are known as *problem oriented*, or *nonprocedural languages*. This term distinguishes generators from procedural languages, in which step-by-step instructions must be devised by the programmer.

■ **4GLs (Fourth-Generation Languages).**   Program generators opened the way toward introduction of higher-level programming techniques, known as *fourth generation languages (4GLs)*. This name distinguishes between the new methods and compilers, which are said to represent third-generation languages. In essence, 4GL methods are additions to DBMS software packages. Query language commands are joined into sequences that execute complete programs. To retrieve and report information under established database techniques, a user must enter each command manually. Under 4GL methods, sets of commands can be established in advance and followed automatically by the system. As in RPG methods, nonprocedural techniques are used to specify functions and data content. Programs are generated by special software. Examples of 4GL packages currently available include Focus, RAMIS, and Oracle.

■ **5GLs (Fifth-Generation Languages.)**   *Fifth generation languages* represent a break in the technological continuity that started with binary coding and has run through program generation. The continuity has concentrated upon easing the process for generating coding sequences that implement algorithms. An algorithm is a set of instructions that are followed in a sequence. A frequently cited example of an algorithm is a recipe for cooking or baking. Fifth-generation programs follow the principles of mathematical *logic*. The purpose of logic programs is to evaluate decision situations rather than simply to process data and deliver information. Under these methods, the user states a set of processing rules and facts that implement those rules. Fifth-generation techniques are sometimes referred to as *natural language* programming because the user can state facts and rules in his or her own terms for comparison of conditions by the computer.

Fifth-generation techniques also are referred to generally as *artificial intelligence*. This term stems from the ability of software to relate a series of facts and rules and, on the basis of these relationships, to propose answers or solutions. Two languages that have been used extensively for pioneering efforts in artificial intelligence are LISP (LISt Processing) and PROLOG (PROgramming in LOGic).

This has been a brief overview to help provide you with background information that will prove valuable to you as an end user. In particular, if you use a microcomputer, you will find it valuable to understand and be familiar with the types of software that put the computer at your service. Within the knowledge base you will need as an end user, an important next step is to understand the processes followed in developing and implementing custom programs through use of programming languages like those described above.

## Developing Custom Programs

The term *custom program* usually designates programs written especially for a specific user application. The custom program represents one of three broad types of application programs that deliver information to users:

- Off-the-shelf application packages are implemented in the form provided by vendors, without alteration.

- Modified application packages are off-the-shelf programs altered by users to meet specific needs. The time and expense needed for modification must be less than for developing original programs.

- Custom programs are designed and developed completely to meet a user application need.

Off-the-shelf packages are a major factor in implementation of user applications. However, custom development still is required widely. One factor: All off-the-shelf packages require custom development initially.

The efforts and costs associated with program development can be extensive. In the early years of computer use, common problems emerged that led computer-using organizations to seek standard solutions. Problems centered around the inability of users and technicians to communicate well enough to identify and solve problems. Also, it proved difficult to estimate the time and costs anticipated for systems and program development. Cost overruns became legendary, running to a surplus of more than $40 million on at least two major projects.

Today, almost all computer-using organizations use a standard set of procedures for program development. Variations exist among organizations in the exact makeup and degree of formality for these procedures. But all sets of programming procedures are patterned after the generic decision-making or problem-solving process described in Chapter 2 of this book. As an example, the presentation that follows establishes and illustrates a five-step procedure:

1. Identify and define problem
2. Design solution
3. Write code
4. Test and debug program
5. Document procedures and train users.

## Identify and Define Problem

The identification and definition established for a problem must be from the user viewpoint. The solution, the finished computer application, then will be evaluated by how well it meets the user's needs. Therefore, effective communication and understanding must be established between end users and the computer professionals who develop systems.

## Design Solution

Design begins with definition of results to be delivered. For example, if a program is to produce reports as outputs, sample reports might be created through use of word processing software. The user should evaluate these samples and determine whether they meet the need. Prospective solutions should be revised and/or modified until they satisfy users. After that, an algorithm is developed. That is, a set of steps is outlined that will be the basis for final design and implementation of a program for implementation and ongoing operation by users.

## Write Code

A programming language is selected and its instruction set is used to write source code. The program is compiled or tested against interpreter software. This step includes the testing of code as each program module is written. Testing of the entire set of programs that will implement an application is handled in the step that follows.

## Test and Debug Program

The term *bug* is rooted in computer-industry history. When an early computer broke down, investigation showed that an insect was trapped in the mechanism and caused a short circuit. Since then, problems that inhibit operations have been known as bugs. Program bugs are errors in use of a language or in logical design of processing that cause malfunctions when programs are run.

Some program bugs are identified and corrected by the programming language itself. Error messages are generated to identify any coding errors. Then, when a program is compiled or has been processed successfully by an interpreter, it is used to process a set of test data devised by the programmer. Test data are selected specifically to make sure a program can handle all conditions for which it is designed, and that it will reject data items that it is not designed to handle.

**Document Procedures and Train Users**

When they are complete and operational, all programs become tools for users. To be applied effectively, programs must be supported by specific instructions for all procedures to be followed. For medium- or large-scale systems, some specific training of users also is necessary. Programmers often participate in this training.

As programs are put into use, they rely on resources within the computer system. Specifically, all modern application programs interact with operating system software. These interactions are described and illustrated in the discussion that follows.

## Operating Systems

In the days when all programs were dedicated to individual applications, the work of setting up the computer and loading software and data was handled by human operators. The entire computer was set up and run to handle a single application at a time. This process was tedious and time consuming. So, a series of tools now known as system software was developed to handle the routine functions of monitoring the condition and status of computer equipment and to maintain processing schedules by retrieving and loading both programs and data as required. Today's computer operators oversee processing facilities by interacting with the operating system rather than by carrying out physical requirements for setting switches and pressing buttons.

That's the picture for large systems. At the microcomputer level, the operating system is an essential part of the user's knowledge. Each microcomputer operator must have some contact with the operating system. On larger computers, professional operators handle these functions; on microcomputers, the user must handle these functions personally. Therefore, all operators and users of computers of any size must be familiar with the makeup and functions of operating systems. The descriptions that follow are based upon the functions and components of PC DOS (Personal Computer Disk Operating System), the most popular piece of system software presently in existence.

An operating system is a group of programs—as many as 25 to 30 separate units for a microcomputer—that are incorporated within three functional modules. These are the *control module,* the *processing module,* and *utilities.*

**The Control Module**

The control module, as its name implies, actually oversees operation of the computer. It consists of a set, or system, of programs that perform three major functions, or operating sequences:

• Executive coordination
• Job control
• Input-output management.

■ **Executive Coordination.**   The executive function also is referred to as the *supervisor*. This program monitors the execution of application programs. Functions performed may include processing requests for input or output support. This set of programs also controls the retrieval of data from secondary storage, the display of file content on a user's video screen, and the recording of files on secondary devices upon instruction from the user. If a system has multiple users, the executive programs include a priority-setting capability that is used to assign services to meet requests.

■ **Job Control.**   Responsibilities of job control programs encompass a number of operations, including system security, memory allocation, and time required for program execution.

To illustrate, think back to the database system at a typical college, described in Chapter 7. This can run a number of applications concurrently. Included would be a registration system, a system for determining graduation requirements, tuition collection, and others. The job control programs determine how many programs can be processed at the same time and how much memory will be allocated to each. Through a built-in priority scheme, this software also determines which users can have access to files and services provided.

In addition, job control software applies the *defaults* specified for the system. In this context, defaults are the devices and programs applied routinely, unless authorized users override these factors. Defaults will include designation of file devices and printers used routinely, unless others are activated.

Users direct job control software through entry of a set of commands known as a *job control language*. These are instructions that permit computer operators to specify which jobs are to be run, which devices are to be used, what priority is to be assigned, and so on.

■ **Input-Output Management.**   You use this set of programs when you enter data from a keyboard or direct a system to read files from storage. Similarly, these programs work for you when you instruct a system to write a file back to storage or to print a document.

These programs also handle the ''housekeeping'' functions associated with storing and maintaining files. Suppose you instruct a microcomputer system to create a file for a text document. Your word processing software activates an input-output portion of the operating system called *BIOS (Basic Input-Output System)* that passes along the name you have entered. The software enters the name into the file directory and assigns a starting address for that file. Each time you update your file, the system assigns and keeps track of the disk space used. Should you overload a disk or ask for a file that doesn't exist, the program will display status or error messages to guide you.

## The Processing Module

The programs within this module support the running of applications. Included are programs that control access to programming languages. In addition, these

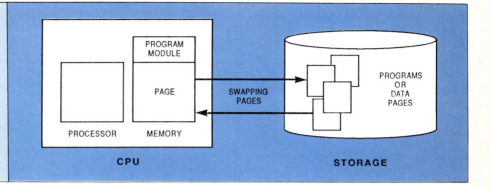

Virtual memory software treats peripheral storage as an extension of main memory. Programs are organized into modules, or segments, and data files are set up as pages.

programs support user access, program execution, and links with communication channels. If a computer provides multiprogramming capabilities or is part of a multiprocessing network, this is the software that applies and monitors the necessary controls.

If a computer has *virtual memory* capabilities, a virtual operating system is needed that includes necessary controls within this module. Virtual memory software applies a storage allocation technique that treats disk files as extensions of main memory. The software identifies needs for programs and data to support operations and *swaps* the needed instructions and information into main memory to support processing of multiple programs concurrently. That is, virtual memory capabilities are associated with systems that provide interactive service, and access to multiple application programs and files. These requirements generally call for extensive swapping of data and program segments from secondary storage to memory. Virtual storage software expediates these swapping operations by applying uniform addressing methods for both memory and peripheral devices.

Real-time and time-sharing services also are administered by this module of the operating system. These capabilities make it possible for the computer to switch back and forth among multiple user jobs and application programs instantaneously to take advantage of all available processing cycles. Terms such as *multitasking* and multiprogramming often are used to described these capabilities.

## Utilities

The idea of software packaging started with utilities. Application programmers discovered that certain routine operations were being coded repeatedly. Included were programs used to sort files, to format reports on a printer, to copy programs and files for backup and protection, and to format disk or tape media for recording of data.

You interact with utility programs when you format a disk for use, erase existing files, ask the system to display a disk directory, or move data content from one file to another.

Most of the time, a user has little or no awareness that an operating system exists. This is as it should be. But operating systems are necessary and, as a user, you will have to call on operating systems for service at some points in your work. Therefore, an understanding of what operating systems are and what they can do can be of great value.

## Firmware: Self-Help Tools Built Into Computer Equipment

As computers gained the ability to control more and more of their own operations, attention was focused on some special problems associated with operational controls. Although other areas also drew attention, the need is illustrated particularly well in the procedures for turning a computer on and making it available for service.

When a computer is turned on, it has no way of operating until software is loaded into memory. The problem centers around how the first, startup instructions get into the computer. The method devised for most modern computers is to store the basic, required instructions permanently in memory chips that are activated as soon as power is supplied to a computer. These chips are known as *read-only memory (ROM)*. The combination of ROM chips and the instructions they contain are known as firmware.

When you turn on a microcomputer, for example, power is provided to one or more ROM chips. Stored instructions begin by applying a checkout routine. That is, the processor is activated and caused to write data to and read data from every available location in main memory. The firmware instructions also check out all of the devices connected to a computer. The system checks to see if communication channels have been opened to disk drives, printers, and video monitors. On some personal computers, a BASIC program interpreter is made available to the user if no disk is inserted. As part of the ROM program, the system is instructed to look for and read the content of a disk in the main drive. The firmware then looks for and loads the operating system if it is available.

The idea is that startup begins from nothing and builds software capabilities one step at a time. This is known as a *bootstrap start*, or *booting* the system.

## Putting Software to Work

To illustrate the services provided to users by system and application software, the narrative that follows tracks a user session with a microcomputer from start through productive operation. The descriptions apply to PC DOS.

When you turn on the power, the computer begins the booting process by reading and executing the instructions stored in a ROM BIOS (Basic Input-

**Insight**

## Which Is the Best Software Package?

Thumbing through a microcomputer magazine can be a treat. Many people who adopt the microcomputer as an everyday tool become ''gadget hounds.'' Enthusiasm takes over. They are ready, at any time, to browse the marketplace for new or improved additions to their systems. A microcomputer magazine meets this craving. Infinite varieties of exciting new gadgets are offered in an endless stream of ads. It seems as though every page offers some new package that promises to solve your problems or enhance the effectiveness of your computing tool.

In particular, microcomputer users seem to be interested continually in new and/or improved software packages. Which package can help you? Which should you buy? These have turned out, literally, to be billion-dollar questions, since computer owners are spending billions of dollars to satisfy their curiosities or to search for solutions.

Software selection can follow several patterns:

One approach can be called the *buddy routine.* You ask a local computer guru which software you should select. The answer generally is a description and name of the package the guru uses or has seen demonstrated. This approach tells you what the guru knows and recommends, an answer that may not correspond with your own best interests.

A second approach is similar. This is the *purchasing department choice.* A decision has been made that uniformity is necessary within the organization. An in-house guru has made a selection and everyone else has to live with it. You have no alternative. Your best bet is to find features within the pre-selected package that can be useful to you.

The next selection process exposes you to a different element of chance. This method is known as the *fire sale.* A need is identified. The cheapest solution, which may or may not deliver the best tool for the job, is selected.

If you are free to reach your own decisions, your best bet is to follow the decision-making process described in Chapter 2 of this book. Start by defining your needs. Be aware that price can be a factor, but need not be the main factor. You are out to satisfy yourself, not to conform to someone else's selections or to implement an answer that has met someone else's needs. Describe the use to which you will put any given package. Compare a number of packages. Rate these packages on how well they do your specific job. Select those which qualify according to your requirements. Then, buy the package that gives you the greatest ''bang per buck,'' the one that provides the best combination of services and costs.

Output System) chip. These instructions apply a hardware check to be sure that all hardware devices are in working order.

After the hardware is checked out, the system goes through a process of *initialization* that includes loading and following instructions within the control module of the operating system. Under the BIOS procedures, the system first checks its A drive for the presence of a system disk. If a disk is available in the A drive, the operating system is read into memory. If no operating system is available and there is no disk in the A drive, the system will load a BASIC interpreter from firmware. If there is no disk in the A drive and the system has a hard disk, generally designated as the C drive, the operating system is read from this location. Note that the hard disk stores data and programs permanently in magnetic coding and is internal to the system.

Initialization steps, which are performed by the operating system, include a check of hardware configuration as a basis for supporting the system that is available. Included are checkouts to determine the amount of memory area available, the type of monitor (monochrome or color), the number and types of disk drives available, and the availability and type of printer that may be connected to the computer. This information is recorded during the initialization process as a basis for control of ongoing operations. For example, on reading a program from storage into memory, the system will note the size of the program and check to be sure there is enough memory available.

When initialization is complete, the operating system displays a prompt to identify the active drive and to indicate that it is ready for use. The prompt will be an A† for a diskette drive and a C† if the hard disk is the default drive. At this point, the user calls up an application program or package. For example, an entry of WP might serve to call up a word processing package. When the menu appears, the system is ready for use.

In summary, software capabilities have made it possible for computers to become the focal point of a trillion-dollar information industry. Without software to enhance ease of use and value, computers would have remained complex wonders accessible to relatively few, highly trained technicians. With friendly software, computers and people have been drawn together in what has become an informational-based revolution. As an information user, you rely on layers of software positioned between your keyboard and your computer's internal processing capabilities. An understanding of these software functions enhances your potential as a computer user.

## Chapter Summary

- Software provides the key that enables people to use computers. Programs that comprise software contain the instructions that run computers.

- Software includes programs that function at different levels, or layers. Operating systems control computer equipment. Programming languages are used to write instructions for the processing of applications. Application programs control processing of user jobs. The structured relationships of the different levels of software is part of the overall design for comptuer architecture.

- Within the architecture for any given computer, application programs represent the entry and operating point for users. Application programs are user tools.

- Application programs are written in programming languages that provide instruction sets that can be understood both by people and by computers. The computer translates programming language instructions into the machine language needed for processing. Machine languages consist of binary coding.

- Programming languages used for applications are mainly compilers and interpreters. A compiler accepts source code from a programmer and creates machine code in a separate program file. An interpreter processes the source code written by the programmer and translates each instruction at the time of execution.

- Among the most widely used programming languages are FORTRAN, COBOL, BASIC, Pascal, Ada, C, and RPG.

- New programming tools include fourth-generation languages that operate from the types of query commands provided within database packages and fifth-generation languages that can implement logic processing techniques.

- Custom programs should be developed under control of a step-by-step process. Steps in the programming process include: 1) Identify and define problem, 2) Design solution, 3) Write code, 4) Test and debug program, 5) Document procedures and train users.

- Operating systems are composed of multiple modules, including the control module, the processing module, and a set of utilities.

- Programs that are used frequently or that are used to boot a computer in preparation for service are stored on special memory chips and are available at all times. These programs are known as firmware.

## Questions for Review

1. How does software serve to make a computer friendly to users?
2. What is computer architecture and what role does software play within the architecture of a computer?
3. What is the role of operating system software?
4. Identify and describe the operation of two types of programming languages. What are the major differences between them?
5. What are application programs and how do they relate to operating systems and programming languages?
6. What are the main features and application areas for the FORTRAN language?
7. What are the main features and application areas for the COBOL language?

8. What are fourth generation languages and why have they been developed?

9. What are fifth generation languages and why have they been developed?

10. What is firmware and what purposes does it serve?

## Questions for Thought

1. What does the DOS disk do? Explain its purpose and functions as though you were training someone who had never encountered a computer before.

2. Where would microcomputers be today if they did not have operating systems? Explain your answer.

3. What are the differences between and the respective strengths and weaknesses of compiler and interpreter programs?

4. What do utility programs do and what are their major values?

5. Picture a world in which computer programs still had to be written in machine language. Describe this situation and tell what you feel would have been the impact upon the growth and development of the computer industry.

## Terms

| | |
|---|---|
| Ada | default |
| artificial intelligence | fifth generation language (5GL) |
| assembler | firmware |
| assembly language | fourth generation language (4GL) |
| BASIC | FORTRAN |
| BIOS (Basic Input-Output System) | initialization |
| boot | instruction set |
| bootstrap start | interpreter |
| bug | job control language |
| C | logic |
| COBOL | multitasking |
| compiler | natural language |
| computer architecture | nonprocedural language |
| control module | object code |
| custom program | operating system |

| | |
|---|---|
| parameter sheet | structured programming |
| Pascal | supervisor |
| problem oriented | swap |
| procedural | syntax |
| processing module | system software |
| read only memory (ROM) | Unix |
| RPG (Report Program Generator) | utility |
| run | virtual memory |
| source code | |

## MINICASE

**Situation:**

On the basis of his school work, which involved completion of an introductory course on computers in business and a laboratory course on microcomputer applications, Stepan Polanski has been hired part time at a local computer store. Stepan enjoys the work of demonstrating microcomputers and software application packages. He feels he learns as much or more than the prospective customers.

After about a month on the job, Stepan notices that he keeps answering the same question over and over. He demonstrates two or three application packages on microcomputers and notes that the prospective customer is interested in the results and fascinated by the equipment. Then comes the question: ''You've got me interested. What do I do next if I want to install this stuff in my business?''

Stepan thinks it would be a good idea for the store to offer a three-hour seminar entitled ''What do I do next?'' The program would be aimed at customers with no previous computer experience. After some conversation, the owners of the store decide they like the idea and instruct Stepan to prepare an outline for the course.

**Decision Making: Your Turn**

1. From the information you have, identify and describe the problem to be solved.
2. Identify alternatives that could be followed to avoid or solve the problem.

3.  On the basis of the limited information you have: a) Identify additional information you would gather if you were dealing with this problem in a real situation. b) Identify the solution that appears best on the basis of the information that is available and explain your reasons for this selection.
4.  What lessons are to be learned from this situation?

## Projects

1.  Visit the computer center on your campus. Interview an operations employee and determine which operating system(s) are used and the language programs supported. Find out if each language is a compiler or an interpreter.
2.  Look through your school catalog to see which computer languages are taught. List the languages offered and explain what types of students should be attracted to each course.
3.  Find an advertisement for a 4GL package and describe one application for which it might be useful.

# Chapter Outline

End-User Perspective

The Point: The Ability to Store Information is Vital

The Need for Storage Methods

Physical Data Storage Techniques
*Data Formats, Data Storage Techniques*

Storage Device Capabilities
*Tape Drives, Magnetic Disk Drives, Mass Storage Devices, Optical Disk Drives*

Selection Trade-Offs for Storage Devices

Effective Use of Storage
*The Right Device for the Job, Investments in File Protection Pay Off, There's Never Enough Storage Space*

Trends in Storage Technology

Chapter Summary

Questions for Review

Questions for Thought

Terms

Minicase

Projects

CHAPTER **10**

# Storage Methods

## Briefing Memo

TO:      Information Users
FROM:   T. Rohm, W. Stewart

Stored information is recognized as a primary asset for almost any computer-using business organization. For people who depend upon information, computer storage devices can be as important as vaults are to banks or financial specialists. Therefore, the configuration, use, and protection of storage media and devices play critical roles in the effective, efficient use of information and computer systems that process information.

This chapter will add to your knowledge of information resources and their use by helping you to understand the relationships between information resources and the devices on which they are stored, maintained, and protected. An appreciation of the need for and value of storage devices has been chosen as the topic to introduce you to a series of chapters that deal with the functions and applications of computer hardware.

## End-User Perspective

Juanita had been feeling good about the day's prospects. She had come to work at 7:30 a.m. to get a headstart on what she knew would be a busy schedule. It was the first of the month and also the end of a quarter. For a staff assistant in an accounting firm, this meant that there were payrolls to process AND quarterly corporate tax forms to prepare.

Before she went to check the message board, Juanita booted her firm's supermicrocomputer system. Then she went to the safe file to pick up the client data disks she planned to run. Juanita was just reaching for the drawer of the safe file when the whole 500-pound cabinet jumped off the floor and bounded back down, adding to the crescendo of noise and shaking that left no doubt; a major earthquake had hit.

Juanita knew she was going to fall. She pushed with her legs to get out of the way of the heavy safe file. About 30 seconds later, she got up and did what she had been trained to do: She moved to the office doorway, where she would have the greatest structural protection. When the building settled, Juanita walked out of the front door of the small office building, where she met Bob Darlow, one of the partners in the firm. Juanita and Bob waited for about 15 minutes, then felt safe to return to the building when there were no more earth tremors.

As they entered their offices, Juanita remembered turning on the computer. She rushed to see what had happened. Bob was right behind. Both suffered what they later called an aftershock as they read the message on the computer screen: "DISK SYSTEM IN ERROR." Further checking confirmed their fears. The vibrations of the earthquake had shaken the rotating hard disk against the read/write heads. The magnetic coating had been stripped away. The disk was destroyed and all its files were lost.

Bob immediately began to check the damage with Juanita. "Did you back up the software files before you left last night?" The answer was affirmative. "Were all of the client files on which you worked copied to diskettes?" Again, the answer was affirmative.

"We're not as bad off as we could have been," Bob said. "If this thing had hit near the end of the day, we'd have lost everything you did. If the client disks were in the machine, we could have lost some master files. Call the repair service and tell them we need a new hard disk as soon as possible. In the meantime, you can do some work with diskettes on the small jobs. Let this be a lesson to both of us. Our whole business rides round and round on that disk. We are only as secure as the backup procedures that we follow."

"I'll never again complain about the time and work involved in preparing file copies," Juanita said as she headed for her telephone.

## The Point: The Ability to Store Information is Vital

Bob was right on two counts. First, he was right in saying his own business spun around on the disk within his computer system. Second, the accounting firm was lucky that the hard disk was destroyed before processing started and after content had been backed up the night before. The exposures involved in operation of computer storage devices should be vital concerns for all computer users. In your own use of the computer, the reliability of the service you receive will depend on the backup and protection you provide for the storage media you use.

## The Need for Storage Methods

In describing the processing cycle, storage often is listed last—input, processing, output, and storage—because storage takes place at the end of a processing sequence. From a user's perspective, however, storage is at the hub of each computer application. Many applications use stored data as inputs. Certainly, processing can't take place without programs and data retrieved from storage devices. The same is true for output. Almost all printed outputs come from stored files.

Therefore, as far as the user is concerned, storage capabilities are central to a workable computer application. Information stored on computer files has become a business asset in much the same way as buildings, machinery, or

The mechanisms of a mass storage device are shown in this photo. Data are stored on strips of magnetic material maintained by individual cartridges. Cartridges are withdrawn as needed and their storage strips are wrapped around a rotating drum for read and write operations.

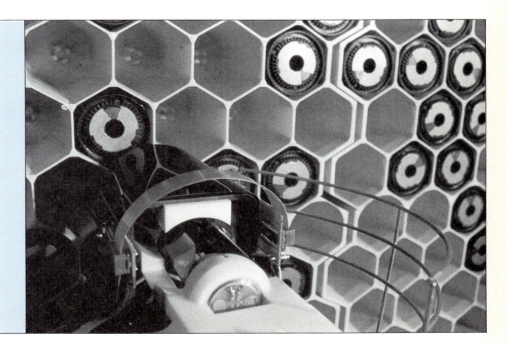

From the user's perspective, the storage function is at the hub of the information processing cycle.

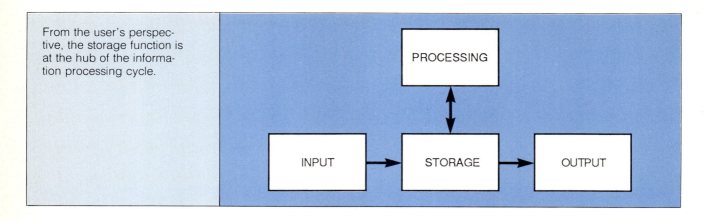

money. It is important that this asset value be recognized and that appropriate protective measures be devised and applied.

Originally, computers and the files they processed were separate entities. This was a carryover from the days of punched-card accounting. Computer files and programs were stored initially on punched cards, then on magnetic tapes. With either storage medium, both vulnerability and potential value of information were minimal. The danger of destruction was small because files were mounted onto processing devices only when they were to be used. Immediately after use, new files were created and could be set aside for safekeeping. Usefulness also was limited because there was little opportunity to integrate

Storage capabilities such as this bank of tape drives are keys to making information available to computers and their users.

and analyze data files that were kept on shelves in the next room or in vaults at a remote storage site.

Disk storage capabilities greatly increased the asset value of data and information stored by a computer. The added value came from the ability to analyze and compare stored data available for on-line access. Also, the ability to retain files under direct computer control represented a greater convenience in the use of computers for business applications.

Before disk files were introduced, it was impossible to use computers for direct support of business transactions. With disk files, computers became integral operating tools for most businesses. Many businesses could not handle present volumes or operate at current levels of efficiency without on-line disk storage capabilities. But these efficiencies have brought a price: The very ability to remain in business can depend on the protection applied to information files and to the media on which they are stored. The common-denominator requirement for using computers to build and retain information assets proved to be storage capabilities. Subsequently, storage devices have become more important as users have begun accessing databases directly.

## Physical Data Storage Techniques

Almost all of the programs and information files needed to operate computers and process applications are retained on devices classified as *secondary storage* or *peripheral storage*. These terms describe devices and methods used to store data or programs external to but accessible by a computer's processor. This means that data in secondary storage are not available for direct processing. Program and data records must be copied into main memory, which is part of the central processing unit, before processing can take place.

Program and data files needed to support an application generally require more storage space than is available in main memory, particularly if memory is allocated to the support of multiple applications. Therefore, secondary storage devices must be able to write and read large volumes of data at speeds that support the needs of the applications processed. To assure these capabilities, planning is required:

- Data formats
- Data storage techniques.

### Data Formats

Another requirement for secondary storage devices is an ability to handle data in formats that are compatible with the internal processing standards, or architecture, of computer processors. Any given circuit and corresponding storage position in memory or on a peripheral must be compatible. It would be impossible to interchange data without this compatibility.

The most basic form of coding for computer-processed data is the bit. Any computer processes and stores data as a series of bits, or *bit stream.* Within these bit streams, groups of bits, known as bytes, form a *character set* that represents the smallest item of data that can be processed. Industry standards center around two sets of byte codes used by the majority of computing and data communication systems. These are ASCII (American Standard Code for Information Interchange) and EBCDIC (Extended Binary Coded Decimal Interchange Code).

ASCII code was a standard of the telecommunications industry before computers entered the scene. When computers were designed initially, little thought was given to the prospects of data communication. Accordingly, computer architects devised their own coding schemes, of which EBCIDIC, developed by IBM, is most popular. As described in Chapter 5, techniques have been developed for converting from EBCDIC computer codes to ASCII and back again to support data communication. Many microcomputers, designed with data communications applications in mind, use ASCII as their standard code for both processing and communication. However, it also is true that both methods still exist separately and that storage devices must support the coding method used by the computer they support.

ASCII code is used in different versions for varying applications. For example, the communication version of ASCII coding uses a seven-bit character format. However, as shown in the accompanying illustration, the format used for microcomputers has an eight-bit character set. The EBCDIC code, also shown in an accompanying illustration, is based on an eight-bit byte structure. Both formats can be extended to include additional bits for automatic validation, or *parity checking.* Parity checking enables a computer and/or storage system to determine that each character processed consists of a valid number of bits.

Parity checking is handled by operating system software. The program counts the number of bits in each byte processed or stored. Parity checks can be either odd or even. Under an odd-parity routine, the computer makes sure that each byte has an odd number of bits. If the bit pattern is even, the parity bit is switched on prior to data transfer. Under an even-parity plan, the procedure is reversed; the number of bits must be even. Parity checking can be particularly important for storage devices because of the sensitivity of data media. A small speck of dust on a tape or disk surface can cause a misreading of data and can destroy the accuracy of files and/or processing. Invalid reading operations must be corrected before processing takes place.

## Data Storage Techniques

As you know, data are organized for processing according to a series of logical structures that include field, record, file, and database. A logical structure organizes data in a format that makes sense to the user and fits into an application in a way that implements user needs and designs. These logical structures, in turn, must be translated to physical organization structures to control the

The main code formats for processing and communicating data are EBCDIC and ASCII. Both these codes are shown in the top chart, which also includes corresponding numbers and letters. The inclusion of parity bits into EBCDIC code formats is illustrated in the bottom diagram. The format shown is for an odd parity system.

| Character | EBCDIC | 8-bit ASCII | Character |
|---|---|---|---|
| 0 | 1111 0000 | 0101 0000 | 0 |
| 1 | 1111 0001 | 0101 0001 | 1 |
| 2 | 1111 0010 | 0101 0010 | 2 |
| 3 | 1111 0011 | 0101 0011 | 3 |
| 4 | 1111 0100 | 0101 0100 | 4 |
| 5 | 1111 0101 | 0101 0101 | 5 |
| 6 | 1111 0110 | 0101 0110 | 6 |
| 7 | 1111 0111 | 0101 0111 | 7 |
| 8 | 1111 1000 | 0101 1000 | 8 |
| 9 | 1111 1001 | 0101 1001 | 9 |
| A | 1100 0001 | 1010 0001 | A |
| B | 1100 0010 | 1010 0010 | B |
| C | 1100 0011 | 1010 0011 | C |
| D | 1100 0100 | 1010 0100 | D |
| E | 1100 0101 | 1010 0101 | E |
| F | 1100 0110 | 1010 0110 | F |
| G | 1100 0111 | 1010 0111 | G |
| H | 1100 1000 | 1010 1000 | H |
| I | 1100 1001 | 1010 1001 | I |
| J | 1101 0001 | 1010 1010 | J |
| K | 1101 0010 | 1010 1011 | K |
| L | 1101 0011 | 1010 1100 | L |
| M | 1101 0100 | 1010 1101 | M |
| N | 1101 0101 | 1010 1110 | N |
| 0 | 1101 0110 | 1010 1111 | O |
| P | 1101 0111 | 1011 0000 | P |
| Q | 1101 1000 | 1011 0001 | Q |
| R | 1101 1001 | 1011 0010 | R |
| S | 1110 0010 | 1011 0011 | S |
| T | 1110 0011 | 1011 0100 | T |
| U | 1110 0100 | 1011 0101 | U |
| V | 1110 0101 | 1011 0110 | V |
| W | 1110 0110 | 1011 0111 | W |
| X | 1110 0111 | 1011 1000 | X |
| Y | 1110 1000 | 1011 1001 | Y |
| Z | 1110 1001 | 1011 1010 | Z |

BIT VALUES: 9 8 7 6 5 4 3 2 1

TRACK NO.: 4 6 8 1 2 P 3 7 9

Characters across top: 0 1 2 3 4 5 6 7 8 9 A B C & $ * . / ,

*THE P BIT POSITION PRODUCES ODD PARITY.

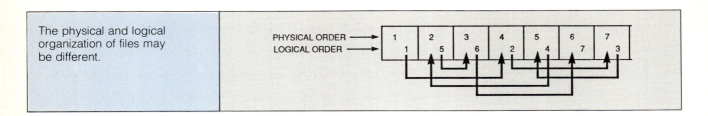

The physical and logical organization of files may be different.

recording and reading of data on peripheral devices. Physical organization designs center around the method of access to be applied in storing and using data files. Three basic approaches are available for organization of data for storage:

- Sequential
- Random
- Indexed.

■ **Sequential.**   Until the late 1950s, all computer data were stored sequentially. Initially, data were stored on punched cards that were arranged in sequence, one after another in *decks*. A deck of cards was a program or a data file. Individual decks could contain many thousands of cards. Each time data from a given deck were needed, all of the cards had to be fed through the computer. If processing led to changes in record content, completely new decks had to be punched by a peripheral machine.

When magnetic tape was introduced, records were stored in what were called *card images*. Each punched card had a capacity for up to 80 columns, or characters, of data. It was common practice simply to transpose records from card formats to tape versions, with the records placed end to end. To this day, the term *sequential file* still means that records are recorded one after another, along the length of a ribbon of tape. Sequential files are recorded in the same order that data are output by the computer and must be read into a computer in the same order in which they are recorded. Each time a sequential tape file is processed, the entire file must be read.

It is possible also to record and read data sequentially on disk files. Though this is done rarely, the same rules would be applied. Sequential files are recorded and read in order and must be processed in their entirety each time they are run.

To process data, it often is necessary to sort records into a desired order if they are kept in a sequential file. For example, suppose a company maintains a sequential employee master file according to identification number. When new employees are hired, they may be assigned numbers that fall within the existing sequence. If so, it is necessary to sort the file to bring it into processing sequence.

Sequence must be maintained for operations that involve processing of data from or changes to master files, those which support the applications and model their organizations. In the payroll example, weekly earnings information would be processed against a master file to compute earnings, deductions, and tax accounts for government agencies. For this operation, two separate sequential files—with earnings and master information—would be read by the computer. When the computer finds a match between earnings and master records, processing takes place. Clearly, the order of records in the two files must match. Any new records, then, must be placed in sequence through use of a sorting operation. Similarly, if an application required a list of employee names in alphabetic order, it would be necessary to sort the master file alphabetically before processing could take place.

Sequential files place restrictions upon the processing that can be performed. Sequential files are inflexible to use because they must be processed in their entirety each time. This feature means that batch processing is necessary for the handling of sequential files. It is impractical to handle interactive or real-time applications with sequential files. However, other applications are well suited to sequential file organization. Typical examples include payroll processing and bank account files. Payrolls are processed against master files of employees that are organized by employee name or number. Bank account master files typically are organized and transactions are processed according to account number sequences.

**Random.**    A *random file* means just what its name implies. Records can be placed ramdomly within a designated storage area. Retrieval also is random in that the computer can find any individual record directly, without having to read the entire file in sequence. Because records can be retrieved directly, this method also is known as *direct access*. When a record from a random, or direct, file has been updated, it is rewritten to its storage location.

Random storage files are maintained predominantly on magnetic disk devices. Access to individual records is possible because data items and records are stored on *tracks*, circular, concentric rings around the hub of a flat, round platter, or disk. For reading or writing operations, a magnetic head of a disk

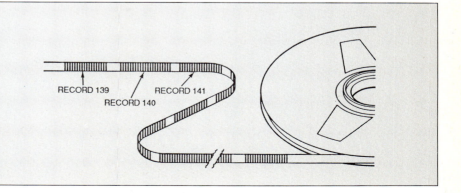

Within a sequential file, records are stored in the same sequence in which they are entered and recorded. Gaps are left between records or groups of records. These gaps provide the space needed to permit stopping and restarting of the tape drive as records are read into or output from a computer.

drive is positioned over a track. Records are read individually as the disk rotates under the head.

To support random file organization, records can be identified and located on disk surfaces in either of two ways. One method uses *relative addressing;* the other uses an *address algorithm* to calculate the address for each record.

Relative addressing relates the physical position of each record to the position of the first record in a file. For example, if a file begins at location 103 on the disk, a record with a key value of 5 would be at location 108. This approach makes it possible to place a sequential file on disk and to use its key values as relative addresses. Such an approach would make random access possible for sequentially organized files.

The second addressing method inolves application of a series of computations, or an algorithm, to the key value of the record. The product of the computation is the address. If key values are selected carefully, it is possible to use disk space more efficiently with computed addresses than with relative addressing. This is because relative files often require that gaps be left in storage space. For example, suppose a bank wanted to assign account numbers to correspond with the alphabetic sequence of customer names. When this is done, a typical practice is to leave 10 blank spaces between names. In this way, added names can be fitted into the gaps to preserve the alphabetic order. However, if the account number is used as a relative address, only one space in 10 on the disk will be occupied. This is inherently inefficient.

Despite these potential drawbacks, the introduction of random file tech-

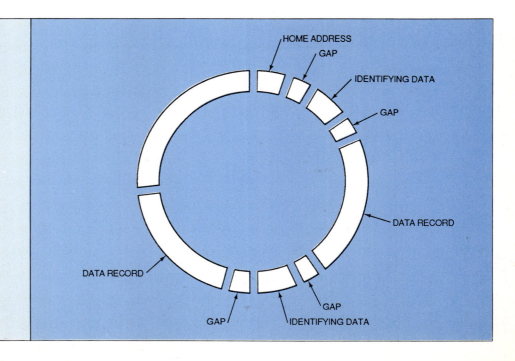

This diagram demonstrates how data records are positioned on the tracks of disk devices for random access. In this example, record positions are relative to the location of a home address for the track.

HOME ADDRESS

GAP

IDENTIFYING DATA

GAP

DATA RECORD

DATA RECORD

GAP

IDENTIFYING DATA

GAP

niques in the late 1950s and early 1960s represented a major breakthrough for business systems. The ability to access data randomly meant that businesses could process transactions interactively, as they took place. Computer utilization grew explosively. For computer professionals, random file techniques also represented a challenge to find techniques for better utilization of storage space and greater flexibility in the processing of applications.

**Indexed.**   In terms of file access methods, an *index* is a directory that contains physical addresses of records for a given file or database. The principle is similar to the function of an index in a book. To find information you want, you consult the index for a listing of the topic or key word in which you are interested. The index refers you to the page on which the desired information appears. Within an information storage system managed by a computer, an index is a separate file that serves a directory for locating records in other files. Records on indexed files are found with an initial reference to the index, then direct access to the record itself.

   With indexed file techniques, it is possible to add records to files without concern for physical location. Index entries are developed automatically as records are created. With the index in place, records can be processed in any desired order. Also, if sequential outputs are needed, records can be accessed sequentially through reference to the computer-maintained index.

   Because of the flexibility permitted and the ability to expand files conveniently, index access is the most popular file organization method today. Indexing techniques also are important to the implementation of database storage systems because of this flexibility.

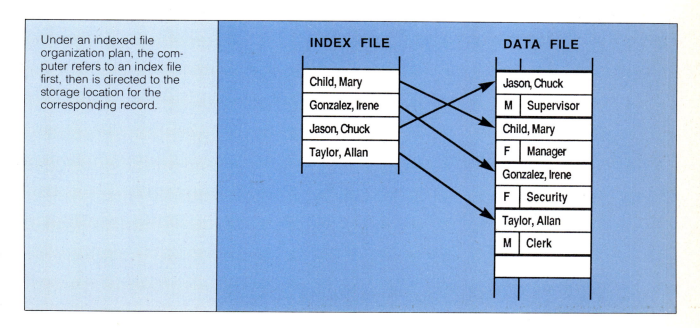

Under an indexed file organization plan, the computer refers to an index file first, then is directed to the storage location for the corresponding record.

INDEX FILE

Child, Mary
Gonzalez, Irene
Jason, Chuck
Taylor, Allan

DATA FILE

Jason, Chuck
M | Supervisor
Child, Mary
F | Manager
Gonzalez, Irene
F | Security
Taylor, Allan
M | Clerk

# Storage Device Capabilities

The data access method selected for support of a computer system generally controls choice of the kind of device that will be used. In general, sequential files are stored and processed on magnetic tape drives. Random and indexed files are maintained primarily on magnetic disk devices, though optical storage methods are gaining acceptance and hold great future promise. These four types of storage devices—tape, magnetic disk, mass storage devices, and optical disk—are reviewed in the discussions that follow.

## Tape Drives

The operating principles of *tape drives* are familiar to most people. Just think of the recording systems used in audio tapes, tape cassettes, or video cassette recorders (VCRs). A long ribbon of acetate is coated with a magnetic material on which either analog or digital signals can be recorded. In the case of computer tapes, of course, recording is digital.

Computer tapes must be of high quality because tape movement is far more rapid than in other recording systems. Also, storage *density*, measured by the number of bytes recorded on each inch of tape, is extremely high. When tape drives first were introduced for computers, the standard recording density was 200 bytes per inch (bpi). This standard was advanced rapidly to 800 bpi. More recent models have capacities of 1,600 and 6,250 bpi. Recording density is important because this capability affects overall performance. Tape transport rates, the speed at which tape moves past the read-write head, are comparable for most tape devices. Therefore, the more data that can be recorded per inch, the faster the system will operate.

Magnetic tape is a high-capacity storage medium. At 6,250 bpi, a 2,400-foot reel of tape holds a lot of data.

The most common form of tape storage medium is the open reel. In use, as shown in an accompanying diagram, a reel is mounted on one of two holders, or spindles, of a tape drive. This reel, which will be used either for reading existing files or writing new ones, is called the *data reel*. An empty reel is provided on the opposite side of the drive. Tape is wound onto this *take-up reel* after it passes under the read-write head. When processing is over, the tape is wound back onto the data reel.

Other tape drives handle tape packaged in a variety of cartridge and cassette sizes, including drives that handle the same type of cassette used in car stereos and portable recorders.

■ **Advantages.**   Tape drives are low in cost and can store data compactly because of their high recording densities. These features make tape ideal for certain applications, described later in this chapter.

On a tape drive, tape is fed from a data reel onto a take-up reel. Tape is transported by a capstan, a powered roller, to run past read-write heads. Loops or buffer mechanisms are provided so that the tape will start and stop smoothly during processing without stretching or tearing the acetate base.

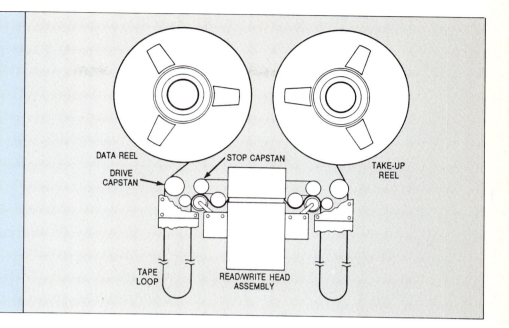

DATA REEL    STOP CAPSTAN    TAKE-UP REEL

DRIVE CAPSTAN

TAPE LOOP    READ/WRITE HEAD ASSEMBLY

■ **Disadvantages.**   Tape drives offer sequential access only because, as shown in the accompanying illustration, data are recorded in a continuous line along the length of the tape. This means that an entire tape must be read and usually rerecorded at each processing step. Tape media are mounted individually and manually by computer operators. Other types of devices provide massive on-line storage and normally require no operator attention.

## Magnetic Disk Drives

Magnetic disks have been likened to record albums. There is a physical resemblance. But the similarities in disk recording for computers are not as close to familiar entertainment media as are tape techniques. One major difference is that the recording tracks on computer disks are not continuous spirals like the tracks on entertainment disks. Instead, as you know, computer disks record data in separate, concentric tracks. The other major difference is that recording is magnetic; recorded information can be erased and rewritten indefinitely. Also, the read-write heads of computer disk units generally do not touch the recorded surfaces. In effect, the read-write head of a disk drive floats on a cushion of air created by the rotating action of the disk. A space of a few thousandths of an inch separates the recording-reading mechanism from the magnetically coated surface.

Many types of disk storage media are available, from microdiskettes that fit into shirt pockets to massive units with large stacks of disks that hold billions of bytes of data.

Disk drives record data on the surfaces of coated platters. Read-write heads move across the surfaces of disks until they are over the recording track that holds the record to be accessed. Some disk drives have a read-write head mounted over each recording track.

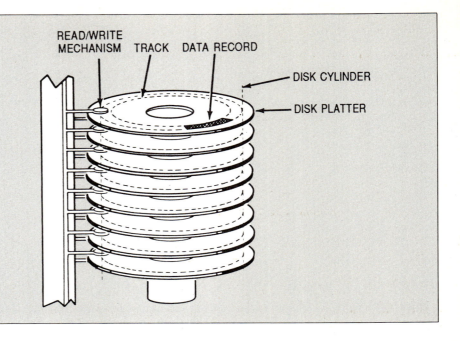

READ/WRITE MECHANISM   TRACK   DATA RECORD

DISK CYLINDER

DISK PLATTER

■ **Diskettes.**   *Diskettes,* also called *floppy disks,* use flexible plastic sheets as their basic structures, or *substrates.* Floppy disks are convenient to use and are inexpensive. Diskettes can be stored in boxes on desktops, in drawers, or in file folders along with the documents they produce. Since the introduction of microcomputers in the late 1970s, diskettes have become smaller in size and higher in capacity. Early systems used diskettes that were 8 inches in diameter and had capacities for approximately 120,000 bytes. Quickly, domination of the market shifted to diskettes of 5.25 inches in diameter that acquired continually increasing capacities. These diskettes had capacities in the range of 120,000 bytes. In 1981, capacities increased, typically to 360,000 bytes. Today, 5.25-inch diskettes offer capacities in the range of 1.2 million bytes (megabytes). More recently, diskettes measuring 3.5 inches in diameter have become popular. These units have capacities in the range of 800,000 to 1.2 million bytes.

*Advantages.*   Diskettes are low in cost; many floppies now cost less than $1 each. Floppies are easy to store and easy to copy for backup protection.

*Disadvantages.*   Storage capacities are limited for many applications. Because they are so portable and so easy to copy, the stored content on floppies can be difficult to protect and control.

■ **Winchester Disks.**   A next step beyond the capacities of floppy disks has come with the introduction of *Winchester disk* drives for microcomputers and minicomputers. Winchester units are of a specific design that includes a sealed device into which no air or moisture can leak and within which recording is done on a *hard disk* that uses a metal substrate. Because of the controlled environment, both speed of operation and storage density can be much greater than for floppies. Winchester drives can accommodate between 10 and 300 million bytes (megabytes) or even more. The disks generally rotate at speeds of 3,600 revolutions per minute (rpm), as compared with an average of 300 rpm for floppies. This means that *rotational delay* in access operations, the time it takes for disks to rotate under the position of the read-write head, is much shorter for Winchester disks than for floppies. A substantial portion of microcomputers now being sold for business applications are equipped with Winchester disk drives.

*Advantages.*   Access is faster and capacities are higher than for floppies. Costs are reasonable for the capacities attained.

*Disadvantages.*   Flexibility and portability of floppies is unavailable on fixed-disk devices. A user is at risk with all storage eggs in one basket. Many users keep all of their software and data files on a single disk and are careless about backup and protection. Vibration or power failure can destroy vital information assets. A single user error can wipe out all software and data files. Special training and care are needed to realize the potential benefits of hard disk storage for small computer systems.

**Disk Packs and Cartridges.**   *Disk packs* and *cartridges* are classified as *removable disk* storage devices. A cartridge contains a single, high-capacity disk platter in an enclosed case that can be mounted on special drives. Disk packs are multiple-platter stacks that also can be mounted on or removed from drives.

Cartridges, packs, Winchester, and floppy drives all are classified as *movable head* devices. This means that the read-write heads of these units move across the surfaces of the disks to execute access operations. Other, high-performance disk devices have a fixed read-write head over each recording track. These units are described below.

Within a disk device, the track is the basic location used to designate physical storage. Any given disk may have between 40 and 400 tracks. On large-scale systems, access operations are according to tracks. Each track has an identified "home address." Positions of records on the track are relative to this home address. Minicomputers and microcomputers add additional breakdowns for disk storage: Within tracks, recording positions are assigned in *sectors,* with each track broken into as many as 16 sectors that can be addressed individually.

Multiple-disk units with movable arms use recording and access patterns designed to minimize access delays due to head movement. Typically, a device has a separate read-write head for each surface in the stack of platters. Movement of all of the heads is coordinated. That is, all heads within an access unit are positioned over the same track of all disk surfaces at the same time. Recording procedures consider these movement patterns.

Groups of tracks at the same position on all recording surfaces of a disk pack are called *cylinders*. For example, cylinder 25 encompasses track 25 on each recording surface. Typically, recording patterns are established in cylinders. That is, file organization sequence would be from one disk surface to another at the same track location. This is more efficient than distribution of data among tracks on the same surface because maximum results can be attained from each disk move.

Cartridge and pack devices provide much higher capacities and access speeds than Winchester or floppy drives. This results partly from higher rotation speeds that usually are much faster than for floppies and also provide much higher recording densities. Individual disk packs now have storage capacities that can run into gigabytes, or billions of bytes of data.

*Advantages.* Access is relatively fast and capacities are high. Removable media can be flexible in that cartridges or packs can be interchanged to support individual applications.

These diagrams demonstrate the recording patterns for storage of data on disk packs. Data are recorded on tracks of individual disk surfaces. Continuous recording is on cylinders that contain the tracks in the same position on each disk surface.

CYLINDER 25

TRACK 25

TRACKS

SECTOR

*Disadvantages.*   Special setup and checkout are needed to load cartridges and packs onto specific drives. Special planning is needed to achieve efficient physical storage of data. Removable-media drives are lower in performance than fixed-disk units, described below.

■ **Fixed-Disk Devices.**   Fixed-disk devices have stacks of disks mounted permanently on drives. The devices usually are sealed to prevent leakage of air and moisture, creating a controlled environment that supports high performance capabilities. Therefore, disk rotation speeds can be extremely high. These units have a read-write head over each recording track. Therefore, access time is as short as a single rotation of the disk.

*Advantages.*   These units deliver high-speed access and high recording densities.

*Disadvantages.*   Costs are relatively high. All data stored in these units are on line and subject to the same hazards as computers themselves. Special procedures and close attention are needed to be sure to back up copies of the files and to establish protection plans for their storage.

## Mass Storage Devices

A special niche in data storage is filled by *mass storage devices.* These units fit well within organizations that have massive amounts of data that experience relatively low levels of activity. One example is the situation of a national credit reference service. A central computer system maintained by this organization has records on many millions of consumers. These records must be available for reference within a matter of seconds and at the convenience of customers who include merchants and banks. Characteristics of these files include low reference and modification rates offset by a need for ready availability.

Mass storage devices contain relatively short strips of wide magnetic tape. These strips are housed within circular cartridges. When a request is generated for a specific record, the tape strip on which it is stored is removed from a storage location and wrapped around a drum from which it is read. Under most systems, the required data are transferred to a disk file for further access and processing. Even though it might take a few seconds to access data on one of these units, the massive storage capabilities and comparatively low costs fit into a number of applications.

■ **Advantages.**   Mass storage devices provide large capacities at comparatively low costs.

■ **Disadvantages.**   Access times are slow.

## Optical Disk Drives

The same technology that makes possible video discs and compact disc audio recordings can be used for data storage within computer systems. Recording and reading on *optical disk* devices are done with laser beams of high-intensity light. The recording surface is plastic coated on a platter of rigid plastic. Data are encoded in the form of small holes, or pits, burned into the disk surface by the laser beam. For read operations, the light beam reads the pitted patterns.

Optical disk units have extremely high storage capacities. For example, a 14-inch platter has a capacity for 1 gigabyte (billion bytes) of data on each side. Access speeds are short because of high rotation rates. However, at this writing, recordings on optical disks are permanent. Computers or special devices can write data. But, once the pits are in the surface, they cannot be erased. Therefore, optical disk devices presently are used for read-only applications. A number of companies are working toward laser storage systems with both read and write capabilities. As discussed later in this chapter, laser units represent an important future potential for storage of data and programs within computer systems. One major application emerging for laser storage devices lies in use of compact disks for read-only memory (CD ROM). These devices are being used to expand and improve capabilities for software storage.

■ **Advantages.**   Optical disk devices provide rapid access and high storage densities—at reasonable cost.

■ **Disadvantages.**   Because of the read-only limitations, optical disk devices cannot be used for applications requiring a capability to change data.

## Selection Trade-Offs for Storage Devices

Many devices are available for use in recording, storing, and retrieving data. The best unit for any given situation is the one that meets the needs of user applications. Therefore, users who are aware of file sizes and access requirements for their applications can enhance the quality of services received and can minimize costs. Trade-offs and selection criteria for storage devices are based upon the factors of speed, density, and cost.

To illustrate, high-density devices provide greater storage capacities than those with lower densities. However, higher costs also may be involved. Therefore, in selecting the best device for a given job, unnecessary costs may be encountered if surplus capacity is purchased. Other factors can include the amount of space to be occupied by storage devices and the cost of renting and maintaining that office space (including air conditioning).

Conversion requirements and costs also can be a factor in storage decisions. For example, suppose an organization with 1,600 bpi tape drives is considering a switch to 6,250 bpi units. Management would have to consider whether it would be profitable to maintain drives with both density levels so that old and new tapes could be used interchangeably. As another alternative, special programs and considerable amounts of computer time could be used to convert all tapes from 1,600 to 6,250 bpi formats.

Equipment selection and trade-offs for conversions present complex situations for which analysis and advice of professionals should be secured. However, as a user, you might be in a position to impact the ultimate decisions about selection of storage devices. As a computer user, you certainly can benefit from knowledge that makes it possible to understand and communicate with qualified professionals.

## Effective Use of Storage

Ultimately, the payoff for effective configuration design and selection of computing devices lies in the performance delivered. The case descriptions that follow illustate situations in which storage devices and user needs have been matched effectively.

### The Right Device for the Job

A large, multibranch bank uses more than 100 fixed-disk drives as storage peripherals. Fixed-disk storage is considered a requirement for the bank's master account files because of the applications supported. In particular, the bank provides 24-hour service at automated teller machines and also for approval of sales on its credit-card accounts. Fixed-disk units are necessary because random access to account records is required and because there would not be time to change removable disk packs. Also, because of the size of the files, the storage density of the fixed-disk units becomes cost effective.

Management realizes that vulnerability is inevitable for a system that relies on fixed-disk storage. An earthquake or tornado that caused exessive vibration could wipe out all the files. Fire also could destroy the on-line file devices. Therefore, a set of procedures for producing backup copies of files and for recording current transactions is essential. The bank has software packages that copy file content rapidly and completely. Each file device is taken out of service for a few minutes and copied completely during the overnight shift, when reference activity is at a minimum. As a further protection, all transactions processed by the system are logged for possible use in rebuilding files. For each transaction, the system records the data entered and copies the account record both before and after the transaction is processed.

The creation of backup copies and transaction logs can be a major expense for a large computer installation. In the case of the major bank, analysis has paid real dividends. The systems specialists in this installation have recognized a special characteristic of both the backup copying and the logging operations: recording operations are serial. Therefore, tape drives, which cost far less than disk units, can be used. The bank writes its master file copies onto tape and stores the copies in a safe location. In addition, transactions are logged onto tape files as they are processed. Should a portion of the files be destroyed, new masters can be built by recapturing the last version of the master file, then processing logged transactions as though they were new entries.

**Investments in File Protection Pay Off**

Jack had been warned to back up the text entered into his word processing and typesetting computer system each half hour, or even more frequently. The system captures new entries in memory. The operator is responsible for saving the text to disk periodically. Jack is a conscientious and hard worker. He came to resent the time spent in backing up files because of the time taken from the main work of inputting text.

**Impact**

## The Electronic Filing Cabinet

Database management system (DBMS) packages have led to use of computers as electronic filing cabinets. The concept of the electronic filing cabinet involves replacement of the traditional filing cabinet with a computer access system. The traditional method is to place paper documents in drawers within rows of file cabinets. The electronic filing approach is based upon computer storage systems accessed through user terminals under control of DBMS software.

Ultimately, it is believed that DBMS packages will become sufficiently effective and efficient so that electronic storage can replace methods for organizing and maintaining files of paper documents. When this happens, the electronic filing cabinet will become a reality of business operation.

Today, business organizations seem to be using traditional filing cabinets in record numbers, with increases occurring at a steady pace. The volumes of paper and the cumbersome procedures they require have created a condition of *information overload*. This means the existing and newly created volumes of information exceed the capacity for understanding by information users. Under document-based methods, each filing cabinet is a separate storage location. Users may have to know the content of hundreds, even thousands, of separate cabinets. Then, there may be tens of thousands of individual documents within each cabinet. Finding needed information becomes a difficult, tedious, physical chore.

Electronic filing methods introduce an exciting prospect for eliminating this type of overload condition. Under DBMS techniques, software tools keep track of locations for needed data. The computer does the searching under software control and delivers needed results right to the user's work station. Information utilization becomes more effective because the user can interact with cross-reference files maintained by software to locate desired information sources. Users operate more efficiently because needed information is located and delivered in fractions of a second. Further, DBMS capabilities can be used to search files or to examine multiple information sources to find exactly what is needed, as it is needed. All of these capabilities, it is worth stressing, are available under security controls devised by people and imposed by computers.

One afternoon, Jack learned a practical lesson about the value of saving his work. He had been working for nearly two hours, since right after lunch, when a power surge wiped out the entire content of memory. Jack's boss, Teri, explained that power interruptions are not unusual. They occur regularly when companies change from one generating station to another for maintenance or load adjustment.

"The interruption doesn't usually matter," Teri said. "The lights might flicker and come right back on. The human eye adjusts. But a power interruption of a fraction of a second makes a big difference to a computer. This is a good lesson."

"It certainly is," Jack replied.

## There's Never Enough Storage Space

Herman had a frown on his face as he stepped into Jose's office. "We've got a problem," Herman announced. "I need another hard disk on my system. We're out of storage space."

Jose laughed, loudly and uncontrollably. He was an old hand with computer systems. Herman, his art director, had just made the change from manual drawing methods to computer graphics.

"I don't see the joke," Herman said. "I've been using the new system for a little less than three months. At first, a hard disk with 20 megabytes seemed like more than I would ever use. Now, I'm down to where I have only 3 megabytes left, and I'll use more than that on the job I'm about to start."

Still smiling, Jose explained that there is no such thing as enough storage space to last indefinitely. "If I bought you 100 megabytes, you'd be out of space in a year," Jose said. "Sooner or later you have to realize that the trick is to manage the capacity you have. Write any files that aren't active onto floppies and free up the space on the hard disk. Also remember that you have all your software on floppies anyway. You don't have to duplicate everything on hard disk. Clean house. You'll find that more than half of what you have on the hard disk can be copied off and saved on floppies.

## Trends in Storage Technology

As demonstrated in the previous discussions, storage technology has changed rapidly and has played a major role in the use of computers. Storage capabilities are vital because storage devices house and maintain assets that are vital to the operation and continued existence of most businesses. These technologies will continue to change and to advance in the future. Prospective users of information systems can, therefore, profit from an ability to anticipate these trends.

At this point, two trends already established can be expected to continue. One is the evolution of optical storage devices, particularly laser units with the ability to erase stored records and reuse disk areas. Some announcements have been made about laboratory breakthroughs in this area. In the near future, optical storage units with full read and write capabilities probably will be introduced and can be expected to have a major impact in the market for computer peripherals.

Even without erasability, optical storage devices are gaining acceptance as high-capacity read-only memory devices. Optical disk devices on microcomputers could hold up to a gigabyte of software and semipermanent data files. As one example, CD ROM technology can accommodate complete merchandise catalogs for large retail chains. Customer selection and invoicing operations could be carried out much more effectively than with printed catalogs and price lists.

The other trend is a merging of memory and storage technology. The breakthrough awaited in this area is the emergence of a *nonvolatile memory* chip, one which would retain stored data after power was interrupted. Nonvolatile memory devices already exist. But so far they have been too costly to be practical for extensive use. However, computer scientists do see the day when a computer system might include an array of 4 to 8 gigabytes of nonvolatile memory.

In an operating environment of this type, present database organization and query approaches might become obsolete. With such capabilities, data could be loaded helter-skelter into a storage device. The computer could search gigabytes of storage on the basis of record keys or content fields—all in a few millionths of a second. Admittedly, capabilities of this type are in dream stages. But these are not impossible dreams. Further discussion of memory devices and nonvolatile storage chips is included in the chapter that follows.

## Chapter Summary

- From the user's perspective, the equipment that stores and retrieves information is at the hub of a computer system.
- The invention of random-access storage devices was the key to making possible direct support of business transactions through on-line computer systems.
- The two principle formats used to organize data for storage on computer peripherals are ASCII and EBCDIC.
- The major techniques for arranging data for storage and retrieval on computer peripherals are sequential, random, and indexed.
- Sequential files record data in sequence, one record after another. These files must be read and processed in the same order in which they are recorded.
- Records within random files can be placed at any point on a disk device, without regard to sequence. Reference techniques are available to make

it possible to retrieve and write individual records, without requiring sequential searches.

- Indexed techniques use separate files that serve as directories to guide the recording and retrieval of records on disk devices.

- The main storage devices used with computers are classified according to the recording media used. The principle types of devices are tape and disk units. Disk drives are used most commonly to support business applications. Disk storage devices come in a number of configurations and capacities.

- Disk drives that store data optically show great potential, which is restricted at present because these units cannot erase and rewrite data once information has been recorded. A number of vendors are working on development of high-capacity optical disk units that will provide capabilities for erasing and rewriting data.

- An important step in the development of business applications lies in determining storage requirements and selecting the best equipment for each computer configuration.

## Questions for Review

1. Why are storage devices said to be at the hub of computer system configurations?
2. What kinds of devices are primary users of ASCII and EBCDIC code formats?
3. What is sequential storage and how does this technique work?
4. What is random storage and how does this technique work?
5. What is indexed storage and how does this technique work?
6. What is meant by recording density and what effect does recording density have on information storage?
7. How are data recorded on tape devices and how are tape files handled during application processing?
8. What storage configuration is used for data recorded on magnetic disk?
9. What are the performance differences between movable-head and fixed-head disk drives?
10. What is an optical disk device and what principles does it implement?

## Questions for Thought

1. Describe conditions under which a microcomputer could make profitable use of a hard disk in addition to one floppy drive.

2. Describe possible coordination or interaction between a hard disk and a floppy disk drive on a microcomputer.
3. Describe at least one application, in addition to backing up master files and logging transactions, for which serial file organization would be suitable.
4. What are the main advantages that have led to popularity of floppy disk drives for use with microcomputers?
5. What are the trade-offs between disk drives with removable media and those with fixed disks?

## Terms

| | |
|---|---|
| address algorithm | nonvolatile memory |
| bit stream | optical disk |
| card image | parity checking |
| cartridge | peripheral storage |
| character set | random file |
| cylinder | relative address |
| data reel | removable disk |
| deck | rotational delay |
| density | secondary storage |
| direct access | sector |
| disk pack | sequential file |
| diskette | substrate |
| floppy disk | take-up reel |
| hard disk | tape drive |
| index | track |
| mass storage device | Winchester disk |
| movable head | |

## MINICASE

**Situation:**

Scott works for an insurance agency that plans to install a microcomputer to handle its client service and accounting applications. A database package will be used and data files will be established for clients and for policies. The clients files are to be used for promotional mailings and special advisory letters. Combinations of data from both files will be used for billings. In addition, a major application that will use the policies file is development of lists of policies that are about to expire. Agents use these lists in their attempts to sell policy renewals.

The ability to mix data from multiple files is important to this system, since most applications will use data from both of the main relations. Scott must choose storage devices for his microcomputer system that will support his application.

### Decision Making: Your Turn

1. From the information you have, identify and describe the problem to be solved.

2. Identify alternatives that could be followed to avoid or solve the problem.

3. On the basis of the limited information you have: a) Identify additional information you would gather if you were dealing with this problem in a real situation. b) Identify the solution that appears best on the basis of the information that is available and explain your reasons for this selection.

4. What lessons are to be learned from this situation?

## Projects

1. Draw and label the different parts of a floppy disk. Note the following components: hub opening, jacket, liner, read/write opening, write-protect notch, index hole, tracks, and sectors.

2. Check PC magazines and literature available through a computer store for information on two or more CD ROM units. Describe the features of this type of device, including advantages, disadvantages, and cost factors.

3. Find out, from magazines or price sheets available from manufacturers, the cost ranges for Winchester disks and floppy disk drive units for microcomputers. Describe the capabilities and costs of one drive of each type. How do performance differences relate to capabilities and costs of each type of device?

# Chapter Outline

## CHAPTER 11

# The CPU Working for You

## Briefing Memo

TO:      Information Users
FROM:   T. Rohm, W. Stewart

The central processing unit (CPU) is the device where actual computing takes place. An understanding of the CPU and its capabilities will become important to you as your work involves operation of a microcomputer or if you decide to buy a personal computer of your own. This is because the capabilities of the CPU determine what you can do with any given computer system. In particular, the size of main memory controls the ability of your computer to use software packages and can limit the amount of data your system can process.

This chapter is designed to give you a level of knowledge necessary to participate in implementation of your own microcomputer systems and/or to converse intelligently about CPU capabilities with computer professionals.

# End-User Perspective

"You've been very quiet, Prof. Chiang," observed Suzanne, the lab assistant in the microcomputer center.

A group was observing the installation and initial demonstration of the first work station in a network of microcomputers that was to serve the business and computer science departments on campus. Suzanne wanted to know: "Is something the matter?"

"Call it pensive, Sue," Prof. Chiang replied. "I was recalling a similar incident just a little more than 20 years ago. I was a lab assistant, as you are today. The university was installing what was then the most powerful computer available, an IBM 7094. A special building was constructed to house it."

Prof. Chiang went on to recall that the 7094, a wonder of its day, had a 64,000-byte memory and a 16-bit word length. In just 20 years, he was observing a microcomputer with a 4-megabyte memory, a 32-bit word length, and virtual access to a 300-megabyte shared storage unit.

"When the 7094 first came out," Prof. Chiang recalled, "people wondered what they were going to do with all that computing capacity. They found out pretty quickly. It wasn't long before systems were designed that needed a lot more power. Systems like the one you see here result from the technologies that answered user demands for faster processing, and for memory capacities that seem to be approaching the infinite.

"Think what we can expect from systems that put many times more power on a desk top?" Prof. Chiang asked.

# The Point: The CPU Is the Power Source

In the preceding scenario, Prof. Chiang and his lab assistant were looking at and talking about a complete computer system. However, all of the measures they applied to performance had to do with one very important part of a computer, the *central processing unit (CPU)*.

In terms of work performance, the CPU can be likened to the generator in a power station. To deliver electricity, you need transformers, relay stations, and other peripheral support. But the generator makes electricity happen. A computer system includes a complex set of devices, all of which play a role in delivering results to users. Computing power resides in the CPU.

As a user, you depend on the CPU available to you to provide the processing capacity you need. The responsiveness of any computer to your instructions or stated needs is governed by the power of the CPU in relation to overall service demands. Thus, as a person interested in receiving and using information, you should be interested in the capabilities of any system you use, including the makeup and operational capabilities of your CPU.

## What Is the CPU?

In considering the makeup of a CPU, keep in mind that you are dealing with electricity and its two basic states, on and off. The CPU is designed to support your processing needs. There will be variations in CPU components for computers of different sizes. But the basic parts will be present in all central processing units. So, the review that follows describes the components of a CPU in terms of processing functions and sequences. Each CPU is made up of three major components:

- The control unit
- The arithmetic logic unit
- Primary storage (main memory).

### The Control Unit

The *control unit* moves data and program commands to the points within the system where they are needed. In normal job sequence, the control unit will begin by accepting input from a keyboard or storage peripheral. Input data items are placed in memory, with a notation made of their locations. When the processor signals the control unit that capacity is available, the data item or program instruction is released for processing. After processing, the control unit

A central processing unit contains a series of interrelated components, including a control unit, an arithmetic logic unit, and a random access memory that provides temporary storage for the operating system, application programs, and data.

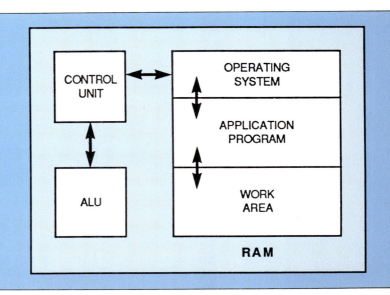

moves the processing results back into memory and also can generate signals to direct the data items to output or storage.

Recall that hardware is machinery that has to be directed through software or human procedures. Now recall that the operating system has a control unit that oversees the movement of data through a system. Hardware and software must be linked to deliver results for users.

## The Arithmetic Logic Unit

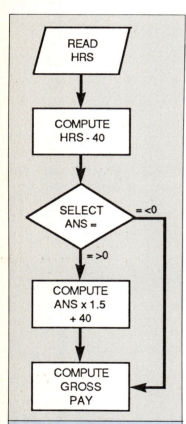

This is an example of a flowchart that represents program processing. The program diagrammed is part of a payroll system. It identifies records for workers entitled to overtime pay and computes gross pay for all workers.

Actual computation takes place in the *arithmetic logic unit (ALU)* of the CPU. From a user's problem solving perspective, the arithmetic capabilities of a computer are the same as those you have used personally. That is, the computer performs addition, subtraction, multiplication, and division. These functions are processed at the rate of millions of operations each second. The processing is electrical and is carried out in binary arithmetic. However, circuits within the CPU translate the binary values into alphabetic and numeric formats that people understand.

The so-called brain power of a computer rests in the logical capabilities of the ALU. *Logic* functions also are binary. The ALU can compare two presented values and can determine if one is greater than, equal to, or less than the other. With negative comparisons, the computer can determine if one value is not equal to, not greater than, or not less than another. The ALU does this by subtracting one value from the other. If the result is positive, the first number is greater than the second. If the result is zero (0), the values are equal. If the result is negative, the first number is less than the second.

Based on results of these comparisons, the computer can follow program commands that direct the course of processing. Application of these functions implements computer logic. Because millions of operations can be performed each second, knowledgeable users can cause computers to produce advanced, sophisticated results.

**Processing Data: A Case Example.** Effective use of the ALU depends on creative design by people. There may be many approaches that will solve the same problem. To find the most effective solution, users must learn to think in terms of capabilities of computing devices. To illustrate, consider a simple computation that is part of most payroll processing systems: determining overtime pay.

Assume employees are paid time-and-a-half for all hours worked in excess of 40 per week. One early processing step is to compare the input field for hours worked with the value 40. If the input field is equal to or less than 40, processing proceeds with multiplication of hours worked by the normal pay rate. If the field for hours worked has a value greater than 40, an overtime computation is necessary.

Under manual systems, many people compute overtime with separate calculations for regular time and overtime pay. Then, the two products are added to derive gross pay. With a computer, a programmer has to learn to think in terms of using the ALU efficiently by requiring a minimum number of logic and computation operations. To determine gross pay with the fewest number of operations, a payroll program typically multiplies overtime hours by 1.5, then adds the sum to 40. This produces an hours-worked total that includes the value of overtime hours. For example, if a worker has 48 hours, 40 is deducted to produce a difference of 8. The value 8 is multipled by 1.5 for a product of 12. This is added to 40 and both regular and overtime pay are derived from a single operation that multiplies 52 by the pay rate. By comparison, many more steps would be required to figure regular and overtime pay separately, then add the computed values. An accompanying illustration shows the logic of this payroll system.

■ **User Support Functions.**   The job of the ALU is to execute the instructions in application programs. This requires interaction with the control unit, which selects and delivers the instructions to be followed and the data items to be processed.

## Primary Storage (Main Memory)

*Primary storage* or *main memory* has been likened to a note pad. To illustrate, think of what you do when you take a math test, you may have a separate sheet on which you work out answers before you mark your test paper. This note sheet also is disposable.

Within a computer, main memory is *working storage,* the equivalent of your note sheet. Main memory exists because it provides a high-speed method for making needed program commands and data items available to the processor. Also, main memory holds interim results of processing until they can be assembled completely for output. To illustrate, consider the example of the overtime pay computation. An employee works 48 hours and is entitled to be paid for 52 hours because of the overtime bonus. The value 52 is an interim figure that is not required in the program output. (Remember: eight overtime hours multiplied by 1.5 equals 12 bonus hours.) This amount is stored only temporarily in memory. The space occupied by this value can be reused as part of the next overtime computation. In this sense, the area of memory used to retain this item is a scratchpad.

The main memory has operating speeds that are as fast as the processor. By comparison, the storage devices from which the commands and data are received are hundreds of times slower. Thus, the reason for memory is to assure productivity of the processor and, therefore, of the entire computer system. Main memory then supports both of the other components of the CPU, the control unit and the ALU, by providing a place where work can be organized and results can be accumulated for continuing use.

■ **User Support Functions.**   It would be impossible for a computer to perform multiple functions or serve multiple users without the storage capability of main memory. On behalf of the user, the supervisor module of the operating system keeps track of the content of main memory and provides the data items and program commands needed by the ALU or by storage and output devices.

Before operating system software was created, programmers had to do this tedious work by "mapping" main memory to keep track of data locations. The operating system now does this work automatically. If a system has multiple users or runs multiple programs concurrently, the supervisor module of the operating system allocates portions of memory, or *partitions*, to support each application program being processed.

The supervisor module of the operating system builds information tables that record the memory locations of groups of data items or program segments. For control purposes, groups of records or portions of programs are subdivided into working units called *pages* or *segments*. The operating system "swaps" pages or segments between memory and storage to support application programs. In memory, detailed searches for individual data items or program commands are addressed to appropriate pages or segments. This approach to management of memory is known as *dynamic allocation*.

## CPU Capacities and Trade-Offs

The architecture of the CPU is a primary factor in determining how much information processing power any computer can deliver. One measure of CPU capacity is the *cycle time* or *clock rate*. These terms describe the electronic pulses that control timing of CPU operations. Processing is controlled by an internal device that generates pulses to control operation of the computation circuits and memory access functions. Larger, more powerful computers have faster clock times. A mainframe might cycle its CPU 50 times faster than a microcomputer.

In addition to architecture, another measure lies in the number of commands and/or data items that can be processed during each CPU cycle. Commands are delivered to the CPU as *binary words*. The number of bits in a processor command determines the *throughput* of a computer, or the amount of processing done in a specific time frame. To illustrate, early microcomputers were structured to process eight-bit command words. By 1981, standardization moved to 16-bit word structures. Today, many microcomputers are executing 32-bit words. Mainframe systems are moving toward capabilities of 64-bit words.

Another capacity factor of a CPU that is used to determine system capacity is memory size. Memory is important to productivity because, the larger the memory, the less time a CPU has to spend swapping data into and out of peripheral storage. Memory sizes have multiplied as costs of microchips have fallen. Early microcomputers had 8,000-byte (8 K) or 16 K memories. Today, 640 K memories are common and memory sizes of up to 4 megabytes (MB) are not unusual. Mainframe systems are being delivered with memories of 8 MB and larger.

Added CPU capacity is one of the major factors in determining the price of a computer. Capabilities for larger memory and word sizes and lower cycle times are being introduced continuously. It is important to match the CPU to the jobs to be supported. Either too much or too little capacity can be inefficient and/or wasteful. Since main memory is particularly critical, and since separate options are available for the type of memory included in a system, this topic is considered next.

## ■ Main Memory: Operations and Options

A primary storage or memory unit is, essentially, a massive grouping (or array) of electronic switches. Each switch functions under the same principles as the ones you use to turn lights on or off. Electronic devices store and process data on the basis of their ability to sense on and off conditions.

The special feature of today's computer memories lies in their magnitude. Think of a microchip about the size of one of your fingernails. Packaged onto this tiny silicon wafer are between 256,000 and 1 million switches that can be set and checked individually to represent data—within cycle times of a few millionths of a second. An array of these chips mounted on a circuit board makes up the memory of a computer.

Today, chips of this type form the basic structure of most memory devices. Individual chips and arrays of chips are manufactured to deliver different capabilities. Some of these capabilities—and their impact upon computer performance—are described below.

### Random-Access Memory

The main memory of your computer works on the same principle as a large post office. A post office supports receipt and distribution of mail through a temporary storage system. A series of partitioned shelves, or pigeonholes, has a location for each address served by the post office. As letters are received, they are ''put up'' in storage positions that represent delivery addresses. When all mail is processed, the letters are withdrawn according to routes and given to letter carriers.

To manage this system, postal workers must be able to go directly to individual pigeonholes within their interim storage devices to insert or remove letters. The same principle applies to a computer's main memory. The control unit and ALU, under program control, must be able to insert data items or program commands anywhere in memory, to keep track of their location, and to retrieve those items as needed.

In a computer memory, each point on every chip represents a pigeonhole that can store one off or on bit value for combination with other bits and use within the processor. Groups of bits are organized to form byte values. Data are recorded by assigning groups of bit and byte positions to hold fields, records, and portions of files.

Memory is a resource that contributes directly to efficient operation of your computer. As a user, you depend upon random-access capabilities of main memory to support the processing that transforms data into the information you need as a problem solver and decision maker.

## Registers and Accumulators

Data items and program segments are swapped into memory in pages that might include 1,000 or more bytes of information. In turn, the ALU may process two to four of these bytes at a time. At any point, the software may interrupt a given program and switch temporarily to another. Obviously, some method is necessary to help the system keep track of where it is in the course of executing each program and/or processing each data file.

Special segments of memory are set up to serve as place markers. These are known as *registers*. The supervisor module assigns registers as part of its job of managing program execution. Each time a program command or data item is removed from memory, the corresponding register is changed to reflect the physical address of the next item to be processed. The function of changing registers to reflect memory addresses for data access is called *incrementing*. A value, or increment, is added to the existing item to represent the address of the next memory location to be accessed.

As each data item is processed, the program may require a memory location in which to store interim results. To handle this requirement, the supervisor module establishes areas in memory that serve as *accumulators*. An accumulator is dedicated to holding interim results for future use. As the program moves on to other calculations, new intermediate results can be written on top of old ones in the assigned accumulator.

In effect, registers and accumulators are the signposts that enable a CPU to meet its responsibilities as a traffic cop.

## Read-Only Memory (ROM)

Most programs, including the operating system, language compilers, and application programs, are stored on peripheral media such as diskettes or disk drives. Software then must be loaded into main memory for execution. The job of bringing software into main memory can lead to considerable processing work load, or "overhead." For one thing, programs compete with data for allocation of memory space. Another drawback is that processing time must be allocated to the swapping of programs.

Certain types of programs are common requirements for many computers. Included are operating systems and language compilers. Requirements for these programs are different from those presented by application software. For example, more than 100 different word processing packages can run under PC DOS. It could make sense to keep the operating system in a permanent location where it would be available to the control unit. The user still would be free to use different application packages, or to change applications at will without giving up the support of the operating system.

To meet these needs, many computers store some software elements that will be needed for long-term use as firmware in *read-only memory (ROM)*. As you know, the BIOS (Basic Input Output System) portion of the PC DOS operating system is kept in read-only memory on the IBM PC and most compatible microcomputers. Several types of devices are used for ROM:

■ **Programmable Read-Only Memory (PROM).**   A *programmable read-only memory (PROM)* is a chip onto which programs or data can be recorded permanently during manufacture. The BIOS system on a microcomputer is a prominent example of the use of PROM units.

■ **Erasable Programmable Read-Only Memory (EPROM).**   An *erasable programmable read-only memory (EPROM)* also is a chip that is used for storage of programs or data. The major difference is that the content of EPROM memory can be changed after manufacture. EPROM content is recorded through use of a special light that establishes data recording patterns. Re-exposure under the same type of light makes it possible to change the content of this memory device.

■ **Compact Disk Read-Only Memory (CD/ROM).**   In the future, it is anticipated that many more software elements will be stored on read-only memory than is done at present. A CD ROM is an optical, or laser, disk used as an adjunct to main memory. *CD ROM (Compact Disk Read-Only Memory)* devices are coming into use for many microcomputers as the number of programs stored in user systems increases. CD ROM can hold massive software and data files at costs far lower than those for PROM devices. Also, removing software from main memory leaves more space for application programs and user data.

Optical disk devices promise to enhance storage capabilities for computer systems. This optical storage unit has a capacity for 1 billion characters of data on each side of a 12-inch disk.

**Nonvolatile Memory**

When computer users and professionals have nightmares, they often center around the frustration that comes with the loss of power, even for an instant, that wipes out the content of main memory. Extensive amounts of work can be lost because current RAM devices are *volatile*. That is, memory content is temporary and is lost when power is turned off or interrupted. The situation is so critical that large computer centers commonly spend many thousands of dollars to install *uninterrupted power supply (UPS)* equipment. UPS systems generally include batteries that have enough stored energy to power a computer through the procedures needed to save memory content to peripheral storage before the system is turned off.

As another, more universal solution to problems of memory volatility, computer architects have been working for some time to develop *nonvolatile memory* devices. These are units that retain their stored content when power is interrupted or turned off. Progress has been made and some devices of this type have been introduced. To date, however, the costs of nonvolatile memory devices have been too high to permit their use as standard RAM components.

■ **Bubble Memory.**   One nonvolatile device that has found limited use for primary storage is the *bubble memory*. The bubble memory is a microchip designed by Bell Telphone Laboratories. Electric current is processed to create magnetic points, or microscopic-sized bubbles, on a silicon base. The positions of the bubbles determine their binary values.

Bubble memories are somewhat slower than integrated circuit chips like those used in most memories. However, they are extremely high in storage density, with capacities of up to 5 million bits per square inch. The main advantage is that these devices are magnetic and can, therefore, retain data when power is shut off or interrupted. The main disadvantage is comparatively high cost.

The greatest application of bubble memory to date has been in portable terminals used for small, temporary files. Some terminals developed for use by journalists have used bubble memory. With these units, for example, a reporter at a sports event can write a story on location and transmit it to the home office through use of a built-in modem. Once the text is received at headquarters, the memory space can be released and reused. This is a high-priority application that requires relatively small memory capacity. The terminals marketed for this application typically contain 32 K or 64 K of bubble memory.

## ■ Representing Data in the CPU

You already know from Chapter 10 that data are represented within computers in binary coding formats such as ASCII and EBCDIC. The character sets illustrated in Chapter 10 also are recognized and used in the CPU. Since coding formats and their structures already have been discussed, interest at this point centers around what happens when these bit structures are processed through the CPU.

Main memory stores and the ALU handles formatted bytes in much the same way as secondary storage devices. The main difference between handling in the CPU and in storage devices occurs in the ALU. The job of the ALU is to apply arithmetic and logic functions to *transform* data. That is, data items can leave the ALU in formats and values that are different from their input state.

## ALU Processing

Transformation occurs in a series of special ALU circuits called *gates*. ALU processing is a highly technical topic that is beyond the scope of this book. However, the principle need not be beyond the understanding of any interested information user.

To illustrate, one of the circuits within an ALU is called an AND gate. AND circuits perform addition by accepting one value AND combining it with another. Repeated processing through an AND gate combines values to perform multiplication. Subtraction is achieved through use of a negative AND, or NAND, gate. Repeated subtraction is used to perform division. Thus, all computer arithmetic is a succession of additions and negative additions that can be combined to achieve other mathematical functions.

Logic functions within a CPU can be performed in OR gates which, as their name implies, are able to make choices on the basis of comparison.

## Binary Computation

All operations within the ALU are performed at the binary level. Since binary arithmetic uses a base value of 2, processing must take place to coordinate computer processing with the values entered and required as outputs by people. People use decimal arithmetic, which is based on values of 10. By contrast, each position, or place, in a binary number has a value of 2. As a result, binary representations of data require many more numeric positions than decimal values.

To illustrate, consider representations for the value 23. As a decimal number, this value requires two positions, known as the units position (to the right)

These simple electrical diagrams show how AND and OR gates are constructed. An AND circuit requires that both open switches be closed. An OR gate passes current when either of two switches is closed.

This diagram demonstrates binary-to-digital conversion for the digital value 23.

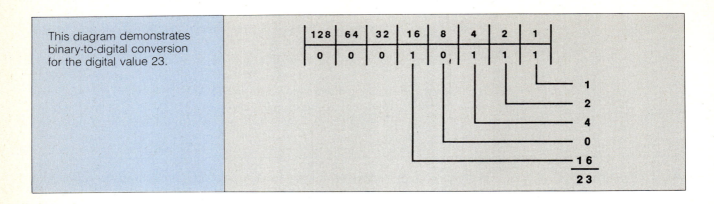

and the tens position. In binary arithmetic, as shown in an accompanying illustration, the place values, from right to left, are 1, 2, 4, 8, 16, 32, and so on. Thus, in binary notation, the decimal value 23 would be transposed to 10111. This binary value represents the cumulative decimal equivalents of 16, 4, 2, and 1, for a total of 23.

Addition of binary numbers works in the same basic way as for the decimal system with which you are familiar. The difference is that carrying of surplus values occurs when a sum exceeds a total of 1 (rather than 9). Thus, addition of 1 and 1 produces a 0 and causes a value of 1 to be carried left. To illustrate, consider the addition of the decimal values 23 (10111) and 14 (01110). As shown in the accompanying illustration, the decimal sum is 37 and the binary sum is 100101, with the carried value to the left occupying the position with a decimal value of 32.

One of the wonders of modern computing is that the circuits needed to perform all of these functions, and the control operations as well, can be incorporated on a single, fingernail-sized silicon wafer. From what you know about the ALU, it can be fascinating to understand and appreciate the power placed at your service by modern electronics technology.

This diagram demonstrates the process of binary addition for numbers with equivalent digital values of 23 and 14 to arrive at the total of 37.

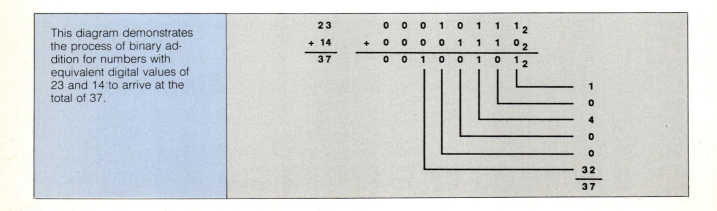

## ■   Classifying Computers

Some 20 million computers now are installed and functioning in business organizations. When you have this many units of anything, there are bound to be differences among them. In fact, there are many types, shapes, and sizes of computers, classified largely according to the design principles and sizes or capacities of CPUs. In terms of design, there are two broad categories of CPU, general purpose and special purpose. Sizes are organized into a range of options, from microcomputers at the lowest level to supercomputers at the top.

## General- and Special-Purpose Computers

As has been mentioned in earlier chapters, the vast majority of computers are general-purpose systems that are adapted to specific jobs through selection of application software and attachment of required peripherals. To illustrate, if you want to produce graphic outputs from a microcomputer, you will have to install a graphics circuit card in the computer itself. This represents a hardware modification. You also will need a software package that translates the numeric values of computers into positions and images on a screen or other output device. Also, as discussed in the chapter that follows, you may want to include a special output device that can deliver graphic images for your use or for distribution to other users.

In most instances, the computer itself is still a general-purpose system. Special-purpose capabilities are added.

In the early days of the computer era, most machines were designed for special users. The original computers were built to handle scientific computation and to support research projects. When business applications came to the forefront, equipment was developed to meet the special needs that were presented. For example, the first computers had character sets that consisted of numbers and a limited group of mathematical symbols. Business computers needed alphabetic characters and symbols used in financial reporting. Business computers also needed to handle and store large data files. Until the 1960s, most computers were special-purpose systems. This changed in the 1960s. The introduction of computer chips and disk storage made general-purpose machines possible by standardizing binary formats that could handle both scientific and business data requirements. General-purpose design has dominated the market ever since.

Recently, however, requirements have emerged that have led to introduction of new generations of special-purpose computing devices, some of which are joined to general-purpose systems in multiprocessing configurations. For scientific applications, an increasingly popular choice has been a *RISC (Reduced Instruction Set Computer)*. These units operate on a small set of simple, basic program commands. Programming is a greater challenge than with higher-level languages, which will not run on RISC machines. However, because of the simplicity of design, extremely high processing speeds are possible. This design makes RISC units ideal for scientific and engineering research jobs that tend to be described as ''number crunching.''

Another type of special-purpose device that is gaining in popularity is the database processor. This is a machine dedicated to storing and retrieving data through an architecture designed to implement database capabilities. Usually, a database machine is a back-end processor that supports a general-purpose system configured to provide time-sharing services to multiple users.

## Classification According to Size

The range of sizes used in classifying computers includes the following categories, ordered and discussed from smallest to largest:

- Microcomputer
- Supermicrocomputer
- Minicomputer
- Superminicomputer
- Mainframe
- Supercomputer.

In large measure, these categories center around the architecture and technology that have been used in the CPU of each type of equipment. It also is true that size and cost tend to be related; larger computers cost more, often thousands of times more, than their smaller counterparts. One reason for classification by size: Users gain guidelines that can be helpful in selecting the right tool for each computing job.

■ **Microcomputer.**   The chief characteristic of a microcomputer is that its processor is a single microchip. Also, main memory capabilities tend to be limited to maximum sizes of 640 K or 1 MB. Most microcomputer work stations have CPUs that process 16-bit word structures and do not have the power needed to act as hosts in multicomputer configurations. Communication capabilities generally are limited to access through dial-up service or as stations on a LAN supported by other, larger devices. Overall, microcomputers tend to be lowest in cost, with price tags starting in the range of $500 and running to perhaps $3,000.

Most microcomputers handle applications for individual users. The most popular software packages include word processing, spreadsheet, and database applications. In addition, many companies use microcomputers for integrated accounting and transaction processing applications that include invoicing, payroll, and preparation of financial statements.

■ **Supermicrocomputer.**   A *supermicrocomputer* is a desk-top work station with advanced technological capabilities that usually include a 32-bit architecture and

A networked executive work station provides capabilities for both stand-alone processing on a microcomputer and also access to large-scale computer capabilities.

main memories of 2 MB or larger. Supermicrocomputers typically have larger screens that deliver better image resolution than standard microcomputers. Although the processor still is a single chip, most supermicrocomputers have high-speed and high-performance capabilities that outstrip those of standard microcomputers. Supermicrocomputers can be configured to function as host devices in networks that include standard microcomputers or terminals. Prices generally are in the range of $3,000 to perhaps $7,000 and, as indicated below, can overlap with the prices and capacities of minicomputers.

Supermicrocomputers and minicomputers are used largely for applications that involve greater volumes of transactions or larger databases than can be handled on microcomputers. These systems also are used for applications that serve multiple users who share data files. Applications may be similar to those for individual microcomputers. However, volumes and complexities require greater capacity.

■ **Minicomputer.**   A *minicomputer* uses a multichip CPU that currently is supported by a memory in the range of 2 MB or larger. Minicomputers are extremely flexible devices that offer excellent communication support capabilities. They are particularly effective as communication controllers or concentrators and often serve as front-end communication and housekeeping ''slaves'' that support mainframe hosts in multiprocessor networks. Minicomputers also are used as central processors within systems configured to serve multiple users in a small- or intermediate-sized business. Prices generally start at about $5,000 and can range up to $100,000 or $150,000, depending largely on the type and amount of storage and other peripheral support that is included.

■ **Superminicomputer.**   A *superminicomputer* often is a central processor or a heavy-duty front-end communication controller in a large multiprocessor system. Capabilities include a large word size and short CPU cycle times. In terms

Superminicomputers like the one shown here provide both user flexibility and processing capacities that rival those of mainframe systems.

of user support and applications, superminicomputers overlap the lower end of the large-scale computer, or mainframe, market. Price ranges can begin at $200,000 and run up into the range of $750,000 or $1 million. Superminicomputers can handle a mix of applications that can support an entire organization. Systems in this category are used for business, research, scientific, and engineering applications—the full spectrum of applications found in business and industrial organizations.

■ **Mainframe.**    A *mainframe* is a large-scale computer. Its CPU features a large word size, a cycle time that is a fraction of that of a microcomputer, memory capacities in the range of 2 MB to 4 MB, and high-capacity communication devices used for direct connection of peripherals and communication networks that provide time-sharing service to large numbers of users. Mainframe computers generally serve as host machines in multiprocessing configurations. Prices range from $750,000 to $2 million. They are used for the full spectrum of business and scientific applications.

■ **Supercomputer.**    A *supercomputer* can be described as a large system that has outgrown the standard classification of mainframe equipment through use of advanced technology to add power and capacity. CPU architectures feature large word sizes and cycle times rated as fast as 80 *MIPS (Million Instructions Per Second)*. As a basis for comparison, fast microcomputers have capacities of perhaps 2 MIPS.

Technologies employed include *superchips* with extremely high processing or memory capacities. For comparison, a typical high-capacity chip is the

Mainframe systems provide capabilities for direct service to on-line users and also provide consoles for control of batch processing jobs.

size of a fingernail and is cut from a silicon wafer that measures perhaps four inches in diameter. A superchip is built onto an entire wafer. This concentration of electronic components, or *component density,* causes intensive heat generation. As a result, some supercomputers are encased in cooling systems that circulate refrigerated water. More recently, supercomputers have been built with *cryogenic* cooling systems that use liquid nitrogen. Cryogenic cooling implies temperatures at minus 250 degrees C and below. The idea: Traditional air conditioning could not keep up with the heat dissipated by some of these units.

Another feature that is being considered for supercomputers of the future is *superconductivity.* This term refers to a state in which conductors lose virtually all resistance to the flow of current, leading to extremely fast operation of electronic components. At present, superconductivity is achieved in special ceramic devices cooled to minus 297 degrees C. The process is expensive, but performance capabilities are multiplied. Supercomputers are being applied to super jobs, such as scientific and space exploration simulations and research support at major universities. Prices generally start at $2 million and can run to $ 4 million or even higher

A major application for supercomputers involves support of scientific and engineering research. For example, new aircraft, space vehicles, and automobiles are modeled before they are built. Designs can be completed in relatively short times and in great detail through the use of powerful computers. Once designs are complete, the computers can control manufacturing or can be used to develop tools for mass production. Supercomputers made available through time-sharing services are used to produce futuristic, animated movies and some dazzling TV commercials. Typical costs for linking a time-sharing terminal to a supercomputer are in the range of $3,000 per hour.

The power of a supercomputer can boggle the mind of an average information user. However, it is a significant comment on the state of the information society that there are waiting lists to receive new supercomputers.

In general, each category of computers filled a special niche at the time of its introduction. Following acceptance, users broadened the application scope for each type of system. Today, the categories form a continuity rather than a series of separate groups. There is considerable overlap between the identified classifications. Thus, the classifications have become less important than the overall principle that it is necessary to match the scope of user needs and budgets with the capabilities of available computers.

## Matching the CPU to its System

Clearly, the selection of a CPU and the components with which it interacts is a job that requires the expertise of advanced computer professionals. One problem is that so much capacity is available that it can be tempting to buy a larger system than is needed.

To accommodate users, most manufacturers design CPUs for *upward compatibility*. That is, a series of CPUs from the same manufacturer can be interchanged. Users can move from smaller to larger units with complete compatibility of operating systems and application programs.

In this environment, planning for CPU and peripheral capacity has become a specialty for a growing group of computer professionals. These people monitor the amount of actual utilization of processor time. In general, a computer system is considered to be approaching saturation of its productive potential when 70 percent of processing cycles go to user work. This level of utilization usually is a signal to begin a process that can take 12 to 18 months and will lead to upgrading of a CPU and its support software. At the other end of the planning spectrum, a CPU is considered oversized for its job if less than 45 or 50 percent of processing capacity is required by users.

This has been a user's overview of CPU features, capabilities, and selection criteria. The topic of CPUs can get far more technical than this discussion. However, you now have a sufficient grasp to ask pertinent questions and, possibly more important, to understand the answers you will get from computer professionals—and to help you get the information you want.

## Chapter Summary

- The central processing unit (CPU) of a computer controls the services that can be delivered to users.
- Each CPU, regardless of the size and capacity of its computer, consists of a control unit, an arithmetic logic unit, and primary storage (main memory).
- The control unit directs the flow of data into, within, and out of the computer. Its role has been likened to that of a traffic cop.
- The arithmetic logic unit performs calculations and comparison, or logic, operations.
- The main memory holds program segments and data in support of processing. Main memory holds data or program instructions only temporarily. When power is turned off, the memory goes blank.
- The design of a CPU is part of a computer's architecture. Design trade-offs center around performance (speed and capacity) as well as cost.
- A computer's main memory must have random-access capability so that individual program instructions or data items can be found and processed.
- To control write and read operations in memory, locations are stored in special areas known as registers. To store interim totals for computations, special memory areas known as accumulators are used.

- Frequently used software routines or data files may be stored permanently within a CPU through use of read-only memory (ROM) devices. Types of ROM units include PROM and EPROM chips and CD ROM devices that utilize optical disks.

- To eliminate problems associated with the loss of data when a computer loses power, vendors are working to develop nonvolatile memory devices that would retain content when power is turned off.

- Computer processing is done with binary values. The ALU has circuits that perform computations and comparisons. The ALU also performs binary-to-digital conversions to accept inputs from and produce outputs for users.

- Computers come in a wide range of sizes and capacities. Common classifications include microcomputer, supermicrocomputer, minicomputer, superminicomputer, mainframe, and supercomputer. The challenge facing users is to match the CPU to the applications to be processed.

## Questions for Review

1. What is a CPU and what is its role within a computer system?

2. What is the purpose and what are some specific functions of the control unit within a CPU?

3. What is the purpose and what are some specific functions of the arithmetic logic unit within a CPU?

4. What is the purpose and what are some specific functions of primary storage, or main memory?

5. What is meant by computer logic and what functions are controlled by logical operations?

6. What are memory partitions and what is their purpose?

7. What are pages and what role do they play in application processing?

8. What are registers and accumulators and what are their functions?

9. What is read-only memory and what is the princpal application for which it is used?

10. What are the main categories of computers and why are the different sizes and capacities necessary?

## Questions for Thought

1. Why is it valuable for a nontechnical user to be aware of the capabilities of different CPU configurations and components?

2. How does a computer achieve complex, sophisticated analysis and reporting through application of simple arithmetic and comparison functions called primitives?

3. What specific types of programs and/or data would a computer manufacturer store on ROM chips?

4. If your microcomputer is a general-purpose system, how is it equipped to solve specific problems?

5. What do you think should determine the size of a computer to be purchased by a business organization?

## Terms

accumulator

arithmetic logic unit

binary word

bubble memory

central processing unit (CPU)

clock rate

compact disk read-only memory (CD ROM)

component density

control unit

cryogenic

cycle time

dynamic allocation

erasable programmable read-only memory (EPROM)

gate

increment

logic

mainframe

main memory

minicomputer

MIPS (Million Instructions Per Second)

nonvolatile memory

page

partition

primary storage

programmable read-only memory (PROM)

read-only memory (ROM)

register

Reduced Instruction Set Computer (RISC)

superchip

supercomputer

superconductivity

supermicrocomputer

superminicomputer

throughput

transform

uninterrupted power supply (UPS)

upward compatibility

volatile

working storage

# MINICASE

**Situation:**

"Hello, Julia, I want to say that I was fascinated by your demonstration of the integrated software package for the PC," Joanne said. Julia was in charge of her company's information center, a facility that assisted users in creating their own computer information systems. It was her job to identify microcomputer hardware and software products that might be useful to employees and help install these capabilities where they could add to personal productivity.

Joanne introduced herself and explained that she was a secretary in the marketing department. So far, most of her work had involved word processing for letters, memos, price quotations, and other documents. Now she was being asked about adding graphics and data tables derived from spreadsheets to her outputs. Also, Scott Jensen, marketing vice president, was interested in building a database that would make it possible to track product sales by customer and region.

"That's an ambitious upgrade," Julia said. "The first thing we need to know is the configuration of the system you have now."

Joanne said she was working with a basic 256 K microcomputer that had two disk drives with capacities of 360 K each.

"The software you are interested in needs a much bigger system," Julia said. "You can't do any integrated processing on the unit you have. You will need at least a full megabyte of memory and a hard disk. This means the company will have to invest either in an upgrade or a new computer. Also, the software itself might cost up to $1,000."

"That's the kind of information I need," Joanne said. "What do we do next?"

**Decision Making: Your Turn**

1. From the information you have, identify and describe the problem to be solved.

2. Identify alternatives that could be followed to avoid or solve the problem.

3. On the basis of the limited information you have: a) Identify additional information you would gather if you were dealing

with this problem in a real situation. b) Identify the solution that appears best on the basis of the information that is available and explain your reasons for this selection.

4. What lessons are to be learned from this situation?

## Projects

1. From sales literature you pick up at a computer store or from personal computer magazines, secure descriptions of systems with two different CPU capacities. One should have a relatively limited memory capacity; the other should be 1 MB or larger. From the literature you review, summarize the capabilities of each system and describe the kinds of applications for which each might be suited.

2. Interview a manager in your school's computer center or other computer professional. Determine how CPU capacities, including the bit size of commands, the clock time for processing cycles, and memory capacity affect the amount of processing a system can do. Report on your findings.

3. If you have access to a microcomputer and have learned how to use it, do the following: Load the DOS program. Remove the DOS diskette. Alongside the A† prompt on the screen, enter the instruction DIR. Do this without inserting a diskette in Drive A. The system will generate an error message on the screen. Note the wording of the error message. Report on what processing took place within the CPU and the DOS program stored in memory to generate this error message.

# Chapter Outline

End-User Perspective

The Point: I/O Devices are Windows to Information

The Need for Input and Output: People and Computers Must Communicate
*Input and Output in Your Experience*

Input Methods
*Keyboard, Speech, Graphics, Document Reading, Magnetic Card*

Output Methods and Devices
*Displays, Printers, Plotters, Film, Audio*

Input and Output as User Applications
*Utility Turnaround Documents, ATM Cards, Touch-Tone Phones*

Chapter Summary

Questions for Review

Questions for Thought

Terms

Minicase

Projects

## CHAPTER 12

# Input and Output Operations

## Briefing Memo

TO: Information Users
FROM: T. Rohm, W. Stewart

As a user, you need the input and output devices of computer systems as your window to an information-centered world. Because the needs of users are extremely diverse, input and output devices are the most numerous—and most varied—of all categories of computer equipment.

This chapter is designed to provide you with an understanding of the capabilities of input and output devices. With this understanding, you will be in a position to gauge your own expectations for information delivery. You also will establish a knowledge base for selecting the most appropriate computer input and output devices for the job at hand.

**End-User Perspective**

"What happened?" Don asked. "I missed the play. I was looking at the scoreboard."

"That's the second time," Anne said. "You're the big-time baseball expert who was going to explain things to me. Then you get so wrapped up in the scoreboard that you miss key plays. Maybe I shouldn't tell you what happened."

After learning that the first baseman had made a jumping catch of a line drive and caught the runner off base, Don checked the scoreboard again. The electronic display showed that the home team first baseman led the league in unassisted double plays.

"That's a statistic I've never seen before," Don said. "Since the introduction of computerized scoreboards, there seems to be some new statistic every time you go to a game."

"There's a new batting average each time a player comes to the plate," Anne said. "I can see where the game must be a lot more interesting with a computer controlling the scoreboard."

"The average fan now has more information displayed than the manager used to have when I played the game," Don said. "If you are trying to figure out the strategy of what's going on, a computerized scoreboard really gives you an inside picture. With the computer running the display, you have a giant information window in front of you—play by play."

 **The Point: I/O Devices Are Windows to Information**

Don's remark can be applied to all computer systems: Input and output devices are windows that provide users with insights into whole worlds of information. You are presented with input-output windows to computer systems many times each day, possibly without knowing it. If you press a "walk" button on a traffic light, you are entering data that says a pedestrian wants to use the crosswalk. When the light changes, you are receiving an output. If you make a purchase in a department store, the tag on the garment you select provides intput to the store's computers on exactly what style, color, and size of garment was sold. The computer responds with output on how much you have to pay for the garment. If you make a credit purchase, your card inputs data that tells the computer you have credit, and the computer outputs a statement about how much you owe.

In summary, input and output devices are the places where users deal with and receive the information potential of computers.

Users accomplish direct input as byproducts of transaction processing through work stations like those shown here. The system displays record formats that guide data entry.

## The Need for Input and Output: People and Computers Must Communicate

Computers are used so widely that the terms *input* and *output* have become parts of everyday language. Input involves capturing data in a form and format acceptable to a computer, as well as entering data into a computer for processing and for updating of files. In other words, input and output are the entry and delivery points within the input, processing, output, and storage cycle.

The input process encompasses an *authorization* function. Authorization means simply that there must be a way to assure that people who enter data are entitled to do so and that data are input to the proper files and systems. Authorization is a function carried out by people and is the point at which information users can assure that results will be accurate, reliable, and timely.

*Data capture* occurs if the input items are recorded on storage media as an interim step prior to entry into the computer. An example of data capture is key entry of data from invoices or orders onto tape or other medium. From there, groups of data items can be processed as batches. *Data entry* is the act of reading captured data into a computer.

Under the procedures for some systems, data capture and data entry can be performed in a single operation that completes *direct entry*. As an example of direct entry, consider what happens when you buy gasoline at a pump with a terminal that reads automatic teller machine (ATM) cards. You pass your card through a reader. When this is accepted, you enter your personal identification number (PIN) into a numeric keypad. A computer has led you through two authorization steps. Then, when you pump your own gas, the computer reads the values recorded on the pump to complete the transaction. You have performed direct data entry as a byproduct of selling yourself gasoline (as distinct from making a purchase through a cashier).

Output encompasses all of the processing, display, printing, or recording functions associated with delivery of information to authorized users on a timely basis. Output can be as simple as a ringing telephone or a changing traffic light

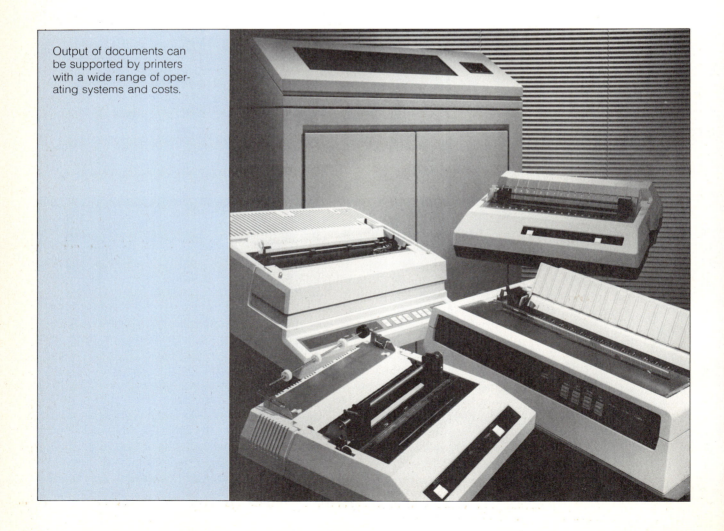

Output of documents can be supported by printers with a wide range of operating systems and costs.

or as extensive as a report that contains more than 100 pages of manuscript or financial data.

## Input and Output in Your Experience

To understand the input and output functions, consider the procedures you follow to enter, edit, and output a document on a microcomputer with a word processing package. Your input device is a keyboard, the most widely used input method for business computer applications. A direct input function is completed each time you touch a key. This action demands a response from the control unit of the CPU. Under control of the input-output module of the operating system, the control unit places each keystroke in memory. The supervisor program allocates memory and keeps track of your work so that each keystroke is added to the text area set aside for your job.

At the same time as your keystroke is recorded in memory, your input is *echoed* in the form of an output—a display on the video screen of your microcomputer. Thus, in response to your actions as a user, the computer performs direct input and output to support each keystroke. Later, your inputs will cause the system to save your text to a disk device and, when you are ready, to generate a printed output.

Inputs can cause more extensive operations as well. For example, when you edit a text document, the computer responds by reformatting the entire text file to make room for the characters you insert or delete.

Nothing happens until people tell computers what to do. No value results until accurate, reliable outputs are delivered to designated users on a timely basis. Input starts with a user action and output represents a response to user inputs.

## Input Methods

Input generally involves some manual action by a user or operator. This means that input is one of the most costly functions within a computer system. The manual nature of input also means that this function is subject to human errors. In turn, the user is challenged to design and apply controls that assure quality and accuracy of information. Methods for control are stressed in the discussions that follow, which identify and describe a number of input methods:

- Keyboard
- Speech
- Graphics
- Document reading
- Magnetic card.

**Keyboard**

The principle of *keyboard* input needs no elaboration. A user depresses keys that represent the letters, numbers, or symbols to be entered. Many types and varieties of keyboards are available. The most widely used is the alphanumeric keyboard like the one found on typewriters and microcomputers. This style of keyboard sometimes is called "QWERTY" after the positions of the alphabet keys at the left of the top row of letters.

User input also can take place with numeric keypads like those on Touch-Tone telephones, cash registers, or automatic teller machines. The functions are the same as those for typewriter-style keyboards, except that only numbers and two symbols are available.

With any keyboard device, keystrokes are recorded in memory and echoed through displays. For telephones, audible tones are created for direct entry of dialing signals into switching computers. As appropriate, the entered data are recorded on a magnetic medium for later entry or processed immediately to complete the input process.

■ **User Control.**    As with all input operations, users have the greatest responsibilities with and concerns for control over validity and accuracy of data. The quality of input governs the quality of processing and output. In other words, users get out of a system only what they put in. For this reason, authorization and validation of inputs are critical controls that should be applied to the level necessary to meet user needs.

Many techniques are used to apply authorization controls. To illustrate, consider what happens when a user processes a transaction at an automatic teller machine (ATM). To initiate input, the user enters a plastic card with an encoded account number. The computer checks to be sure that the account is active and valid. After the card has been accepted, a second check is performed to be sure that the card is not lost or stolen. The user enters a personal identification number (PIN). When this entry is accepted, the user can follow procedures that can involve depositing or withdrawing money.

For every entry of money values made by a user, the computer requests *validation* of the information. A validation operation controls the correctness and accuracy of input. A correctness check might verify that the transaction is being processed against the proper account. An accuracy control determines that the values entered are exact and can be used for processing. An accuracy control, for example, might verify that the amount of a deposit or withdrawal is right. The user presses a key to indicate that the amount is correct or another key to indicate it is incorrect. If the amount is incorrect, the user has a chance to correct the entry.

The ATM technique uses interactive validation. For entry of batches of data, operators sometimes enter all fields twice. One operator captures the data, another keys the same data into the same stored file. The computer checks to be sure values match. If the entries don't match, the field is marked and must be checked and corrected before input is accepted.

Another validation technique is to produce an output listing of data entries and to read these against the source documents to assure accuracy.

Immediate display of information reflecting data input helps to assure the accuracy, reliability, and quality of data resources. In this photo, a user receives immediate, graphic feedback to validate the processing of inputs.

If entries are made through a Touch-Tone telephone, the system can read back the input values for user validation through an audio response capability (described below).

No information can be any more accurate and reliable than the inputs that are processed. The computer industry has a longstanding saying to describe this principle: "Garbage in, garbage out."

## Speech

Today, users literally can talk to some computers to achieve data input. The term *speech recognition* identifies three approaches to spoken input. One method uses a limited, defined command set. That is, the user speaks only certain words or numbers. These are input and processed in much the same way as program language or application commands. An example can be seen in automated warehouse distribution systems. An operator examines storage location instructions written on packages and speaks into a microphone. The operator uses a limited set of phrases and numbers as working commands. The system responds by setting the switches needed to deliver articles to the location described in spoken commands.

A second method is still in work in developmental laboratories and is expected to become available in the near future. Under this method, users address computers in normal vocabulary. For example, you can dictate a letter directly to a computer, eliminating the need for direct keyboarding or dictation transcription. The computer translates spoken words into data or text through use of an internal dictionary, enters the data or text into memory, and also displays the translated input on a screen or generates a printed output. Instead of being limited to a brief command set, this approach has capacities for handling a vocabulary of tens of thousands of words.

Speech also is being processed by computerized communication systems in its natural form. For example, telephone messages can be accepted and stored on magnetic media by *voice store and forward* devices. The user receives a notice that a message is waiting and retrieves the recording through use of a Touch-Tone telephone. Speech represents valid input under these systems. Processing takes place for files that *digitize* the sounds for computer storage. Outputs are in audio form.

■ **User Control.**    Speech input can be used for a variety of purposes. One application is for file inquiry. If the data accessed are not confidential, authorization is not a problem. If entries are to be processed and will modify the content of user application files, users may be required to speak an identification number, also called a *password*, to authorize access. Accuracy can be checked by causing the system to repeat audio instructions or by displaying a translation. Then, the system can request that the user validate the input through a spoken or keyboard entry.

## Graphics

*Graphic* inputs can be completed by drawing images or pointing to positions on a sensing device and instructing the software to create lines or shapes at the indicated locations. Note that these inputs involve images and are different from data inputs that are translated to graphic outputs by special software like the modules included in spreadsheet packages.

The most widely used graphic input device is the mouse, a device with a rolling ball that is moved on a desk top. As the mouse moves, the motion is mirrored through movement of a cursor or locator arrow on a video display. The mouse has one, two, or three buttons, or switches, that can be used to communicate with the system. With the mouse, a user can select from menus of lines or shapes that can be included in the image being created. The mouse also can be used to select tones or color values from a *palette,* or graphics menu.

Additional graphics input devices include the tablet, light-sensing stylus, touch screen, and TV camera. A *tablet* is a flat surface on which an artist can draw with a pointed instrument. Positions and lines traced on the tablet are echoed on a display screen. Artists or designers can draw directly on a screen with a pen-like, light-sensing device. A bright cursor is sensed by the user, who can draw lines or mark points to create images directly on a display screen with a pen-like *stylus.* A *touch-screen* system displays images for user interaction. Instead of entering data through a keyboard, the user performs input by touching portions of the displayed images. A TV camera can be used for direct input into systems that record the images on magnetic media and permit users to manipulate or change those images.

Graphic images can be input directly to computers through support from special software and imaging devices, such as graphics tablets.

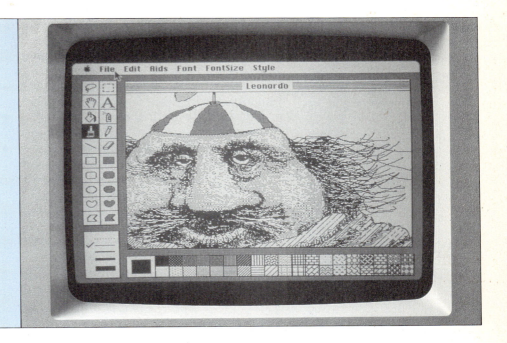

**User Control.**   Graphics data are not subject to the same kinds of authorization and validation controls as those for text and numerical input. The reason is that the user interacts with the system at all times when input takes place. The user is in control. The user decides when a graphic input is satisfactory because there are no standards of accuracy for images—acceptability lies in the judgment of the user. Graphic inputs are creative and are not subjected to the kinds of accuracy checks applied to text and numbers through comparison or balancing operations.

## Document Reading

Techniques for direct *document reading* input attack the basic problem, identified above, that manual techniques are slow, costly, and prone to error. The idea of document reading is to encode data in graphic or printed form on documents that are known to be accurate. Then, these imprints can be read automatically into a computer—with assured accuracy—at a fraction of the cost associated with key entry. Common techniques for document reading input include the following:

- The coded labels used by supermarkets to enter product descriptions and cause the computer to enter descriptions and prices are part of a system known as *universal product code (UPC)*. The bars, or lines, on the labels—and the spaces between them—are readable by laser devices built into checkout counters.

- *Optical character reading (OCR)* devices read printed, typewritten, or handwritten entries on sheets of paper, labels, garment tags, or sales slips. This method also is used for input under some credit card sales recording systems. You have experienced this method if you have made a department store purchase in which the salesperson reads the tag on a garment with a pen-like device, known as an *optical wand*. The wand is a fiber-optic device that senses and reads printed information. Full pages from typewritten manuscripts or printed books can be read directly into computers by special OCR units called *page readers*. Devices also exist that will read handwritten numbers and letters from special sales slips directly into computers. A large shoe store chain uses this technique in thousands of retail outlets to record information on styles of shoes sold.

- The coding of numbers at the bottoms of checks and deposit slips issued by banks implements a technique known as *magnetic ink character recognition (MICR)*. The information on the check identifies the account number of the depositor and the bank and/or branch where the account is held. Without a capability of this type, it would have been impossible for banks to process the more than 40 billion checks currently written each year in the United States.

- Another example of document input, *optical mark reading,* will be familiar to every student. A major application is test scoring. Students mark positions on an answer sheet to indicate responses to questions. The answer sheets are fed through reading devices that identify answer selections and compute scores. This method also is used for opinion surveys and other applications that require gathering of data that can be represented in multiple choice formats.

■ **User Control.**  A major advantage of document reading systems is that control can be maintained by the originator of the input media. That is, computers or printing devices can be used to generate documents or imprints of known accuracy. These documents, in turn, can be used with extremely high levels of reliability. For example, check reading devices in banks operate at accuracy levels of better than 99 percent. However, there are costs and controls necessary in preparing the documents to be used for input. Users and systems designers should verify that the costs of preparing and distributing the documents are more than offset by the savings realized through improved input efficiency.

## Magnetic Card

Hundreds of millions of wallet-size plastic cards are designed for automatic computer input applications. These cards contain stripes of magnetic material that are encoded for automatic reading by devices attached to computers. Stores, restaurants, and hotels secure credit approval through machines that read this magnetically encoded information. Cards used for access to automatic teller machines operate on the same principle, as do most gasoline credit cards.

The same method is used to encode identification information on employee badges. These badges can be used to control access to buildings or for attendance and production reporting from factory work areas. Magnetically encoded plastic cards serve both for data entry and also as authorization controls, since they enable users to gain access to ATMs and other computer systems.

■  **User Control.**  With plastic cards, considerable measures of control are maintained by the companies that issue the cards and the users to whom they are issued. A potential problem centers around misuse of cards that are lost or stolen. There is extensive underground traffic in stolen credit cards. This means that issuing organizations and users must be alert continuously to avoid misuse of plastic cards. The issuing organizations must have rapid-response capabilities to put cards on hold or to cancel them if they are lost or stolen. Individual users must be aware of the exposure to loss that is involved in use of credit cards and must act quickly to report loss or theft of cards.

## ■  Output Methods and Devices

Outputs are the main reason that information systems exist. All users need outputs. End users apply information to perform their jobs. Managers base decisions and plans on information outputs. Also, computer professionals require outputs that are used in building and maintaining systems.

Outputs, as you know, are generated under control of software that determines format and content. Hardware devices, reviewed below, determine speeds and formats available in producing outputs. For each category of device, a discussion is presented on capabilities that can lead to user selection of specific features or capacities. Output devices are reviewed according to the following categories:

• Displays
• Printers
• Plotters
• Film
• Audio

### Displays

Output displays are temporary presentations that can be read by users and can be used for interaction between a user and a computer system. *Video displays* like those built into most microcomputers illustrate just how temporary displays tend to be. The displays are formed by electronic beams that scan the inside surfaces of display tubes. A display is formed in an operation that takes one-thirtieth of a second. To keep the display available for your viewing, it must be "refreshed" with a new scan pattern that is repeated 30 times each second. If the scan pattern stops, the display disappears.

Video displays are the most popular form of visual output. However, there are other methods that include *light-emitting diode (LED)* displays, *liquid crystal displays (LCD)*, and *plasma* devices.

Light emitting diodes form images through points of light that can be set to off or on conditions. LED displays are rugged and relatively inexpensive. They are valuable for situations in which outputs are in the form of data only (without graphics requirements). A popular application for LED displays is for mobile terminals in police cars. Many scoreboards in sports stadiums use LED principles.

LCD devices form images by applying electric currents to surfaces that respond in patterns that form numbers and letters. Most digital watches use LCD techniques. At this writing, LCDs are used for most lap-top microcomputers.

Gas plasma displays are felt to be a wave of the future as output devices. At this writing, their use is limited by the fact that they are more expensive than the other methods. However, plasma displays have a number of advantages: They are bright and clear and also are flat and convenient to mount. This type of display is being used in some models of lap-top computers. Acceptance is expected to increase strongly as prices decline.

Display outputs from computers can range from this LCD screen of a portable computer to large scoreboards in stadiums.

■ **Capabilities.**   The main selection factor for display devices is visibility for the user. This factor has led to experimentation and to some alternatives that are worth considering. To illustrate, when microcomptuers were introduced, most displays presented white characters against black backgrounds. Users complained of eyestrain. This led to introduction of displays with green letters. Some displays also use amber letters against a black background. Still others present black-on-white images that attempt to replicate the clarity of printed documents.

Another factor in display selection is *image resolution*. This factor centers around the way images are formed. A computer-generated display is produced by marking or illuminating a series of points on a screen. The closer together and the better defined these display points are, the clearer the image they form. A number of alternatives are available for screens with different resolution capabilities. A user or a professional who establishes standards for a using organization should consider trade-offs of image clarity, brightness, and cost from the user perspective. Users should be provided with units that are comfortable to operate under the working conditions involved. For example, a user who spends less than an hour a day at a terminal will have different eyestrain conditions than a person who is at the keyboard all day long.

## Printers

A *printer* is an output device that forms readable images on paper. Printers are used primarily for character outputs (letters, numbers, and symbols), though rough graphic images can be formed through a series of imprinted dots. Printers come in hundreds of makes, types, and sizes that can be grouped according to three major categories: character, line, and page.

■ **Character Printers.**   *Character printers* imprint one character of information at a time. The major use for character printers is within microcomputer work stations. The most widely used type of character printer is called a *dot matrix* printer. The print mechanism forms characters as a matrix of points on a character-sized imprint area. Wires, or pins, embedded in the print head are pushed forward to form images. The wires strike a ribbon to create an impression. The quality of matrix imprints varies with the number of pin positions in a printing mechanism. The greater the number of pin positions, the greater the clarity of printed impressions. Among character printers, dot-matrix devices are the highest in speed (up to 280 characters per second) and lowest in quality. For this reason, they sometimes are called *draft printers*.

Another type of character printer has characters that are formed in metal or plastic. Usually, these images are mounted on a mechanism that moves or rotates into position over the intended print area. The character images strike a ribbon to form an impression. These units, often called *letter quality* printers, produce images that are higher in quality than matrix printers. However, operation is slower, with speeds ranging between 10 and 75 characters per second.

An in-between level of performance and print quality also is available with *near-letter-quality* printers. These use a matrix print head with a large number of pins. Characters are formed through multiple striking actions of the print head. This results in an impression quality that is in between draft outputs from matrix printers and letter-quality units. Output speeds are also at intermediate levels. Available models generate text at speeds of up to 100 characters per second.

■ **Line Printers.**   *Line printers* get their name from the fact that they imprint complete lines in a single operation. Some line printers have a matrix print head at each print position along the width of a line. Others use a chain containing one or more character sets. The chain rotates behind the paper and is struck by a series of hammers mounted in front of the paper. Ribbons in front of the hammers form images.

Line printers are high-speed devices generally used in conjunction with relatively large computers. Some of these devices are used with super-microcomputers, but most support larger systems. Output speeds range from 100 to 2,000 complete print lines per minute.

■ **Page Printers.**   A *page printer* generates entire pages of output with each operating cycle. These devices also are called laser printers or *xerographic printers* because of the technologies used. Virtually all page printers are adaptations of the same technology used in office copiers. That is, impressions are created on light-sensitive drums that attract a magnetic-based imaging material. The image then is transferred from the drum to paper. On office copiers, images are formed by exposing original documents to light-sensitive drums. On computer page printers, the images are formed by a beam of laser light that scans the surface of the drum to form the image.

When they first were introduced, page printers were extremely high in cost and output speed, with initial units handling between 5,000 and 20,000 lines of text per minute on continuous rolls of paper. More recently, wider ranges of capabilities have been added. Today's high-speed laser printers form images on sheets of paper at rates of up to 7,200 pages per hour. These units can imprint both sides of the paper and can collate and staple full documents.

At the low end of the page printer scale are units designed for use with microcomputers. Outputs range from eight to 20 pages per minute.

A special feature of laser-type page printers is that they can reproduce and mix both text and graphics on the same document. Because of this capability, laser-imaging printers are used widely for desktop publishing applications. This feature lets the computer print the form and complete text and data entries at the same time. This particular application can save the organization the expense of printing and storing supplies of preprinted forms.

An important characteristic of page printers lies in image quality, which is determined by the density of imprint dots in the image area. Measurements are in number of dots per square inch (DPI) of image area. Models now on the market range from 300 DPI to 2,500 DPI. Greater image quality usually carries higher costs.

■ **Capabilities.**  The main factors that affect printed output capabilities include speed, image quality, and line width. Speed and image quality are discussed above in connection with descriptions of individual types of units. Line width is a factor that must be related to individual applications. In general, computer printers handle standard paper widths of 8.5 and 14.75 inches. The wider widths often are needed for spreadsheet applications and financial reports. In evaluating printers, users should consider the types of documents to be issued.

Still another factor is the availability of printers with color output capabilities. Because they were expensive when they first appeared, these devices are not in general use. However, they are dropping in cost and growing in popularity. Currently, color printers are used only for special applications.

## Plotters

*Plotters* are output devices that draw images and characters by controlling movement of a pen-like stylus across a sheet of paper or drawing film. Plotters come in models that produce one-color images or that have multiple writing devices, each of which draws in a separate color.

Each plotter has a mechanism that drives a stylus back and forth along the width of the drawing surface. In addition, to do complete drawings, it is necessary to move the stylus along the length of the drawing surface. Existing plotters handle this requirement in two different ways. One technique, used in a *flat-bed plotter,* is to move a bridge-type structure lengthwise over the paper. This means that the same drive device supports movement in two directions. Another technique is used on *drum-type plotters.* This has a drive mechanism that goes back and forth in one plane only. The other dimension of movement is achieved by mounting the paper on a rotating drum and moving the paper back and forth to achieve the other movement directlon. Drum-type plotters tend to be less expensive while flat-bed units tend to deliver greater precision in drawing images.

Plotters are used to generate graphics that can support business applications and also to produce engineering and architectural plans and drawings. Graphic outputs like those produced from spreadsheet packages can be generated on plotters.

■ **Capabilities.**  Plotters tend to operate slowly. Speed generally is not a factor in selection of these devices. The most important criteria generally are the precision with which images can be drawn and a determination of whether color is needed or whether monochrome images are acceptable.

## Film

Applications with high-volume outputs often use *COM (Computer Output, Microfilm)* devices. These units record pages of output as miniature images on photographic film. The film used can be in rolls or in sheets called *fiche.* COM devices can record data directly onto film through use of laser beams. Another method is to focus a camera on a video display from which each page-sized image is photographed.

Other types of film outputs also are gaining use for special applications. For example, some graphics computers can output color images to slides or to movie film. Many TV commercials and animated films now are produced on computers and recorded on videotape or motion picture film.

Still another type of film output is used in publishing. For example, many newspapers now use computerized typesetting and page makeup. The makeup programs are used to position type and illustrations on pages. When images are stored in computers, it is possible to output directly either to film that is used to create printing plates or directly to printing plates.

■ **Capabilities.**   The most critical capability for microfilm is to reduce the bulk of stored records. Documents that would occupy complete file cabinets can be recorded on a few rolls of film. Another value is that film provides *archival quality.* That is, the images on properly processed film are permanent. This can be an advantage over paper records that fade or disintegrate over time.

The main disadvantage is that microfilm cannot be viewed directly by users. Special magnifying readers are needed. Also, it is expensive to make enlargements from microfilm if full-sized documents are needed.

Output speeds and image sizes are of special importance in selecting devices that generate output on film. For example, most COM devices are attached to mainframe systems. Speed is a factor because of the amount of output to be generated and also because higher output speeds minimize processing demands on mainframes. Slide, motion picture, and publication film can tie up computing equipment for comparatively long periods. For example, a computer might have to generate images at 2,500 DPI for a newspaper-sized sheet of film. Without high-capacity processors and large memories, a single page could tie up a computer for an hour or more. High-volume graphics outputs require extensive CPU, memory, and storage capacities.

## Audio

*Audio response* is an output capability under which computers speak to people. Two approaches are used. Under one, the computer stores a series of sounds actually recorded by human voices. The audio segments are combined to form spoken messages. Under the other approach, an *audio synthesizer* is used to generate the sound of a human voice electronically.

Either type of output is driven by software that reads data and text files and reproduces words or numbers in voice-like sounds. This capability is used for applications that involve low output volumes (speech outputs are many times slower than high-speed printing). Another factor is user convience. For example, a number of banks provide a capability under which users can call a special number to connect them to a computer. When the user enters an account number on the telephone keypad, the computer reads the balance amount.

An advantage of this approach is that tens of millions of Touch-Tone telephones can function as computer terminals.

■ **Capabilities.**  As indicated, the main capability lies in user convenience. A relatively inexpensive peripheral device can put computers directly in touch with information users via telephone.

## Input and Output as User Applications

This review brings you to the end of a group of chapters dealing with computer hardware and software. This and preceding chapters deal with specific types of hardware components. In concluding this section of the book, recognize that each component is part of a larger entity, a computer system that encompasses the functions of input, processing, output, and storage. The system, in turn, must be configured to support user needs and company applications. Human knowledge and imagination can play major roles in bringing together the hardware components needed to support processing of specific jobs. Some illustrations of applications that make creative use of hardware and software capabilities are described below.

### Utility Turnaround Documents

A *turnaround document* is a computer output document that can be used for later input. Many public utility companies issue customer bills that have identification numbers and amounts recorded in optical character recognition (OCR) fonts. When a customer sends in a portion of the bill with a payment, the computer-generated bill becomes an input document. Accuracy is high and costs of processing input are low.

### ATM Cards

Bank customers who elect to use automatic teller machine (ATM) services receive a plastic card for input authorization. For this application, an important feature of the ATM card is that it is set up to permit customers to authorize deposits to and withdrawals from their accounts.

This capability has been recognized as an opportunity. Recently, a number of retailers and oil companies have elected to make it possible for customers to use ATM cards for purchases. In the oil company application, a customer passes an ATM card through a special terminal. When the card is accepted, the customer enters a personal identification number provided by the bank. The terminal reads the purchase information from the gas pump. This transaction causes the integrated system that ties together the bank's network with the oil company's to withdraw money from the customer's account and deposit it to an account maintained by the oil company. The transaction is complete, or ''perfected,'' right at the gas pump. The customer gains convenience. The company gains immediate access to cash.

Because the transaction withdraws money from the purchaser's account, this application is known as a ''debit card'' purchase. The debit card is different from a credit card, which is used for charge purchases to be billed to the customer and paid for later.

**Touch-Tone Phones**

A large manufacturing company has installed a computer-controlled crane that moves heavy objects or containers of parts to points throughout the factory. The computer treats the entire factory as a large checkerboard and can move parts to any position on the factory floor under user direction. Users wanted to be able to interact with the computer from any point in the factory. It would not have been satisfactory to require users to go to a limited number of keyboard-operated terminals. Instead, the in-place telephone system, with stations all over the factory, was adapted for this job. Production employees or supervisors who require parts to be moved simply pick up the nearest telephone and punch in the job number and the location to which the bin of parts is to be moved. The computer picks up finished work, moves parts to storage, then moves the bin to the next location when a worker is ready to perform a production operation.

A well-known business executive has been quoted as saying: "Nothing happens around here until somebody sells something." That certainly is true for the organization as a system. For a computer information system, this idea can be paraphrased: "Nothing happens until a user creates an input and no value is received until an output is delivered." It also is true, of course, that no outputs could be delivered without processing and that systems rely on storage capabilities to maintain essential data resources. Putting it another way: Input, processing, output, and storage are a set. All elements are necessary. But each element also has its own identity and makes its own, unique contribution in providing information to users.

## Chapter Summary

- Input and output devices are the channels through which people and computers communicate.

- Input encompasses two functions: data capture into a form compatible for computer processing, and data entry to place data within the computer for processing. For some applications, these functions are combined to complete direct data entry.

- Output encompasses processing, display, printing, and recording associated with delivery of computing results.

- Input methods and devices include keyboard, speech, graphics, document reading, and magnetic card reading.

- Regardless of input form, it is necessary to establish controls to assure the accuracy of information through the processing and output operations within the overall system.

- Output methods include displays, printers, plotters, film, and audio. Each method presents a series of capability ranges and trade-offs that figure in selection and computer system configuration.
- Some applications depend heavily on input and on-line devices for implementation. Examples include use of turnaround documents for utility bills, use of ATM cards for direct payment in retail purchase transactions, and use of Touch-Tone telephones for applications involving data input and audio output.

## Questions for Review

1. What functions are involved in computer input and what is the purpose and result of each?
2. What is direct data entry and what are its results?
3. What forms of output are available?
4. What procedures are followed for keyboard input and how can controls be established over entered data?
5. How is speech used in data input and what options are available?
6. How can graphic data be entered into a computer?
7. What is meant by document reading and what are some techniques for input from printed documents?
8. What range of options is available for printed output and what are the trade-offs among these alternatives?
9. What are plotters and how are they used in computer output?
10. What are audio outputs and what are some of their uses?

## Questions for Thought

1. What are the major trade-offs between keyboarding and document reading as input techniques?
2. Why is it vital to establish control over data accuracy during input procedures and at what points should accuracy be tested and verified?
3. Why is an ATM card used in retail transaction called a ''debit card'' and what are the advantages of debit cards over credit cards to retailers?
4. What are the advantages and limitations of speech as an input method?
5. What are the trade-offs between draft, near-letter-quality, and letter-quality printers for computer output?

## Terms

| | |
|---|---|
| archival quality | magnetic ink character recognition (MICR) |
| audio response | |
| audio synthesizer | near-letter quality |
| authorization | optical character recognition (OCR) |
| character printer | optical mark reading |
| Computer Output, Microfilm (COM) | optical wand |
| data capture | output |
| data entry | page printer |
| digitize | page reader |
| direct entry | palette |
| document reading | password |
| dot matrix | plasma |
| draft printer | plotter |
| drum-type plotter | printer |
| echo | speech recognition |
| fiche | stylus |
| flat-bed plotter | tablet |
| graphic | touch screen |
| image resolution | turnaround document |
| input | universal product code (UPC) |
| keyboard | validation |
| letter quality | video display |
| light-emitting diode (LED) | voice store and forward |
| line printer | xerographic printer |
| liquid crystal display (LCD) | |

## MINICASE

**Situation:**

John Kinnear, president of EatRite, Inc., is both proud and confused by the rapid growth that his company has enjoyed. John and two employees started the company three years ago in a tiny warehouse space. The line of health foods marketed by EatRite has caught on well enough so the company is planning to move into distribution and processing quarters five times as large as those presently occupied.

Kinnear recognizes that he will have to computerize at least some of his operations. He is not concerned about the computer itself. Working with a consultant, he has selected a minicomputer and software that can support input and output devices situated throughout his facility. He is concerned at the moment with picking the input and output devices to be used for the following applications:

- Accepting orders over the phone from customers, who operate retail stores and chains
- Processing purchase orders for suppliers
- Checking in receipts of supplies and goods through use of a fiber-optic wand that reads labels on boxes and/or packages
- Reporting on production completion by workers on a new packaging line to be opened
- Preparing invoices for customers.

**Decision Making: Your Turn**

1. From the information you have, identify and describe the problem to be solved.
2. Identify alternatives that could be followed to avoid or solve the problem.
3. On the basis of the limited information you have: a) Identify additional information you would gather if you were dealing with this problem in a real situation. b) Identify the solution that appears best on the basis of the information that is available and explain your reasons for this selection.
4. What lessons are to be learned from this situation?

## Projects

1. Go to the computer center at your school and make a list of the different input and output devices you see. List these devices according to their function, input or output. Identify each device according to the type of input or output performed, using the categories presented in this chapter as a basis for your classification.

2. Look at some computer publications. Choose a device with a specific category and capacity, such as a low-priced laser page printer. Identify a number of manufacturers who market products that fall within this category. Compare performance characteristics (speed, quality, and cost).

3. Visit a local computer store for demonstrations of two microcomputer output devices. As an alternative, if you have access to a microcomputer, print a document such as a spreadsheet or letter on two different types of output devices. Report on what you saw and what you learned.

# Computer Information Systems

Computer information systems don't just happen. People have to build them. Analysis of information needs, as well as design and development of systems was at one time the sole domain of computer professionals. Today, users play key roles. Methods have been devised to enhance communication between users and computer professionals to enable users to take an active role in building their own systems. Chapter 13 discusses a four-step life cycle for the development of computer information systems, as well as some of the alternatives available to users.

Chapter 13          Systems Development

# Chapter Outline

# Systems Development

## Briefing Memo

TO: Information Users
FROM: T. Rohm, W. Stewart

Even with "user friendly" systems and off-the-shelf software packages, user applications don't happen automatically. Systems must be developed carefully. Since user needs vary widely, systems development methods should be flexible enough to adapt to individual situations.

An important feature of the chapter is that it establishes a perspective by differentiating between development of large-scale systems for organizations and those you might want to implement for your personal needs. This chapter also provides the information you can use to plan for and develop applications to meet your own needs.

## End-User Perspective

"This could be a good opportunity for you, Tina," Tom Wrightman explained. 'Our application will give you a look at a total system. The assignment should fit in with your studies and your future plans."

Tom was referring to Tina's position as a student in the information systems program at Central State. Tina was being invited to develop a microcomputer system to handle integrated accounting applications at Vitamin Distributors, Inc., where she worked part time running a payroll system.

"We've ordered everything that the computer store people say we need," Tom explained. "We'll upgrade our microcomputer with a hard disk. The software package is the newest one. We should be able to start processing invoices, controlling inventory, and preparing our general ledger at the beginning of the year, less than a month from now."

Tina became alarmed. "Not so fast, Tom," she said. 'Do you understand what's involved in developing a new application?"

Tom remained optimistic. "This isn't a new application," he said. "The software is standard. All we have to do is set it up and run with it."

"Hardly," Tina responded. "This is not a trivial job. To begin, it will be necessary to match the processing design of the programs with your own system. It would be highly unusual to find a perfect match between your procedures and the standardized program. If there are differences, you have to decide whether you want to change the way you run your company or to modify the standard program. Whatever you decide, changes will be necessary and they will take time. This is unavoidable, even if all that's involved is to document your present procedures and compare them with the programs you have bought.

"Even after your needs are identified and modifications to your system take place, initiating a new system is still a lot of work. You have to create your files, then load your data. This could take months. Your business isn't as small as you think. You have 2,000 customers and almost 10,000 products. Even if you knew what information you wanted in your files, it could take months to set the system up.

"What I suggest," Tina continued, "is that we start work as soon as possible and figure out what we need. Your interest in this project will be a big advantage. You will be the main user of this system. Your involvement is necessary to success in its development."

# The Point: End-Users Need to Be Involved

Tina's final words hold the key to effective development of information systems: All systems should be designed to serve their users. If systems are to be effective and adopted by users, users must be involved. Not only must user needs guide systems development, but they must serve as the basis for evaluating effectiveness of information systems.

When it comes to systems development, users are the customers of computer professionals. The users are buying services—and a system that will meet their information needs. As knowledgeable customers, it is the responsibility of users to know enough about computers and information systems to make their needs understood by the computer professionals, to assess the value of their purchases, and to estabish and get approval for budgets to be spent. Then, it is up to users and computer professionals to work together to make sure that plans and budgets are coordinated and followed. This requires close monitoring of systems development activities. This chapter describes the systems development process and what users must know to assure that their information needs are met.

## What Is Systems Development?

*Systems development* is an organized, orderly, controlled process for creating or modifying information systems to meet the information needs of users. A

Systems development is handled best as a team effort that involves users, systems analysts, programmers, and other computer professionals.

*process* is a planned series of steps that can be controlled—and directed to produce a specific set of results. Systems development requires a special type of process to deal with the necessities for user participation and for support by computer professionals. To achieve this level of coordination, systems development projects should be team efforts.

## Lessons From History

Systems development techniques have evolved from recognition of necessity in the information systems field. During the early days of computer use in business, most systems were developed under an "ad hoc" approach. Basically, this meant that systems were developed a step at a time, with no long-range plans and goals. Needs and problems were addressed as they were recognized. If a computer professional didn't understand a user requirement, questions were asked. If the *systems analyst* or programmer was satisfied that there was no problem, he or she went ahead independently.

This proved to be unproductive. The systems analyst is a computer professional who helps users solve problems and to devise information systems that are responsive to their information needs. To do this, a systems analyst receives requests from users, researches existing systems and procedures, identifies opportunities for improvement, collaborates with users to design new systems, then oversees the technical aspects of new-system implementation.

During the era when business-oriented users spoke a different language from technically oriented analysts, there was a tendency for each party to function independently. One result was that many systems were designed on the basis of misunderstandings. Systems were developed that were elegant technically but which did not solve the user's problem. Experiences of this type occurred with sufficient frequency so that it became apparent that effective systems development required close cooperation—a team effort.

These lessons about the need for teamwork proved costly. During the 1950s and 1960s, many projects involving development of major information systems overran their budgets by millions of dollars. It was estimated, for example, that one major computerized reservation system overran its original budget by some $40 million dollars. A pioneering banking system developed overruns of even greater magnitude.

Another alternative to a project structure has been a "do it yourself" approach. Users would attempt to design and implement systems without assistance from computer professionals. This method can sound simple at the outset. But, as in the scenario about Vitamin Distributors, this approach can lead to pitfalls and unexpected problems. The lessons of history establish that the best solutions for systems development needs lie in teamwork between users and computer professionals.

Without cooperation between systems analysts and users, experience has shown, it is virtually impossible to maintain schedules and to produce systems that are useful to users.

## Systems Development and the Decision-Making Process

Information systems development, as indicated above, requires an orderly, controlled process. Individual systems development projects generally are set up to include a series of steps at which progress can be checked and decisions made on the quality and value of proposals for improving existing systems or replacing them with new ones.

This means that each step, or stage, in the systems development process provides an opportunity for profitable use of the decision-making process introduced in Chapter 2 and reviewed in a number of subsequent chapters. The decision-making process, recall, involves four basic steps:

- Identify and define the problem or need.
- Gather information and evaluate alternatives.
- Select the best course of action.
- Implement the decision and evaluate results.

This decision-making structure helps to shape and implement a step-by-step approach that represents a practical approach to the development and management of systems within organizations. The systems development approach works because of built-in reporting and review requirements designed to assure that decisions will be considered carefully. Reviews at key points in the development cycle make it possible to alter systems plans or to terminate projects that run into problems before major expenses are incurred for a system that is not useful or does not meet the needs of users.

Information systems must support the operational and decision-making activities of users. Therefore, user review and evaluation are keys to successful development projects.

In organizations that require large systems, systems development may be part of the *capital budgeting* procedures. Capital budgeting is a planning process for the control of major investments. Responsibility for capital budgeting generally is assigned to a committee of top managers. In many organizations, the creation of new information systems involves expenditures that qualify in the same category as construction of new buildings or the purchase of new manufacturing equipment.

## A Systems View

Each information system, as you know, consists of four elements: people, procedures, data, and equipment. There can be a tendency, for example, for project team members to become preoccupied with equipment or procedures (particularly programs). However, the problems encountered most commonly relate to people or data. Members of a systems development team must recognize that all four elements are vital and that attention to these elements must be balanced and must reflect the relationships among them. System elements and their relevance to systems development are described below.

**People.**   People make up the project teams that develop systems. Team members include users, managers, and computer professionals. Users function both as customers and as advisers who identify the requirements for a system and determine, at each step in development, whether the project is on the right track. The managers involved in specific projects usually are involved in the departments or organizations for which a system is being developed. Computer professionals on project teams include systems analysts, application programmers, and systems programmers—the technical support specialists responsible for operating system and equipment configurations.

**Procedures.**   In an operational company, there will be existing procedures for conducting business. These must be understood thoroughly before improvements to the existing information system can be made. In most systems development efforts, new or modified procedures must be developed. If suitable software exists, programs generally must be documented for the benefit of the computer professionals and users who will work on the system. Also, users must indicate whether and what modifications may be necessary for existing software packages. To be effective, users must be involved actively in defining results and evaluating alternatives.

**Data.**   Data resources must exist to support current user operations. These data resources must be evaluated as a basis for a review that determines whether new data items must be added or whether the existing data files must be modified. In this sense, users take on responsibility for building and maintaining the data/information resources that represent a major asset for the using organization.

■ **Equipment.** Computer equipment is in a state of continuous flux as new, smaller, more powerful devices are introduced. In particular, current systems development projects often involve introduction of new tools for direct user operation. Included are terminals and microcomputers. Advances in data communications capabilities mean that many new systems involve the implementation of networks.

The comparison between creation of an information system and construction of a building holds true even after a system is in operation. Just as all buildings require maintenance, systems also require monitoring and modification. In one dramatic example, a large midwest bank surveyed recipients of reports produced by its computer center. The finding: More than 50 percent of the printed outputs had outlived their usefulness. These reports were no longer used, though they had once served a purpose. Savings by eliminating the unneeded applications ran to tens of thousands of dollars annually.

Development and operation of computer applications is a big investment. It pays for organizations to monitor and manage these activities. A systems development approach is essential for the development of an effective, efficient computer information system.

## Systems Development Life Cycle

The *systems development life cycle (SDLC)*, is a formal series of stages through which a system progresses. This traditional approach has been adopted by most medium- and large-sized organizations. For smaller systems like those you may encounter with microcomputers, the SDLC can be modified to correspond with the need. Also, life-cycle processes vary among organizations. Some life-cycle processes have as few as four stages. Others may have as many as 10 or 12. However, the same principles apply for almost any major systems development effort.

Each life cycle consists of a series of stages during which specific activities are completed by project team members and reviewed by management. At each review, management can authorize the project to continue, direct that changes be made, or even terminate the project. The life cycle discussed below is organized into four stages:

1. Planning
2. Analysis and design
3. Implementation
4. Post-implementation.

This flowchart identifies the sequence of steps and decisions within the systems development life cycle.

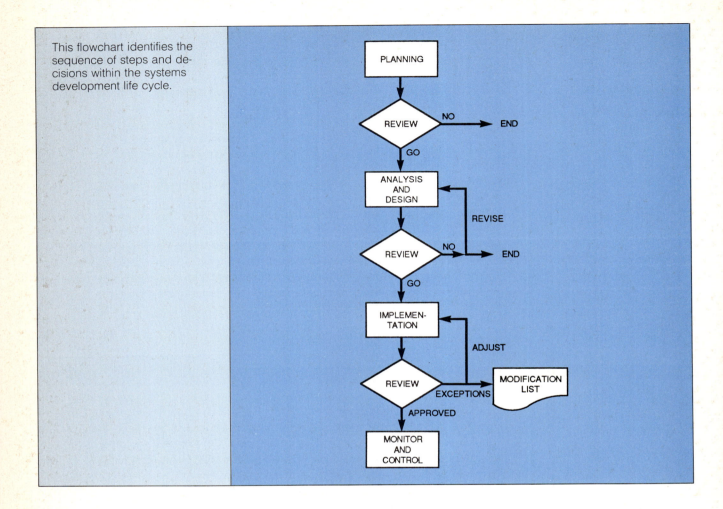

**Systems Development: Case Example**

As a basis for illustrating the systems development life-cycle descriptions that follow, consider a typical situation:

Carol, assistant purchasing agent for Machine Tools, Inc., a regional distributor of heavy duty machinery, reports on a systems development opportunity to Teri, the purchasing agent:

"I think this situation calls for a systems development study: I've been monitoring the time sheets for the staff that handles receiving and accounts payable reporting. Right now, we have two people on that job. They file copies of purchase orders, then match them with receiving reports when the goods arrive. When vendor invoices are received, they check to be sure that we have everything we ordered. Problems are directed to my attention. If everything matches, the invoices are approved for payment."

When Teri nodded, Carole continued: ''Volumes are growing. The payables clerks are keeping up with receiving reports. But they are falling behind on clearing invoices. We are losing some money because we are missing discounts. Some vendors allow cash discounts for early payment. We aren't clearing the invoices quickly enough to take advantage of some of these opportunities. In addition, overtime is beginning to mount. Between the two people, we are running 15 to 20 hours a week of overtime.''

Teri agreed. She reviewed a report Carol had prepared and referred it to the Systems Services group for consideration. The handling of this request for systems service is covered following descriptions that follow of each of the stages in the SDLC.

## Planning Stage

During the *planning stage,* a potential systems development project is defined. The planning step can be short and simple if it turns out that a project is not worthwhile. If a proposal has merit, this stage can include a detailed study on the feasibility of a computer application. If users and computer professionals agree on feasibility, they may develop a complete plan of work and schedule for a development project.

Possible reasons for terminating a project after a short review include discovery that the service already is available on an existing system without the knowledge of an inquiring user. Another possible reason for early termination is that a system to produce comparable results already is under development.

The planning stage of a systems development project starts with a review between users and systems analysts of user information needs and the feasibility of meeting those needs with computers.

Also, if the user's request can be met through use of a standard application package on a microcomputer, a full-blown development effort would not be needed. Instead, users could be assisted in development of their own application, as described later in this chapter.

During this initial stage, a rough, preliminary estimate is made to determine whether projected results of the proposed system offer potential benefits to the using organization. If benefits are identified, rough estimates are made about the cost of developing the system and realizing the benefits. The principle is that the user must be aware of benefits and costs and, at each stage of a project, must be willing to commit that the expense and effort are justified by the projected results. Without user commitments—support from computer professionals—effective systems development becomes highly doubtful.

■ **Case Scenario.** At Machine Tools, Inc., Carol's report on the receiving and accounts payable situation is referred to an experienced systems analyst, Raul. Raul studies the report, reviews documentation within the computer center on existing applications, and calls Carol for an appointment.

When they get together, their first step is to define the need. They develop a short, simple statement of need that establishes the overall objective for the investigation: "Develop a better method for tracking receipt of ordered materials, validating vendor invoices, and processing accounts payable. The resulting system should minimize staff time and take maximum advantage of available discounts."

This statement, Carole and Raul agree, sets goals for a potential systems project. Their next step is to determine whether a computer can help achieve those goals. Raul is ready for that question. He points out that computer applications already exist for issuing purchase orders and paying invoices. The recording of receipts and the checking of invoices are in-between steps that remained manual because they were small at the time systems were developed.

Raul says that it would be feasible to establish a computer file with records for open purchase orders. Receiving information could be entered into this file by inspectors in the receiving department. When invoices arrive, the accounts payable staff could check receiving information at terminals. If invoices match receiving records, payments could be authorized immediately. Problem situations could be referred to Carol, who could access computer files in resolving them.

"No sweat so far," says Raul, who adds that the elimination of overtime would more than cover the cost of setting up the needed files, programs, terminals, and procedures.

Raul and Carol plan another meeting. In the interim, Raul is to prepare a set of specifications for the new system. These will be sent to Carol for review with Teri before they get together again.

"It's all up to you," Raul stresses. 'Only the user can tell whether a system is worth developing and whether the costs of development are offset by benefits. Only users can measure the end-result benefits of any system."

## Analysis and Design Stage

The *analysis and design stage* involves two activities that are critical to the success of systems development:

*Systems analysis* is the study and documentation of existing information systems. The study typically begins with outputs. Analysts collect all reports or forms generated by an existing application. After outputs are understood, analysts review inputs and storage files. Their purpose is to identify sources for all of the inputs that must exist to produce the outputs. After outputs and inputs are identified, analysts document the processing that takes place within the system.

Systems analysis generally is a team effort that involves participation by users and computer professionals. A number of tools and techniques are used in systems analysis and design. These are identified and described later in this chapter.

The results of systems analysis serve as a basis for *systems design.* Systems design is an activity that applies the decision-making process to devise new systems that will deliver improvements over existing systems. Systems analysts and users identify alternatives for new or different equipment and procedures, as well as for modification of data files. New designs are evaluated in the light of the statement of need that guides the project. Design alternatives also are evaluated in terms of anticipated benefits and costs. The result of the design activity is a detailed specification that outlines the equipment, procedures, data, and people contributions to a new or modified system. These design specifi-

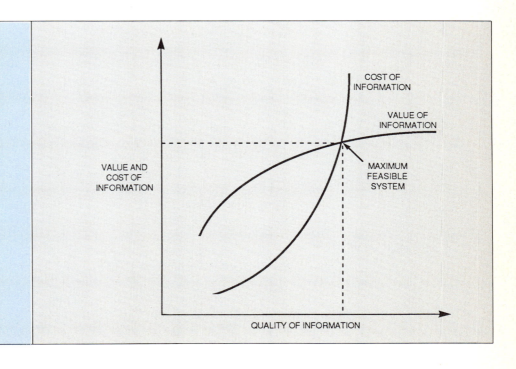

Trade-offs between the value and cost of information are illustrated in this graph. A system is feasible as long as the curve for values is higher than the curve for costs. The point at which the curves intersect is the maximum feasible system.

cations are reviewed, modified as necessary, and (when they are accepted) are used as guides in development and implementation of the new system.

The first result of the analysis and design phase should be a determination of whether to proceed with implementation of the system. If so, the project team must develop detailed specifications that state user needs. This *user specification* document becomes the basis for programming and other technical activities needed to implement a system.

■ **Case Scenario.**   To start the analysis process, Raul asks Carol to guide him on a *walk-through* of existing procedures. A walk-through is a structured review of an existing system or of documentation for a new system. A person who knows the system well identifies the elements of the system, how they are applied, and what results are produced at each step. The purpose of a walk-through is to create (or validate) documentation of application specifications and procedures.

Together, Raul and Carol observe the use of files of purchase order copies in the purchasing department. Then they review the procedures for receiving materials, recording descriptions on receiving report documents, and transmitting these to purchasing. As they go, Raul collects copies of all documents used. The walk-through continues through the procedures for receiving and processing vendor invoices.

This activity takes several days. After each portion of the system is reviewed, Raul documents his observations with a flowchart that describes the procedures on a step-by-step basis. Raul asks Carol to verify the procedures, with special attention to the steps within the system at which decisions are made or processing takes place.

''We have to understand two things,'' Raul explains. ''First, we have to identify processing steps and be sure controls are maintained in any new systems we develop. Second, we have to understand data transformations. These are the points at which data items are combined or changed through computation. Your job as the user is to verify that all of these steps are correct and necessary. Also, it is up to you to say whether any changes are needed or whether suggested changes will work. Without your knowledge of the basic business functions, it would be impossible to develop an effective system.''

Once Raul and Carol are satisfied that they have documented the existing system, including computer procedures for processing purchase orders and for paying vendors, they turn their attention to potential changes and improvements. Using the flowcharts they have developed, Raul points out that the documents used in the receiving and accounts payable operations duplicate applications and files that already exist on the computer. Instead of referring to purchase order documents, Raul explains, personnel could call up records from the existing database. Instead of handwriting receiving information, the inspectors in the receiving department could enter the same information directly into computer terminals. With this information in the computer, terminals could be used to compare records for purchase orders and receiving reports. Review of vendor invoices could also be performed with records displayed at terminals.

These findings are reviewed with technical support personnel in the computer center. Specifications are developed for extending the company's database management system to include a new relation, or file, to support receiving and accounts payable operations. Technical support people review the information assembled by Raul and Carol and recommend the equipment configurations for the new terminals that will be needed.

Information contributed by these reviewers becomes input to a major management review of the system under development. All of the procedural and technical requirements are summarized in a report that provides a detailed specification of the elements of the new system and their costs. This review is distributed to members of an *information systems steering committee* composed of five management representatives. Together, members of this committee exercise control over all major capital expenses to be committed by the company. The job of the project team is to take a position about the benefits to be derived from the new system and to show how these benefits justify the cost. The presentation must be convincing to succeed. An approval by the steering committee means that the company has committed funding to proceed with implementation of the new system. After steering committee approval, the project is ready to move into the implementation stage.

## Implementation Stage

The *implementation stage* of a systems development project involves translating design specifications into software and testing new programs, hardware selection and installation, and training of users. Users must be involved in contributing information to and approving changes to be made. Users must be trained and ready to operate the new system.

When all of the activities identified above have been implemented, the project is ready to move forward into *conversion*. Conversion is the point in the project where hardware, software, and new procedures are in place; the necessary data resources have been created; and the users assume their new operating roles.

Four main strategies have been developed for conversion:

- Direct cutover
- Parallel
- Phased
- Pilot.

**Direct Cutover.**   Under the *direct cutover* approach, conversion takes place all at once. On a given day and at a given hour, the old system is discontinued and a new one begins. Everything is new all at once—the procedures, the equipment, the data resources, and possibly even the personnel. In general, direct cutover provides the least expensive conversion technique. But this method also involves the greatest risk among conversion options because there is no fallback system if the new system fails.

■ **Parallel.**   Under *parallel conversion,* there is an overlapping between operation of the old system and introduction of the new one. Both systems are operated, side by side, for a planned interval—typically one or two full processing and reporting cycles. During the parallel processing period, the results of the old and new systems are compared and any problems are resolved. When users and managers are satisfied with the reliability of the new system, the old one is discontinued. This is an expensive, but safe, approach to conversion.

■ **Phased.**   Under *phased conversion,* one portion of a new system is implemented at a time. For example, a company with branch locations might elect to install a new system in one location at a time. This enhances the coordination and utilization of key resources, such as technical support personnel and the people assigned to train new users. A schedule generally is established for conversions at each affected location. For each using location, the conversion may be a direct cutover. However, the overall system is not considered to be implemented until all phased conversions are completed.

■ **Pilot.**   A *pilot* approach tests a portion of the system before full conversion and implementation are scheduled. In the situation of a company with multiple locations, for example, one office may be selected as a ''pilot site.'' The new system is implemented at this location and results are observed before further conversion plans are set. This approach provides an opportunity to increase user confidence and commitment—or to modify the system if necessary—before full conversion takes place. Another piloting approach might involve implementation and operation of part of a system before a full commitment is made. To illustrate, a company planning for a system that will encompass invoicing and inventory control might elect to convert the invoicing application first, then add inventory processing at a later date.

The time span for the implementation stage of a project can vary widely. For a large mainframe system involving newly announced hardware, this stage can run for years. For a microcomputer system, hardware and software acquisition can become simple. But the creating of needed files and the training of users still can occupy months.

   The end result of implementation should be an operational system that is delivering specified information to authorized users. The users of the new system should feel comfortable both with the procedures and the information results delivered by the system. Working relationships should exist between users and computer center personnel to assure smooth, continuous service from the new system.

■ **Case Scenario.**   At Machine Tools, Inc., Raul reports regularly to Carol, who is surprised by the amount of detail involved in implementing what she thought would be a simple application. Provision has to be made for the new files within the database. Carol is asked to oversee preparation of test data that is processed against the expanded database to be sure implementation of the new application will not degrade service for other database users. Communication lines have to be established to the work stations where the new application will be used. The personnel involved have to attend training programs in the use of terminals and in some of the basics of database and data communication applications.

Special attention is needed as the new relation is established to support the new application. A decision has been made to use parallel conversion. The old, manual method will be run during the interim when the new system is brought into regular use. This proves to be the best approach for the application and the people involved. The size of the new system is too small to support phased or piloting conversions. Since all parties are new to the use of computers for this application, a parallel approach provides the greatest confidence for the people involved and the greatest assurance of reliability.

Carol is relieved when Raul agrees to make considerable amounts of his time available to help users solve problems during conversion. "This is the time when a computer professional has to be available," Raul explains. "If we're not around when the problems occur, everything we have done can be defeated."

## Post-Implementation Stage

The *post-implementation stage* starts as soon as a new system has been implemented and is said to be in production. An initial issue is to compare the actual results of systems development with the projected benefits identified during the planning stage. Each systems development project is an investment. It makes sense for management to review results to see if the organization got its money's worth.

Another issue that surfaces shortly after implementation is the identification of needed changes to the system. Typically, opportunities for enhancement are identified as users implement the new system. The temptation to make changes during implementation generally is delayed. It is best to complete the designed system, measure results, then make modifications in an orderly, planned set of procedures.

Modifications result from user and managment feedback. In general, three types of modfication requests affect operational systems. One is legal. Changes in payroll or sales tax laws, for example, can require modifications in application software. A second major source of change requirements comes from management decisions or policies. For example, addition of a new line of products or merger of two companies will require corresponding changes in information systems. A third area of changes lies in opportunities uncovered by users and analysts as they become familiar with a system and discover new opportunities for improvement.

System modification generally is done under methods that resemble the SDLC but are less formal and extensive. However, the rule still holds that nothing should happen in the area of systems development without management, analyst, and user involvement and approval.

**Case Scenario.**   At Machine Tools, Inc., it didn't take long for users and analysts to discover new opportunities shortly after the system was implemented. Teri was pleased with the benefits and cost reductions realized on implementation. Once she was aware of the potential for computer processing, she found an improvement opportunity that would make her own job easier: Part of her responsibility was to approve and sign purchase orders before they were issued. When questions came up, Teri had to check on current inventories and previous costs for ordered items.

It would be easier for her, Teri reasoned, if the information on stock levels and purchase prices was included in the documentation she reviewed. Accordingly, she initiated a request to add terminals to the work stations of the staff members who processed requisitions. Teri asked that a notation on inventory level and last purchase cost be added to the requisition that was attached to the purchase order. In this way, her decision support information would be included in the documentation she reviewed routinely.

Systems development proceeds in cycles. As an application is used, new requirements are bound to arise. These may be in the form of opportunities in the form of new, efficient, and effective technologies available. Other requirements for modification may include actions by competitors or responses to equipment or operating system upgrades within the computer center. The one constant about information systems is change. This characteristic of the systems development field is reflected in the fact that most systems analysis tasks now involve modification of existing systems, rather than development of entirely new applications. However, regardless of the challenge presented, the systems analysis tools reviewed below can help to improve the effectiveness and efficiency with which organizations use computers to meet user information needs.

## Systems Analysis and Design Tools

Systems analysis and design tools support the communication necessary among members of a systems development project team. Use of these tools should result in mutual understandings among users, computer professionals, and managers. To promote the necessary understanding and to support decision making, a series of special tools has been devised. Some of the most widely used tools are reviewed briefly in the discussions that follow. The specific choice of tool(s) depends on the nature of the systems problem.

### Questionnaires

As its name implies, a *questionnaire* gathers information by asking questions of persons affected by a present or proposed system. Two general types of questions are included. One type solicits specific facts or opinions from respondents. Responses to this type of question can be tabulated as a basis for measuring opinions or desires. The other major type of question is open-ended. That is, respondents are free to give opinions or ideas that might not lend themselves to tabulation.

Because of their role, questionnaires sometimes are called *data collection instruments,* a term that applies to any written guidelines for the gathering of information needed by systems analysts. The same name can be used to describe a printed guide for interviewers, as described below.

## Interviews

An *interview* is a face-to-face meeting for the exchange of information. In systems analysis, interviews are methods for information gathering. Either systems analysts or qualified users interview persons who actually operate a system or use its outputs. The purpose is to determine what is happening and what is needed. Often, interview guides are prepared as a basis for data gathering. Interviewing success requires that persons asked to contribute information be advised in advance of the purpose of the interview and the type of information sought. Appointments should be made under schedules that provide enough time for the interview subjects to gather information that can be useful.

## Flowcharts

A *flowchart* is a diagram that presents a graphic image of the steps for implementing a proposed system. Flowcharts use symbols to represent the functions performed and the events involved in operation of a system. These symbols are presented in an accompanying illustration.

Two types of flowcharts are used in systems development:

• System flowcharts
• Program flowcharts.

■ **System Flowcharts.**  A *system flowchart* depicts the overall structure of a system, including manual procedures, computer processing, and data files. A system flowchart provides a tool for visualizing the flow of information and control within a system. All manual input and review operations are included as an indication that procedures must be developed for performing these functions. Another symbol is used to identify computer processing functions. Each of these entries indicates that a program must be developed to implement those functions.

■ **Program Flowcharts.**  A *program flowchart* provides, in effect, a visual model to detail the processing that must be accomplished within a single program. In a program flowchart, a single computer processing function on a systems flowchart may be "exploded" into a full page of processing steps on a program flowchart.

These are the major symbols used for planning and representing system functions in flowcharts.

**MANUAL OPERATION** — Jobs performed by people

**ON-LINE KEYBOARD** — Device used to communicate with computer

**INPUT-OUTPUT** — Process for either entry of data into a computer or output of information from a computer

**PROCESSING** — An operation carried out on a computer processor, including arithmetic and logic operations

**DOCUMENT** — Printed record (or film image) created by a computer. Also a paper record used as a source of input data

**DECISION** — A point at which the course of processing is adjusted to reflect the status of information within a system

**COMMUNICATIONS LINK** — A channel by which an external device communicates with a computer

**TAPE DRIVE** — A device that records data on and reads data from magnetic tape under computer control

**DISK DRIVE** — A device that records data on and reads data from magnetically coated platters under computer control

**OFF-LINE STORAGE FILE** — A collection of information generated through computer processing on magnetic media or hard copy, ready for use in future computer processing and/or delivery to users

This flowchart demonstrates how standard symbols are used to diagram the functions that comprise an information system.

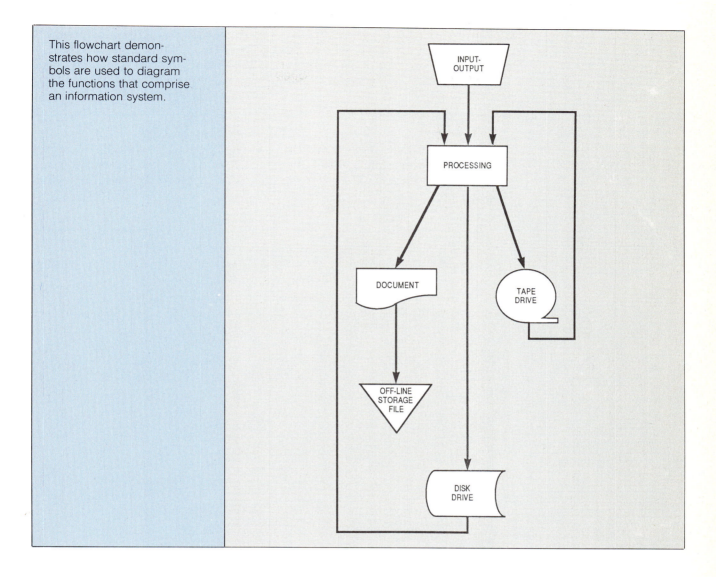

## Data Flow Diagrams

A *data flow diagram* is a graphic presentation tool that diagrams the flow of data through a system and identifies the processes that transform data into information. Data flow diagrams are a modern system tool that has become very popular.

As a point for comparison, flowcharts represent each operation, in sequence. This means that flowcharts show all documents entered into or generated by a system. Also shown on flowcharts are decisions about the control of data. A data flow diagram, by contrast, stresses the points in the system at which data are combined with other items or altered through computation. At each processing point, the *data stores,* or specific data elements needed for processing, are identified. A final set of items in data flow diagrams identifies *external entities,* information sources or users who interact with the system.

## Document Flowcharts

A *document flowchart,* sometimes callled a *paperwork flowchart,* is similar in concept and design to a data flow diagram. The difference is that the document flowchart stresses the creation, modification, and flow of documents through manual procedures rather than tracking data transformations through computer processing.

## Decision Tables

A *decision table* is a tool for defining applications of computer logic within programs. A logical operation, you will recall, is a comparison that results in selec-

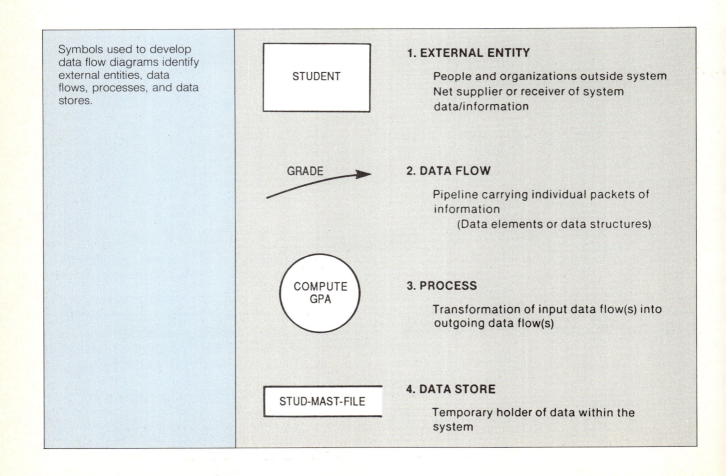

Symbols used to develop data flow diagrams identify external entities, data flows, processes, and data stores.

STUDENT

**1. EXTERNAL ENTITY**

People and organizations outside system
Net supplier or receiver of system data/information

GRADE

**2. DATA FLOW**

Pipeline carrying individual packets of information
    (Data elements or data structures)

COMPUTE GPA

**3. PROCESS**

Transformation of input data flow(s) into outgoing data flow(s)

STUD-MAST-FILE

**4. DATA STORE**

Temporary holder of data within the system

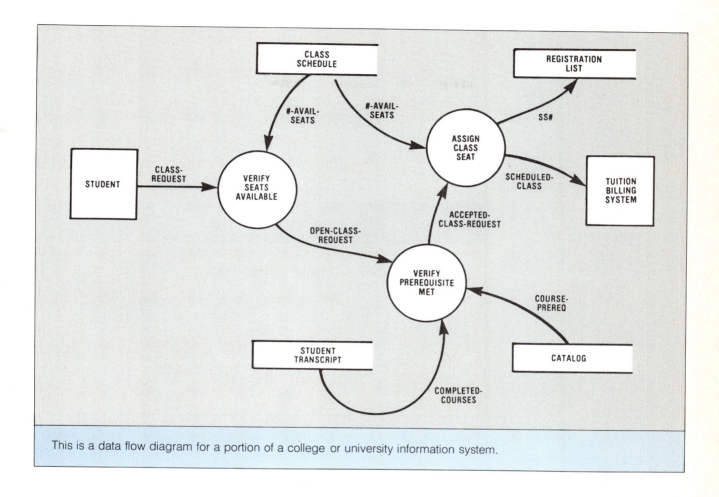

This is a data flow diagram for a portion of a college or university information system.

tion of a processing alternative on the basis of whether one item is equal to, greater than, or less than another. A decision table breaks down complex processing decisions into a series of simple steps. Decision tables then serve as a checklist to be sure the programmer includes all required logic operations in a program under development.

## Decision Trees

A *decision tree* can be likened to a road map that identifies the points within a project, or within an application program, at which decisions have to be made. The decision tree identifies the alternatives for each decision and establishes the relationships among the alternatives that can be selected. Decision trees often are represented in diagrams that resemble the PERT or critical path networks described below in the discussion of project management tools.

A decision table can be represented as a matrix of logical conditions. Computer decisions represent choices between two alternatives, such as yes/no or true/false. Systems analysts specify the conditions to be sensed and the outcomes to be produced.

| | | | | | | | | |
|---|---|---|---|---|---|---|---|---|
| AVG BAL ≥ 1000 | Y | Y | Y | Y | N | N | N | N |
| NUM OVERDRAFTS ≤ 2 | Y | Y | N | N | Y | Y | N | N |
| AVG BAL ≥ 500 | Y | N | Y | N | Y | N | Y | N |
| APPROVE | X | X | | | | | | |
| COND. APPROVAL | | | | X | | X | | |
| REJECT | | | | X | | | X | X | X |

**THE GENERAL FORM OF DECISION TABLE:**

| CONDITIONS | COLUMS REPRESENT LOGICAL COMBINATIONS OF CONDITION VALUES |
|---|---|
| OUTCOMES | X INDICATE SPECIFIED OUTCOME(S) FOR EACH SET OF CONDITIONS |

## HIPO Diagrams

A *hierarchy input, processing, output (HIPO) diagram* is another type of graphic tool used to guide programmers. A hierarchy breaks a large project into a series of detailed parts. For each of these parts, a HIPO chart lists the input, processing, and output requirements. Thus, a HIPO chart is an alternate method for representing a program algorithm.

## Warnier-Orr Diagrams

A *Warnier-Orr diagram* implements an approach known as *structured programming*. Under this methodology, all programs are segmented into a standard set of parts, or "legs." As shown in an accompanying illustration, program legs are devoted to initiating a system, processing, and terminating use of an application.

Within this framework, separate program modules are designated for application steps. For example, in the initiation portion of an application, modules would instruct the computer that a given job is to be processed, open the

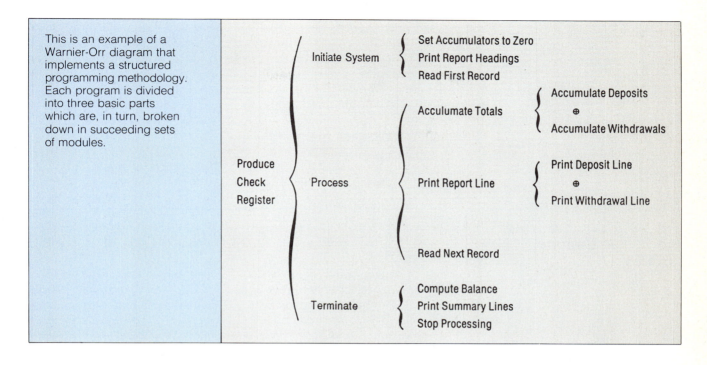

This is an example of a Warnier-Orr diagram that implements a structured programming methodology. Each program is divided into three basic parts which are, in turn, broken down in succeeding sets of modules.

needed files, and read the first record into memory for processing. Then, control is passed to the processing module to process the entered record and to continue the processing sequence. The Warnier-Orr approach helps to manage the programming process by breaking applications into a series of program modules that can be assigned to different programmers. In addition, the modular approach makes it easier to test and debug programs.

## Pseudocode

*Pseudocode* consists of a series of structured English statements that describe the processing steps and logic needed to implement an application program. The writing style of pseudocode statements makes heavy use of verbs or condition descriptions (such as IF or THEN) that highlight the processing to be done. These statements generally correspond directly with the commands that will be written in a programming language after program design is approved.

## Project Management Tools

The main purpose for establishing project methods for systems development is to achieve manageability. From the descriptions above of project structures and systems analysis activities, it is obvious that a lot happens in the course of systems development. The number of work assignments and events involved defines the ability of managers to keep track of everything that happens unless they use some special tools that represent situations graphically. The tools used most commonly to show detailed tasks, planned schedules, as well as actual completion times and dates are described below.

- Project evaluation and review technique (PERT)
- Critical path method (CPM)
- Gantt charts.

## Project Evaluation and Review Technique (PERT)

The *project evaluation and review technique (PERT)* is a method for identifying the key ''events,'' or important points at which activities are completed within major project.

PERT is implemented through use of a diagram, called a *network.* On a network diagram, project activities are represented by lines that connect a series of circles, or *nodes,* that represent events. A PERT event usually is the point at which one activity is completed and another begins. Networks are structured to show relationships and elapsed times between events. However, PERT is not a scheduling technique. Rather, it is a tool to establish a management overview for monitoring and control purposes. Another network technique, described below, adds a dimension for monitoring schedules and assessing the impact of problems or delays.

## Critical Path Method (CPM)

The *critical path method (CPM)* uses a network structure similar to that of PERT. Activities are represented as labeled lines while events are shown as circular nodes. The difference is that one set of lines generally is heavier than the rest. These heavy lines identify a continuous set of events that form a ''critical path'' through the project. The critical path is the sequence of activities that must be completed, in order, to carry on the project. Any delay in completing an activity on the critical path causes a delay in the entire project.

An accompanying illustration shows a network with CPM notations. A PERT network would look the same, except that timing notations would be in estimated number of working days rather than in start and completion dates.

## Gantt Charts

A *Gantt chart* is a time-related scheduling tool that is structured upon a time scale. A series of parallel, horizontal lines is drawn on a flat surface. Along the top line is a series of marks that represents a time scale. Commonly used scales divide the available width of the chart into days or weeks. Each line, or row, on the chart represents an activity or job to be performed. Lines are drawn to represent the beginning, duration, and completion of each activity. If appropri-

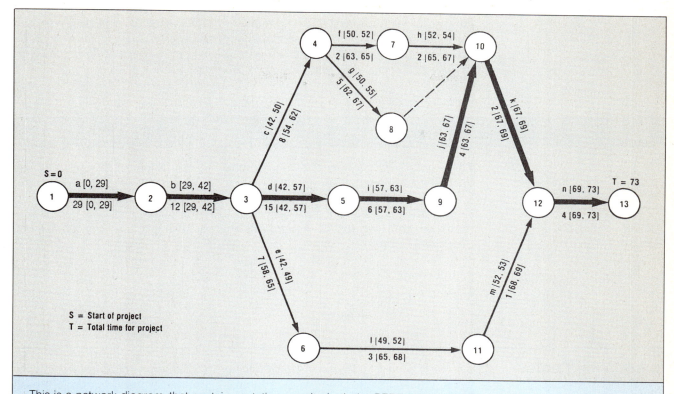

This is a network diagram that contains notations under both the PERT (event duration) and CPM (elapsed time for each event) methods.

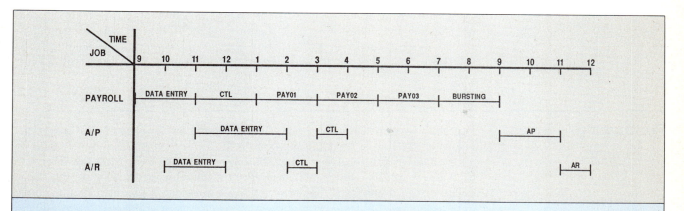

This is an example of a Gantt chart. The application is scheduling for a computer operations center.

ate, the line is identified with the name of the department or person who will complete the work. The lines along a Gantt chart, as illustrated, represent the duration of each activity. The total chart reflects the overlaps and relationships involved in completing the project or production job.

## User-Developed Systems

The advent of user-friendly microcomputers and application packages has opened some potential shortcuts in systems development. One result is a trend known as "end-user computing." That is, if users understand systems concepts sufficiently—and if they can find easily adaptable software packages—they can shortcut the development process through methods like those described below.

- Information centers
- Prototyping
- Application packages.

### Information Center

An *information center* is an in-house facility that provides technical support to users who want to implement their information systems applications. A typical information center will have microcomputer equipment and an assortment of application packages available. In some instances, there may be terminals linked to on-line processing systems available to users.

A user with a problem or need can make an appointment or may just visit the information center. Computer professionals who operate the information center are available to help set up and adapt available applications to specific user needs. For example, a user responsible for preparing spreadsheets can receive suggestions and/or instruction on two or more packages as a basis for selection. Once the package is selected, the information center personnel can help to secure equipment and software and to install the system.

### Prototyping

*Prototyping* can be described as a "toe in the water" approach to systems development. That is, the organization elects to try part or a limited version of a new system before undertaking the major commitment of full implementation. Users can evaluate a system before full development costs are incurred. In the development of a new manufactured product, a *prototype,* is a preliminary model used to test a product before development and/or production plans are finalized. In systems development, prototyping is a technique that uses powerful software tools to test a system on a preliminary basis before full-scale development is undertaken. A prototype system imitates the complete system without requiring all of the expense involved in developing programs and building extensive files.

## Application Packages

The computer itself can be used as a tool for systems development and project management. Software packages introduced recently are built upon the capabilities of the fourth- and fifth-generation tools described in Chapter 9. Recall that fourth-generation methods make it possible for users to communicate their needs through software packages that react to a set of easy-to-learn, powerful commands that extend the query language of a database. Eventually, fifth-generation methods will make it possible for users to address computers in their own, natural language.

The special dimension of application development packages is that they enhance the ability of users to develop their own systems. The user simply names the files needed in a system and the software provides support in the specification and formatting of a series of relations. Through interactive entries, the user creates the database needed to support a new system. Then, through use of an extended command set, the user identifies the processing functions to be conducted and specifies contents of required reports. The software constructs the processing sequences needed to implement the system.

Techniques for end-user computing put information tools directly in the hands of the people who experience and understand the needs that must be met. With the availability of microcomputers and application packages, each manager and/or department can, in effect, establish and maintain its own information processing facilities and systems. This means that information users can acquire an entirely new dimension of capabilities for information analysis and decision support. The former dependencies and delays associated with securing information from a central computer operations facility can be eliminated in many cases.

Though the benefits can be immense, there are also potential drawbacks. When users proceed on their own, the professional support provided by an information systems department may be diminished or eliminated. As a result, the accuracy, reliability, and/or validity of information may suffer from lack of adequate controls or professional attention.

Ideally, a balance should be struck under which users have a strong hand in designing and developing systems to meet their own needs while computer professionals are close by as coaches and quality controllers.

## Chapter Summary

- Systems development is an organized, orderly, controlled process for creating new computer systems.

- The process for systems development, known as a systems development life cycle, consists of a series of stages. The life cycle reviewed in this chapter has four stages: 1) Planning; 2) Analysis and Design; 3) Implementation; 4) Post-implementation.

- The planning stage identifies the project, determines whether the opportunity is worth pursuing, and establishes initial estimates of costs and benefits.

- The analysis and design stage centers upon systems analysis activities that identify existing methods and establish designs for a new system. At the conclusion of this stage, a definitive commitment is sought from top management on whether to proceed with implementation of the new system.

- The implementation stage encompasses all of the activities needed to program the system, establish needed procedures, acquire hardware, and convert from the existing methods to the new ones. Conversion alternatives include direct cutover, parallel processing, phased implementation, and pilot implementation.

- The post-implementation stage is devoted to evaluating results of the systems development effort and to maintaining the system through enhancements or required modifications.

- Tools for systems analysis include questionnaires, interviews, flowcharts, data flow diagrams, document flowcharts, decision tables, HIPO diagrams, and Warnier-Orr diagrams.

- Visual tools that can assist in project management include PERT, CPM, and Gantt charts.

- Tools that enable users to develop systems on their own or with direct assistance from systems specialists include information centers, prototyping, and systems development software.

## Questions for Review

1. What is a systems development life cycle?
2. Identify and describe four stages that can constitute a workable systems development life cycle.
3. What basic principles and concepts help to establish the value of the project approach to systems development?
4. What are the benefits of the planning stage of the SDLC?
5. What are the basic steps in the analysis and design stage of the SDLC?
6. What is the implementation stage of the SDLC?
7. What are the major results of the post-implementation stage of the SDLC?

8. What is system conversion and what are the results of this activity?
9. What is a critical path and what is the value of identifying a critical path?
10. What is an information center and what does it do?

## Questions for Thought

1. What is the purpose and what are the advantages of a project approach to systems development?
2. What is the role of the systems analyst in a systems development project and how does a systems analyst interact with users?
3. What are the major methods for converting from an old system to a new one and what are the reasons for selecting each of the methods as compared with the others?
4. What is prototyping and how can this approach assist in the development of new computer information systems?
5. What is pseudocode and how is it used as a systems tool?

## Terms

analysis and design stage

capital budgeting

conversion

critical path method (CPM)

data collection instrument

data flow diagram

data store

decision table

decision tree

direct cutover

document flowchart

external entity

flowchart

Gantt chart

hierarchy input, processing, output (HIPO) diagram

implementation stage

information center

information systems steering committee

interview

network

node

parallel conversion

phased conversion

pilot

planning stage

post-implementation stage

process

program flowchart

project evaluation and review technique (PERT)

prototype

prototyping

pseudocode

questionnaire

structured programming

system flowchart

systems analysis

systems design

systems development

systems development life cycle (SDLC)

user specification

walk-through

Warnier-Orr diagram

## MINICASE

**Situation:**

You have a part time position as a systems analyst in your school's computer center. You are assigned to work with Sylvia Hidalgo, director of student placement.

Sylvia has a microcomputer with a 640 K memory, a 40 Mb hard disk, and two 360 K disk drives in her department. She also has a printer. She wants to create a database system to be used for placement of students in both part time and permanent jobs. Sylvia's idea is to buy a database package and to set up records for some 2,500 prospective employers. The names will come from a series of directories to be provided by different disciplines within the school.

The database then will be used to address questionnaires to the listed companies to determine if there is interest in student placements. As questionnaires are returned, the database will be updated to reflect job availabilities. Eventually, the database will be used to develop listings for interested students and to match the academic specialties of students with job openings.

**Decision Making: Your Turn**

1. From the information you have, identify and describe the problem to be solved.
2. Identify alternatives that could be followed to avoid or solve the problem.
3. On the basis of the limited information you have: a) Identify additional information you would gather if you were dealing with this problem in a real situation. b) Identify the solution that appears best on the basis of the information that is available and explain your reasons for this selection.
4. What lessons are to be learned from this situation?

## Projects

1. Find a description of another systems development life cycle structure. Compare this other structure with the four-stage SDLC described in this chapter. Analyze and explain the differences and possible reasons for those differences.

2. Based on the Minicase above, devise a questionnaire that could be used to gather information about current operations and future needs from members of the faculty and school administration.

3. Visit the computer center on campus or a commercial computer installation. Through interviews with systems analysts, develop a simple written description of an existing system that has required modification since its implementation. Describe the modifications and the purposes they have served.

# Glossary

**accumulator.** A register that accumulates the results of computations.

**Ada.** A high-level computer language named after Lady Ada Augusta Lovelace, a British noblewoman and mathematician.

**algorithm.** A well-defined, step-by-step procedure for accomplishing a task and/or solving a problem.

**alphanumeric.** A character set that contains letters, digits, and special characters such as punctuation marks.

**ALU.** See arithmetic/logic units.

**analog signal.** A data communication signal that is continuous wave patterns. Contrast with digital signal.

**API (a programming language).** A high-level computer language developed for interactive problem-solving.

**applications program.** A sequence of instructions written to solve a specific problem or accomplish a specific task.

**arithmetic/logic unit (ALU).** The section of the CPU that handles arithmetic computations and logical operations.

**array.** An ordered set of data items. Also called a table or matrix.

**artificial intelligence.** A field of computer science that studies how computers can be used to solve problems that appear to require imagination, intuition, or intelligence.

**ASCII (American Standard Code for Information Interchange).** A 7-bit or 8-bit standard code for information interchange among data-processing systems, communication systems, and associated equipment.

**assembler.** A program that translates assembly language programs into machine-executable code.

**assembly language.** A symbolic programming language that uses convenient abbreviations rather than groupings of 0s and 1s.

**asynchronous transmission.** Transmission of data over a communications line at random time intervals.

Asynchronous transmission is one bit at a time. Contrast with synchronous transmission.

**auxiliary storage.** See secondary storage.

**BASIC (Beginners' All-purpose Symbolic Instruction Code).** A programming language commonly used for interactive problem solving by users who may not be professional programmers.

**batch/sequential processing.** A method of processing data in which data items are collected and processed in a group or batch.

**binary system.** The numeric system used in computer operations. It is a numbering system with a base of 2 and uses only the digits 0 and 1.

**bit.** A binary digit (either 1 or 0).

**buffer.** A temporary storage location for data transferred between computer devices such as for output sent from the CPU to a printer.

**bug.** A mistake or malfunction in the hardware or software.

**bulletin board.** An electronic database for users to post messages and programs for other users.

**bus network.** A data communication system where each node attached to the network communicates using a common channel or bus.

**byte.** Set of bits (usually 8 bits) that represent a number or character.

**C.** A high-level programming language that is both easy to use and operationally very efficient.

**card punch.** See keypunch.

**card reader.** A device that translates the holes in punched cards into electrical pulses for processing by a computer.

**cartridge.** A storage device that contains a single, high-density disk platter or a tape in an enclosed case. A cartridge is removable from its drive unit.

**cathode ray tube (CRT).** An output device that displays computer output as an image on a television-like screen. Also called a video display.

**CD ROM.** See compact disk read-only memory.

**cell.** Individual areas on an electronic spreadsheet where constants (numbers), text and formulas are stored and displayed. They are formed at the intersection of a row and a column.

**central processing unit (CPU).** The hardware component that executes software instructions, performs arithmetic and logical operations, and communicates with input, output and secondary storage devices.

**character printer.** An output device that prints one symbol (number or letter) at a time.

**coaxial line.** A communications cable for high-speed data transfer. Cable television line is the most familiar use of coaxial cable.

**COBOL (Common Business-Oriented Language).** A high-level programming language generally used for accounting and business data processing.

**code.** To express a problem solution in a programming language.

**COM.** See computer output, microfilm.

**command driven.** Describes software applications where the user directs the program with specific software commands.

**compact disk read-only memory (CD ROM).** A special high-density storage device which uses optical or laser technology for reading and writing data.

**compatibility.** The degree to which programs can be run on a different computer system without modification.

**compiler.** A computer program which translates high-level computer languages into machine-executable object code.

**computer.** A collection of electronic equipment devices connected to one another for coordinated use in supporting information processing.

**computer architecture.** The components that make up the total computer hardware system including the peripheral devices.

**computer information system.** A total system of people, procedures (including computer programs), data and equipment needed to accept data as input and to deliver information required by users.

**computer output microfilm (COM).** A storage medium where data is stored on a microfilm.

**computer professionals.** Individuals who develop, operate and manage computer sysems and deliver results in the form of computer output.

**computer system.** The combination of computer equipment and sets of instructions (procedures) that enable a computer to deliver information needed by people.

**concentrator.** A device that systematically allocates communication channels among several terminals. It is a special type of multiplexor.

**control program for a microcomputer (CP/M).** A general-purpose portable operating system used on microcomputers.

**control unit.** The CPU component that directs the execution of software instructions.

**conversion.** A process of changing from one computer system or program to another.

**co-processor.** An additional CPU added to a computer system to help with specific applications, such as a graphics co-processor to perform graphic functions.

**copy.** A software command that reproduces an existing character, string of characters, or file.

**CP/M.** See control program for a microcomputer.

**CPU.** See central processing unit.

**create.** A software command that develops a new data file.

**CRT.** See cathode ray tube.

**cursor.** The blinking light on a video display that indicates where the next character will appear.

**custom program.** A software program designed for a specific user or organization.

**data.** The raw materials (facts and concepts) from which information is processed.

**data communication.** The electronic transmission of data, usually over communication channels such as telephone/telegraph lines, coaxial cable or microwaves.

**data dictionary.** Identifies and defines the data elements of a database and their relationships.

**data element.** A unit of information consisting of one or more bytes. Also called a field.

**data entry.** The process of inputting data into a computer system.

**data flow diagram.** A graphical presentation of the flow of information through a system.

**data item.** See data elements.

**data model.** A plan for organizing, storing, and manipulating data within a data base.

**data processing.** Operations performed on data to produce information for users.

**data structure.** A plan for organizing data to reflect data elements and their relationships. The data structure establishes the data file.

**database.** A collection of data integrated according to content and convenience of access. It is a set of related data files.

**database administrator.** A computer professional who is responsible for creating and managing the organization's databases.

**database management system (DBMS).** A set of programs that serves as an interface between the database and three principal users—the programmer, the operating system, and the end user.

**DBMS.** See database management system.

**debugging.** The process of detecting, locating and eliminating errors, or bugs, in a program.

**decimal system.** A number system with a base 10 that uses the digits 0 through 9.

**decision support system.** A system that supports managerial decision making.

**decision table.** A system analysis and design tool for defining decision logic within a program.

**decision tree.** A system analysis and design tool to identify the alternatives for each decision and to establish the relationships among the alternatives.

**density.** The number of characters or bytes that can be stored on a storage medium (tape or disk).

**desktop publishing.** The integration of text and graphics into the same document using a software package which runs on a microcomputer.

**dial-up service.** A data communication term which refers to any transmission that takes place through public telephone networks.

**digital signal.** A signal which represents and transmits data as a series of electrical pulses. The electrical current is on or off, thus representing binary 1s and 0s. Contrast with analog signal.

**digitize.** The process of converting a physical measurement into a digital value.

**direct access.** The ability to store data and retrieve data directly from storage.

**disk drive.** The mechanical device used to access data stored on a disk (floppy, hard or optical).

**disk operating system (DOS).** A set of programs that control the computer hardware and software. DOS is a term associated with the microcomputers. See operating system.

**disk pack.** A single-tiered stack of high-density magnetic disks which are removable from a disk drive.

**diskette.** See floppy disk.

**distributed system.** Geographically dispersed computer equipment linked together by a data communications network.

**document flowchart.** A method for tracing the creation, modification, and flow of documents usually through manual (as opposed to computerized) information systems.

**document reading.** An input method that recognizes and interprets various characters directly from hard copy sources. Specific methods of document reading include Universal Product Code, Optical Code Reading, Magnetic Ink Character Reading and Optical Mark Reading.

**DOS.** See disk operating system.

**dot matrix.** A method of forming characters and images from a matrix of printed dots.

**duplex line.** A data communications channel in which data can be transmitted in both directions at the same time.

**EBCDIC.** See extended binary coded decimal interchange code.

**edit.** The process of changing a document from its original form.

**EDP.** See electronic data processing.

**electronic data processing (EDP).** Data processing performed largely by electronic equipment (computer), rather than by manual or mechanical methods.

**electronic mail.** The process of sending storing, and receiving messages electronically.

**EPROM.** See erasable programmable read-only memory.

**erasable programmable read-only memory (EPROM).** A ROM chip that can be erased and reprogrammed.

**expert systems.** A computer system which simulates a human expert in a specific field.

**extended binary coded decimal interchange code (EBCDIC).** An 8-bit code for character representation.

**external storage.** See secondary storage.

**field.** A unit of information consisting of one or more bytes. A byte identifies the smallest unit of data suitable for processing. See data element or data item.

**file.** A grouping of related data records.

**film recorder.** An output device for taking graphic output and storing the images on film or videotape.

**flat-bed plotter.** An output device used to produce graphic images where the pen moves horizontally and vertically over a fixed, flat surface.

**floppy disk.** A thin sheet of flexible plastic which stores magnetic data.

**flowchart.** A graphic representation of program logic or a system configuration. The program flowchart depicts the types and sequence of program operations. The system flowchart shows the flow of data through an information system.

**font.** Separate typefaces used in printing characters.

**FORTRAN.** FORmula TRANslator is a high-level programming language used primarily for performing mathematical or scientific operations.

**fourth generation language (4GL).** High-level programming languages that are English-like and often DBMS languages.

**front-end processor.** A small CPU serving as an interface between a large CPU and its peripheral devices. It is used frequently in data communications systems.

**gigabyte (GB).** One billion bytes.

**graphic display device.** A visual display device that projects output in the form of graphics images.

**half-duplex.** A data communications channel in which data can be transmitted in both directions but in only one direction at a time.

**hard copy.** Printed output.

**hard disk.** A secondary storage device that stores data magnetically on a rigid, high-speed disk.

**hardware.** Physical equipment such as semiconductor chips, cables, or disks.

**heuristic.** An exploratory approach to solving problems that identifies "rules of operation."

**hierarchical input, processing, output (HIPO).** A graphical tool to guide programmers that breaks complex programs into their component parts and indicates their input, processing, and output requirements.

**hierarchical model.** A tree-like structure for organizing data—a database structure.

**high-level languages.** English-like coding schemes which are procedure-, problem-, and user-oriented.

**high resolution monitor.** A video display that presents images at a fine level of detail. It is used extensively for displaying graphic images.

**HIPO.** See hierarchical input, processing, output.

**Hollerith code.** A method of data representation named for the man who invented it. It represents numbers, letters and special characters by the placement of holes in 80-column punched cards.

**hybrid model.** A combination of data structure-types (hierarchical, network, and relational models)—a database structure.

**hybrid network.** A data communications network that combines different network types (bus, ring, star, etc.).

**impact printer.** A printer that forms characters by physically striking a ribbon against paper.

**index.** A directory referencing records in a data file. It contains a list of key names and physical storage addresses where specific data records can be accessed.

**indexed-sequential.** A file organization technique in which records are organized in sequence and an index is maintained, thus allowing both sequential and direct-access processing.

**information center.** An in-house service facility that provides direct support for users.

**information system.** An organized set of people, equipment, procedures (manual and/or automated), and data that deliver information to users.

**information utility.** An external supplier of large data libraries, such as a news information service, a stock quotation service, and airline scheduling service.

**initialization.** A set of operating system procedures for setting up the computer system for use. It includes checking the hardware configuration, and setting different computer systems variables to predetermined values.

**input.** Data that is submitted to the computer for processing.

**insert.** A word processing function for entering text into existing text.

**integrated software.** Applications software that combines applications such as word processing, electronic spreadsheet, data base management, and data communications as a single software package.

**interpreter.** A computer language translating program that translates into machine code and executes a line of source code at a time. Compare with compiler.

**JCL.**  See job control language.

**job control language (JCL).**  A set of commands with which the user directs the computer operating system.

**key.**  A data file field that identifies specific records. It is used to locate a particular record within a file.

**keyboard.**  An input device with which users enter data and programs into a computer system. Its principal feature is a set of keys representing letters, numbers, special symbols, and functions.

**keypunch.**  A keyboard device that punches holes in a card to represent data.

**kilobyte (KB).**  Approximately one thousand (1024) bytes.

**label.**  A name or identifier for columns or rows of spreadsheet data or for graphic display details.

**LAN.**  See local area network.

**large-scale integration (LSI).**  Process of concentrating multiple integrated circuits onto a single semiconductor chip.

**laser printer.**  A type of nonimpact printer that combines laser and electrophotographic technologies to produce images on paper.

**LCD.**  See liquid crystal display.

**LED.**  See light-emitting diode.

**letter quality.**  A print quality that compares with that produced by a good typewriter. A letter-quality printer produces text that is clear and sharp. Contrast with near-letter quality and draft printer.

**library programs.**  User-written or manufacturer-supplied programs that are frequently used in other programs. They are written and stored on secondary media and called into main storage when needed.

**light pen.**  See light-sensing stylus.

**light-emitting diode (LED).**  An output display that forms images through points of light.

**light-sensing stylus.**  An input device that senses a bright cursor generated by the computer on its display screen. It is used to write or draw images on the display screen.

**line printer.**  An output device that prints one line at a time.

**liquid crystal display (LCD).**  A display where images are created by passing electric current through a liquid crystal solution.

**list.**  A software function that displays the contents of a file.

**local area network (LAN).**  A data communications network that connects computers and peripheral devices within one building.

**logical design.**  The user's view of a database structure, which may be different from the actual, physical storage structure.

**LSI.**  See large-scale integration.

**machine language.**  The only set of instructions that a computer can execute directly. It is a language code consisting of 0s and 1s.

**macro.**  A single software function which when invoked executes a series of instructions.

**magnetic ink character reader (MICR).**  An input device that reads characters printed in magnetic ink.

**mail/merge.**  A process that prints individualized form letters. Names and addresses from an address file are merged with text from another file.

**main memory.**  See primary storage.

**mainframe.**  The CPU of a large-scale computer.

**management information system (MIS).**  A computer information system that supplies information to managers to support their planning, organizing, and controlling functions.

**mass storage devices.**  A class of secondary storage devices capable of storing large volumes of data at low prices and slow access speeds.

**megabyte (MB).**  One million bytes.

**memory.**  A holding area for programs to be executed and for data to be processed.

**MICR.**  See magnetic ink character reader.

**microcomputer.**  A desktop computer with a single processor chip.

**microprocessor.**  The CPU of a microcomputer.

**microwave transmission.**  A data communications channel which utilizes high-frequency, electromagnetic waves to convey data.

**minicomputer.**  A computer with the components of a full-sized system but having a smaller memory. It is often used as a communications and network server, database machine, or single-function computer.

**modem.**  A data communications device that modulates a digital computer signal into an analog signal for transmission over telephone lines. It demodulates the analog into a digital signal.

**monitor**.    See video display.

**mouse**.    An input device used to move a cursor around a video display.

**multiplexor**.    A data communications device that consolidates multiple inputs into a single stream of data.

**multiprocessing system**.    A multiple CPU configuration in which multiple programs are processed simultaneously.

**multiprogramming**.    See multitasking.

**multitasking**.    A process where a single CPU switches back and forth among multiple-user jobs and application programs.

**nanosecond**.    One billionth of a second.

**natural language**.    A language that permits users to program computer applications in their own language phrases (English).

**network**.    A system of linked communication devices configured to support the interchange of data.

**network model**.    A database structure similar to a hierarchical structure, but that permits complex relationships between data elements.

**node**.    A data communications station, communications computer, or terminal.

**nonprocedural languge**.    A high-level language that is problem oriented and that directs the computer in what to do, not how to do it.

**nonvolatile memory**.    Memory units that do not lose their contents when the electricity is turned off, such as bubble memory.

**numeric**.    Number data (as opposed to alphabetic).

**object code**.    Machine code program generated from source code by a compiler.

**OCR**.    See optical character recognition.

**offline**.    Pertaining to equipment or devices not under the control of the central processing unit.

**online**.    In direct communication with the computer.

**operating system**.    A collection of systems software that manages the execution of programs, scheduling, and input/output control. It controls the operations of the computer system.

**optical character recognition (OCR)**.    The process of reading numbers, letters, and other characters, and converting the optical images into appropriate electrical signals.

**optical disk**.    A storage device which uses laser technology to read and write data.

**output**.    Information that comes from the computer as a result of processing data.

**page printer**.    An output device that prints entire pages of output with each operating cycle.

**parallel transmission**.    Each of eight lines carries a separate bit of data simultaneously. The result is transmission of a complete byte of data at a time.

**partition**.    In multiprogramming, an area in primary storage which is assigned for one program. It may be fixed or variable in size.

**pascal**.    A high-level computer language which follows structured programming concepts.

**peripheral**.    Any input, output, or secondary storage device of a computer system.

**physical design.**    A description of how data is physically stored on a secondary storage device and how the data is accessed.

**plotter**.    An output device that creates characters and graphic images by automatically controlling pens.

**port**.    An element of a computer system through which the CPU communicates with its supporting peripheral devices.

**primary storage**.    Memory under direct control of the operating system. Also called main memory or core.

**printer**.    An output device used to produce permanent (hard copy) computer output.

**processor**.    See central processing unit.

**program**.    A series of instructions which direct the computer to solve problems and to accomplish tasks in a step-by-step manner.

**PROM**.    See programmable read-only memory.

**programmable read-only memory (PROM)**.    Read-only memory that is programmed by the user.

**protocol**.    Rules and standards governing data communications between computer systems.

**RAM**.    See random access memory.

**random access**.    A process for finding and recording individual data records.

**random access memory (RAM)**.    Any memory that supports direct or random access such as main memory and disk storage systems.

**read-only memory (ROM).**  Permanently programmed and nonvolatile memory that can be read but not written upon. See PROM and EPROM.

**record.**  A collection of data items, or fields, that provide information about a specific person, place, or thing.

**register.**  A central processing unit component used for temporary storage for the ALU.

**relational model.**  A database structure which organizes data as a series of interrelated tables.

**ring network.**  A data communications system where nodes are connected in a circle or loop.

**ROM.**  See read-only memory.

**save.**  A software function for recording a file from primary memory to a secondary storage medium.

**scanner.**  An input device which "reads" information into the computer from images that are printed or drawn on paper.

**scroll.**  A process that moves lines of text on a display screen up or down. As text is moved upward, lines at the top of the screen disappear, and new lines are added at the bottom of the screen.

**SDLC.**  See systems development life cycle.

**secondary storage.**  A data storage medium outside the computer such as magnetic disks and tapes. Also called auxiliary or external storage.

**sector.**  Part of the structure for storing data on most disks. Disk tracks are divided into individual addressable sectors.

**select.**  A database function for picking out a group of records from a database which meets user specifications.

**sequential file.**  Data records stored in a specific order, one after the other.

**serial transmission.**  A data communications term where the bits are sent one at a time in sequential order.

**simplex line.**  A data communications channel through which data can be transmitted in only one direction.

**software.**  Any program written for the computer.

**software package.**  A set of standardized computer programs, procedures, and related documentation designed to accomplish specific tasks.

**sort.**  A software function that arranges records into a specified order.

**source code.**  English-like program instructions before they are translated into machine-readable object code by a compiler.

**spreadsheet.**  A software program that organizes numbers, text, and formulas into a matrix of cells.

**star network.**  A data communications system where all nodes are linked to a central node. Data transmitted from one node to another must be handled by the central node.

**stylus.**  See light-sensing pen.

**supercomputer.**  The fastest mainframe computers.

**superconductivity.**  A process where electrons flow through a material without any resistance. Computer chip manufacturers are attempting to increase computer processing speeds by incorporating superconductivity into advanced chip designs.

**synchronous transmission.**  Transmission of data over a communications line at a fixed rate and in rhythm with a clock signal. Contrast with asynchronous transmission.

**systems analysis.**  A detailed investigation of a system for the purpose of determining what must be done and the best way to do it.

**systems analyst.**  The computer professional who performs the system analysis.

**systems design.**  Alternative solutions to problems (defined during system analysis) are designed, their cost effectiveness determined, and a final recommendation made.

**systems development life cycle (SDLC).**  A formal series of stages through which a system progresses. The stages include planning, system analysis and design, implementation, and control.

**systems software.**  Computer programs that control the internal operations of the computer. Operating systems, language translators (compilers, assemblers and interpreters), and utility programs are systems software.

**tape drive.**  A secondary storage device that reads from and writes data onto tape.

**template.**  An electronic spreadsheet designed for a specific application with labels and formulas already entered. The user enters only key numbers and names.

**terminal.**  An input/output device, usually a keyboard/video display or keyboard/printer device.

**track**.    A horizontal row stretching the length of a magnetic tape on which data can be recorded; or one of a series of concentric circles on the surface of a disk; or one of a series of circular bands on a drum.

**transmission rate**.    A measure of data transfer speed which is often expressed in number of bits per second (BPS).

**turnaround document**.    An output document that is used later as an input medium, such as a utility bill stub.

**uninterrupted power supply (UPS)**.    A device that provides electrical power to a computer system during a brownout or blackout.

**universal product code (UPC)**.    A code consisting of 10 pairs of vertical bars that represents the identity code of most supermarket items and their manufacturers.

**UPC**.    See universal product code.

**UPS**.    See uninterrupted power supply.

**user friendly**.    A term used to indicate ease of use. Software and hardware are considered user friendly when the user does not require extensive training to operate them.

**utility programs**.    Systems software which performs specialized, repeatedly used functions such as sorting, merging, and transferring data from one I/O device to another.

**video display**.    A terminal capable of displaying output on a cathode ray tube (CRT).

**virtual storage**.    An extension of multiprogramming in which portions of programs not being used are kept in secondary storage until needed, giving the impression that primary storage is unlimited. Also called virtual memory.

**volatile storage**.    Temporary storage where data is lost when the power is interrupted.

**Warnier-Orr diagram**.    A method for designing and documenting information systems using a structured programming approach.

**Winchester disk**.    A high-speed, high-capacity magnetic hard disk which is housed in a sealed unit to protect it from dust and moisture.

**xerographic printer**.    An output device that uses optical images to print entire pages of text and graphic images.

# Index

access and DBMS, 147
accumulator, 254
Ada, 205
ADD instruction, 58
ad hoc approach, 298
address algorithm, 230
agricultural-crafts period, 7
algorithm, 230
alternatives, evaluation of, 34–35
ALU. *See* arithmetic/logic unit
analog signal, 180
analysis and design stage, 305–307
analytic graphics, 124, 125
AND gates, 257
append function, 162–163
applications, 32
applications program, 49–60, 203–204, 321
  *See also* database management systems
  and databases, 148
  for data communications, 189
  defined, 57
  for electronic spreadsheets, 111
  for graphics, 134
  languages for, 204–205
  for payrolls, 61
  for PC DOS, 254
  standards for 60–63
  and systems development, 303–304
  for word processing, 88
archival quality, 286
arithmetic/logic unit (ALU), 250–251
  binary computation, 257–258
  processing in, 257
artificial intelligence, 206–207
ASCII, 173, 185, 226
assembler, 201
assembly languages, 201
asynchronous transmission, 186–187, 188, 189
ATM systems, 15
  as computer information system, 28–29
  direct entry into, 274
  input and output applications, 287–288
  keyboards on, 46, 276
  magnetic cards for, 281
  networks for, 183
  storage devices for, 239
attributes, 149
  in relational model, 155
audio response, 286–287
audio synthesizer, 286
automated warehouse distribution systems, 277
authorization function, 273

automatic teller machines. *See* ATM services
automobile technology, 4–5
auxiliary storage, 50, 225

backspace function, 84
backup copies. *See* storage
banks. *See also* ATM services
  DBMS use for, 163
bar graphs, 132
BASIC, 59
batch processing, 229
batches of data items, 52
baud, 186
Baudot, Louis, 186
benefits, confirmation of, 37
binary codes, 201
binary digit. *See* bits
binary system, 252, 257–258
  and telephone communication, 53
BIOS (Basic Input-Output System), 210, 254
bit stream, 226
bits, 149
  and CPU, 252
  start bits, 187
  and storage, 226–227
boldface function, 87
booting. *See* loading
bootstrap start, 212
Bricklin, Dan, 96–97
broadband lines, 177
bubble memory, 256
buddy routine, 214
budgets
  capital budgeting, 300
  electronic spreadsheets for, 112
  software, 61–62
buffers, 182, 187
bugs, 208
bulletin boards, 192
business meetings, graphics for, 126–127
bus networks, 183–184
bytes, 149. *See also* gigabytes
  stop bytes, 187

C., 205–206
capital budgeting procedures, 300
capture function, 78
card punch. *See* punched cards
card reader, 228
cartridge, 235–237
cash registers, 46
CD ROM, 238–242
cells, 100
Census, 1890, 8–9

centering function, 87
central processing unit (CPU), 13, 246–268.
    *See also* arithmetic logic unit;
    main memory
  capacities, 252–253
  classifications of, 259–263
  defined, 249–253
  matching system and, 263–264
  memory sizes, 252
  representing data in, 256–258
  trade-offs, 252–253
channels, 182
character printers, 283–284
character sets, 226
character spacing function, 87
child nodes, 156, 158
circuit board, 253
clock rate, 252
coaxial lines, 177
COBOL, 202, 205
code, 208
coherent beam of light, 178
color printers, 285
columns in spreadsheets, 100
COM (Computer Output, Microfilm)
    devices, 285–286
COM 1 ports, 181
command driven software, 83
communications
  hardware, 52–54
  ports, 182
  protocols, 185–188
  software, 188–190
compact disks for read-only memory, 238, 242, 255
compatibility, 264
compilers, 201, 204
component density, 263
components, 44
compute function
  for DBMS, 161
  with electronic spreadsheets, 108–109
computer, defined, 15
computer architecture, 203
computer graphics. *See* graphics
computer information systems, 15–29
computer output, microfilm (COM), 285–286
computer professionals, 14–15
configuration of components, 56
contracts, 72
control module, 209–210
control program for a microcomputer (CPM), 318, 319
control unit, 249–250